TECUMSEH'S CURSE

Indigenous Wisdom, Astrology and and the Deaths of U.S. Presidents

by Karen Christino

What is life? It is the flash of a firefly in the night. It is the breath of a buffalo in the wintertime. It is the little shadow which runs across the grass and loses itself in the sunset.
– Crowfoot, Blackfoot

ISBN 13: 978-0-9725117-6-6
ISBN 10: 0-9725117-6-8

Published by Karen Christino
Brooklyn, New York, U.S.A.

Table of Contents

List of Charts and Figures

Introduction

On December, 2020, two of the brightest objects in the night sky, the planets Jupiter and Saturn, came together. To the untrained eye, two spots of light were simply aligned with one another in a darkly shimmering void. Yet throughout history, cultures around the globe have memorialized this planetary conjunction in myths, legends and stories.

Astronomer and astrologer Johannes Kepler was fascinated with the celestial pairing and associated it with the birth of Jesus Christ, and it's been linked with the beginning and end of the Inca Empire. Other earthly echoes of this important sky event can be noted in Maya calendars, the ritual destruction of Japanese Shinto shrines, and the prophecies of the biblical Daniel. Why have so many peoples regarded the meeting of Jupiter and Saturn as a momentous event?

250 years ago, Jupiter and Saturn represented the outer-most reaches of our astronomical vision, and to the ancients, they were unequalled, meting out periods of 20, 200 and even 800-year intervals, significant cycles that astrologers have been studying for over 2,000 years. As Jupiter and Saturn represented "the greatest" celestially, they were often symbolically linked with the change in power from one ruler to another. In America, the conjunction has forecast tumultuous changes in our presidency.

U.S. presidents elected in the "zero" years of 1840, 1860 and so on have regularly died in office, and many astrologers have correlated the 20-year Jupiter-Saturn conjunctions with the presidential deaths. These cyclical deaths are also sometimes referred to as "Tecumseh's Curse." The celebrated Shawnee chief Tecumseh had fought against William Henry Harrison, the first president to die in office. According to legend, Tecumseh's brother, Tenskwatawa, after his defeat at the battle of Tippecanoe, predicted death and destruction for Harrison and his successors every 20 years.

Tenskwatawa, also known as the Shawnee Prophet, had taken a number of Harrison's men prisoner in the battle. He supposedly released a few back with an important message: "Your leader will become a great man in his country. He will meet his death in a zero year, and every 20 years thereafter the leader of your country will die in office." This is quoted in several different accounts but never attributed to an original source or reference work. It's not included in serious studies of the people or time. Usually the

Prophet makes the statement. Sometimes it's Tecumseh when he's dying. In one account it was Tecumseh's mother after she learned he'd been killed. So it's most likely not an accurate quote.

But beginning in 1840, seven out of nine presidents who were elected every 20 years have died in office. Ronald Reagan may be an exception as he was shot but survived. George W. Bush had a live hand grenade thrown at him but it did not explode, though the 9/11 attacks occurred on his watch. A new presidential term began in 2021.

What is it about the Jupiter-Saturn conjunctions that resonates so strongly with the United States' presidents? Is it an astrological cycle, an actual curse, or a myth?

Since this is also a Shawnee story, we'll look at the lives of the leaders Tecumseh and the Prophet, Shawnee history, beliefs and practices, and Indigenous astrology. We'll then examine the zero-year American presidents and the astrology of the presidential deaths to gain a better understanding of what may happen in the future.

Part I: THE HISTORY

Chapter 1: Centuries of Upheaval

For it is with yesterday that we learn for tomorrow.
– Edward Benton-Banai, Ojibway

To understand the significance of a curse connected with Tecumseh, it's useful to look back at the roots of Shawnee culture.

The Shawnee homeland was the Ohio River Valley, which they called their heart. Millennia before, the area was occupied by the Adena people, who built dome-shaped burial and ceremonial centers from around 1,000 to 200 BCE in what are now parts of Ohio, Indiana, West Virginia, Kentucky and Pennsylvania. The structures they left are often referred to as mounds, and the area was home to the most numerous and varied mounds on the continent.

Burial mounds were often part of a grouping that included circular structures made from earth and timber, topped by platforms and surrounded by water-filled moats. It's believed they were religious and celebratory gathering centers and probably also served as town squares, where storytelling, games and community meetings took place. The Adena may have imported maize and squash from Mexico. They left pottery, artwork, inscribed stone tablets and artifacts of copper, suggesting a large trading network. Many of the structures were destroyed after white colonists arrived and began clearing and farming the land.

The Hopewell people lived in this area from approximately 500 BCE to 750 CE, overlapping with the Adena, and their influence, too, was wide-ranging. They continued the tradition of building earthworks, and theirs were larger and more complex, featuring geometric shapes and walled walkways. Some

1 Adena mound, Miamisburg, Ohio

were flat-topped, reminiscent of the more familiar ancient stone structures of Mexico and Central America. Excavations of these sites have revealed mica, shark's teeth, obsidian, copper and shells, pointing to contacts and imports from the east coast to the mountains in the west.

2 Hopewell mound, Hillsboro, Ohio

The Shawnee are often associated with the Fort Ancient culture, a designation that is fading, but considered to have developed later, around 1000 to 1750 CE in the Ohio River Valley. Their mounds were walled and smaller, and the cycles of the Sun and Moon could be viewed from them. In 1824, the Shawnee Prophet confirmed that his people believed the ancient structures in the area were built by their forefathers or other Indigenous peoples in the area before the arrival of the whites.

The Shawnee were an Algonquian people, a vast group speaking similar languages that included Nations like the Mohegan, Chippawa, Kickapoo, Lenape (Delaware) and Miami, who lived in what is now the northeast United States coast, Great Lakes region and Canada.

The arrival of European colonists brought extensive disruptions. Indigenous people were often decimated by measles, small pox, influenza and other diseases from Europe. By the 1640s, a lively fur trade had developed with the French and British, but the use of firearms and demand for fur made beavers scarce in the northeast. The powerful Iroquois (Haudenosaunee) Confederacy pushed west into the Ohio Valley, fighting many Algonquian groups and the French for control of the market. Colonists from plantations in Virginia and elsewhere also raided Indigenous lands and captured some people as slaves.

The Shawnee left Ohio in the 1670s and 1680s to escape the violence. They were scattered across the eastern U.S., from

Michigan, Illinois, Indiana, Delaware, Pennsylvania, Virginia and the Carolinas to Tennessee and Alabama in a web of widespread communities that retained contact with kin in Ohio and elsewhere. The Shawnee befriended, married and stayed in touch with others from the Gulf Coast to the East Coast and the Mississippi Valley. As migrants, they relied on diplomacy and alliances to share land.

Their diaspora continued from the 17th to 19th centuries, though they consistently identified themselves as Shawnee people. In the 1720s, after Iroquois aggressions ended, many Shawnee returned to their homeland in the Ohio Valley, the center of their world. They often hunted across the Ohio River in what is now Kentucky.

By the 18th century, many colonists had settled in adjacent areas and were expanding to encroach on more Indigenous land. Once abundant resources became scarce and poor harvest years made conditions worse as hunting lands and trade were also diminished. Other Nations in the area posed a different threat, as some groups sold land to white settlers, often without the consent of others with equal or superior rights to it. Many groups were forced to move west.

By the 1740s, the Shawnee were gathering together near the confluence of the Ohio and Scioto Rivers, which would later be known as Lower Shawneetown, near mostly abandoned ceremonial mounds. By 1751, perhaps 1,500 lived there. They grew corn, beans, squash, tobacco and sunflowers, searched the forests for clay and nuts, gathered wild potatoes, onions and milkweed sprouts, found springs, and hunted deer, bear, elk and bison.

The town grew to a large trading center that included other villages, families, individuals and various refugees. French and British traders also resided in the area or visited for the opportunities for commerce and diplomacy. There was intermarriage, at times with Europeans. Some of the many nearby peoples in the area included Iroquois, Lenape, Wyandot and Miami. The Ohio Valley was on the great Seneca Trail that stretched from Alabama to New York and was used by Cherokees and Catawbas from the south.

With personal autonomy and ethnic diversity, the region attracted many who prized their independence and the opportunity to interact. But Shawneetown never unified as a community with any influence.

Indigenous leaders regularly met in regional councils for discussion, compromise and consensus. Shawnee diplomacy attempted neutrality and friendly terms with all, including groups like the French, English and Spanish to the west. Their relationships were loose, and they avoided commitments. But in the 1750s they joined with other Nations for military campaigns against colonists who'd overtaken their territories in parts of Virginia, Pennsylvania and Maryland, pushing the Americans to abandon borderland areas and commit to a permanent boundary.

By this time, a European influence could be seen in Lower Shawneetown and elsewhere, with many Indigenous people favoring western jewelry and clothing. They'd continued trading animal skins and furs for guns, knives, saddles, pots and rum. Although a 1754 trader had described Shawnees as "the greatest travelers in America" (Lakomaki, p. 13), they decided to stay and defend their land: a major change after a century of migration and dispersal. A council of Shawnees retained the common goal of lasting peace. While small-scale violence with colonists had been common, numerous peoples began actively uniting against the English in the early 1760s.

Europe's Seven Years' War had bled into land rights battles in North America called the French and Indian Wars. As the European powers carved up their North American claims in 1763, the French ceded their lands east of the Mississippi to England, and west of the Mississippi to Spain. The Shawnee had aligned themselves with the French, and their defeat led to greater British influence and trade restrictions.

A Lenape (Delaware) war chief named Neolin from Muskingum County, Ohio, had gone on a vision quest in 1761 and encountered the ultimate Master of Life, an extremely unusual and even extraordinary event since Indigenous people usually only experienced contact with the Manitou spirits surrounding them. The Master gave Neolin a clear message: they must reject the whites' influence and vices. Bringing his message to the people, Neolin attracted many followers, one of whom was an Ottawa named Pontiac, who began a Pan-Indian movement with followers from numerous groups. By 1763,

3 Ottawa Chief Pontiac

they had attacked and reclaimed the Ohio Valley from the English.

Throughout the Revolutionary War era, Indigenous people resisted the colonists' increasing expansion into what was then considered the Old Northwest Territory. But nothing prepared them for the consistent and unrelenting onslaught of the colonists. The groups were weakened by their limited hunting and foraging grounds, and the focus on war led to less planting and harvesting. Small pox, measles, flu and other diseases from Europe continued to take many lives. American militia and cavalry, when successful in driving Indigenous groups out of their towns and villages, would burn their fields, stores and homes, destroying the inhabitants' hopes of returning. Indigenous Nations were forced to ally with the English against the colonists and eventually came to rely on them for ammunition and supplies

Some continued to coalesce around the idea of joint action and cooperation against a common foe. But they were simply outnumbered by the growth of European settlements in what is now Ohio, southern Indiana and Kentucky. Notable Indigenous leaders made peace a priority, but there seemed to be no way to assuage the colonists' insatiable hunger for land.

Various Nations, as well as the separate divisions of the Shawnees themselves, had different perspectives on how to resolve the situation. Their strength had consistently been in their loosely-knit alliances and independent spirit. Agreement and consensus were always achieved through discussion and compromise, rather than the authoritarian-style rule of the Europeans. This took time and coordination. And no matter how many agreed to a compromise, it seemed there was always a group who'd seize the moment to make a deal and sign away the rights to a parcel of land that was not solely their own. Surveyors and colonists then rapidly moved in and aggressively defended their claim to the territory.

The Shawnees and their fellows had some notable victories and were periodically able to force the colonists back beyond a certain point. But reclaimed boundaries generally did not remain in place for long. Some Indigenous groups migrated further west to St. Louis or even across the Mississippi, where they were welcomed by the Spanish, who were pleased to have them serve as a buffer. But by the end of the Revolutionary War, the English ceded land rights to the American colonists and withdrew any support of the local Nations, considering them vanquished peoples with no rights. None were even involved in settlement negotiations.

The Shawnee and others remaining in the Northwest Territory agreed that they should defend the boundary of the Ohio River, though there continued to be internal disagreements over what they could realistically achieve and how to go about it. But in treaty after illegitimate treaty, the Indigenous people were forced to cede their rights to what is now Kentucky, then Ohio and southeast Indiana, and finally the large Shawnee village of Chillicothe and much of the homelands they'd occupied for generations. By 1800, the group's efforts were effectively broken by hunger and betrayal and the Shawnee divisions themselves had varying interests and could no longer sustain an alliance. They were impoverished and further dispersed. Well-known Shawnee war chiefs like Black Hoof (Catecahassa) and Blue Jacket (Weyapiersenwah), who had long resisted the colonists' expansion, felt that continued struggle would only weaken their people. They were among those who signed away Shawnee rights and agreed to cooperate with the Americans.

The United States continued its consolidation and development of the area. Indiana was split off of the Northwest Territory, while Ohio moved to become a state. President Washington and Secretary of War Henry Knox put forward a policy of support for the Nations that adopted white approaches to agriculture and farming, hoping to assimilate and pacify them. Imposing

4 Nations of the Northwest Territory

European culture was another way the Americans effectively broke up any possibility of Indigenous unity. The Mekoche division of the Shawnee, hoping for peace and a livelihood, agreed, and some leaders signed for payments from the Americans. This created more conflicts, as many Shawnees could not or would not abandon their own way of life.

Chapter 2: Cultural Affairs

Our Creator sang to us in the wind and the running water, in the bird songs, in children's laughter, and taught us music. And we listened.
– Tenskwatawa

The five divisions of the Shawnee were the Thawikila ("Tha-we-gi'-la"), Pekowi ("Pe'-ku-we"), Kispoko ("Kish'-pu-go"), Chillicothe ("Cha-la-e-kau'-tha") and Mekoche ("May'-ku-jay"). Many historical towns named Chillicothe in Ohio and Missouri are testaments to the Shawnee division, as Piqua and Pickaway are named after the Pekowi division. Traditionally, the Chillicothe and Thawikila tended to political and general tribal matters. The Mekoche were focused on health and wellness, the Pekowi on religion, ritual practices and maintaining order; and the Kispoko were warriors. Each division had its own chiefs, and there continued to be significant differences of opinion within the divisions over how to address American aggressions. But by the early 19th century, due to migrations and intermarriage, the original divisions were mixed and often indistinguishable.

The group followed animals in winter, when men hunted, and formed villages in summer, when women tended crops. Their individual homes or wigwams were made from saplings covered with bark, and they also built larger wooden lodges. They used flat stones to create sweat lodges and tombs for their dead.

The Shawnees were loosely-knit, never compelling anyone to stay. They'd developed autonomy, mobility and lasting kinship networks, and members often travelled to visit distant kin. They also had enduring connections with other Nations, and some of the most cooperative were with the Wyandots and Lenapes in Ohio and the Creeks in Alabama.

The concept of reciprocity was important to Indigenous people, whether in personal relationships, with Nature or outsiders. Gifts created an obligation for a future exchange and ensured continued peaceful relations. Harmony and cooperation were significant values, and they sought to unite people by encouraging spiritual connections, not imposing force. Effective public speaking was prized. A negotiation process could take years of open communications with meetings in lodges or council houses to discuss common concerns. The process was one of collective decision-making, arbitration and mediation as a means of sharing power, unlike the top-down hierarchical model of the Europeans.

Fair compensation was also an important principle. The Shawnee legal tradition allowed for a murder to be balanced with ritual gifts of valuable wampum beads to the victim's family. They sometimes practiced what was called a mourning war: when too many tribal members were lost to disease or battle, they'd raid other groups to kidnap and adopt new ones to replace them. Prisoners of war and others could also be adopted as one of their own, regardless of their background (as similarly shown in the Kevin Costner film *Dances with Wolves* with the Lakota Sioux).

Creditors could seize property with similar value if not paid. Thieves were reprimanded by a chief for repeated offenses, but if the behavior persisted, perpetrators were whipped. For more serious offenses, such as female adultery, the offending party was driven away. Adults generally married after they turned 20.

Civil chiefs ruled during peacetime, were male, and tended to general, tribal and international affairs. In war time, war chiefs took control. The Shawnee also had a tradition of female chiefs. Peace women and war women made decisions regarding planting, the harvest, and war, and could hold much power. (Shawnee Chief Cornstalk's sister Nonhelema was well-known as a powerful female chief as well as for her commanding presence at 6½ feet tall.) Seniors were respected and sought out for their advice.

Ceremonies and rituals were practiced for war. Initially, a council would have to agree to take action. They might practice war dances in advance, including full dress and face paint to instill confidence. Bathing, prayers, anointing with oils, abstention from sex and taking powerful herbs for strength could all be part of their preparation for battle.

The Shawnee creation story explained how they came to be. Kitchie Manitou or the Master of Life (what the whites called the Great Spirit) created twelve Shawnees and sent them to their Island, which rested on the back of a great turtle (called their Grandfather) swimming in vast waters. They called the continent Turtle Island. The Master of Life gave them the Sun, Moon, food and medicine. Whites were created by another spirit, and it was understood that the two were separate.

Our Grandmother (Kokumthena), their primary guardian, taught the Shawnee how to live. She is represented by the Moon, and is only inferior to the Great Spirit. Shawnees were also surrounded by Manitou, who were primal spirits and natural forces, both animate and inanimate, who could be petitioned or manipulated for assistance. (Shawnees considered the magnetic action of a compass to be Manitou, a natural force.) The Indigenous people were inextricably linked to their environment. Human activity could also trigger or signal changes in the cosmic order: the relationship was reciprocal.

People were an integral part of the natural world with a responsibility as trustees. All other creatures have lives and the right to exist, and each plays an important role in the overall scheme of things. Animals and plants were near relations, and clan associations drew some even closer. Nature was to be loved, respected, cared for and cherished for its powers, not controlled. Indigenous people had no biblical fall from grace, and considered they lived in a Garden of Eden, so did all they could to maintain a harmonious relationship. It would violate natural laws to do otherwise. This is quite a different perspective from that of the European Bible, which advises, "...fill the earth and subdue it; have dominion over... every living thing that moves on the earth." (Genesis 1:48, New King James version)

5 Shawnee State Forest, Hillsboro, Ohio

An affinity for Nature was prized. In his meeting with William Henry Harrison in 1810, Tecumseh said, "The Sun is my father, and the Earth my mother; on her bosom will I repose." (Smith, p. 125) Numerous Indigenous groups felt the same way. The great Creek leader and orator Chitto Harjo came to a clear-cut conclusion when he noted that "Anglos will sell their mother." (Chaudhuri, p. 160)

Rivers for the Algonquins were the blood of Mother Earth. Waterfalls, where physical and emotional healing could take place, were also sacred places, as they represented the heart of the river. They were used for meditation and ceremony. Jack D. Forbes, of Powhatan-Renapé and Lenape descent, explains the Indigenous relationship with Nature:

I can lose my hands and still live. I can lose my legs and still live. I can lose my eyes and still live… But if I lose the air I die. If I lose the sun I die. If I lose the earth I die. If I lose the water I die. If I lose the plants and animals I die. All of these things are more a part of me, more essential to my every breath, than is my so-called body. What is my real body? (Forbes, p. 291)

The Shawnee Grandmother was the keeper and grantor of fire. She gave sacred bundles (Messawmi), also known as medicine bundles, as gifts to each clan. These portable collections of sacred and spiritually powerful items were used for ritual and ceremony; they also provided for communications with the Creator. (Many Indigenous people shared these customs, and sacred bundles from the Aztecs and Maya have been preserved.) Individual totem bundles (Pawaka) were earned for personal accomplishments.

Truth bearers or Tipwiwe such as tobacco, cedar, water, fire, the eagle, hawk, the Sun, Moon, the stars, the earth, corn or pumpkin were among the many common items that could communicate the people's intentions, carry prayers to Our Grandmother and help receive her messages. Since Nature speaks directly to individuals, providing signs and directions, the Shawnee also received messages through sacred bundle ceremonies, dances, signs in the sky and other signals or sounds. These messages often benefitted the entire group.

Dreams had special significance, as part of the soul might travel while dreaming. Elders and shamans could help interpret important dreams. Shamans reached transcendental states of consciousness through natural means or the use of hallucinogens, and shared their visions of contact with the spirit world. Other forms of divination may have also been practiced. Shawnee neighbors the Wyandots placed live coals on a piece of bark representing each party to a rumored war. The outcome depended on how the fire ran: if it did not spread, war was not anticipated.

As the inner life was revered, Shawnee girls and boys went on vision quests from the age of seven (which was unusually young) to puberty, praying and fasting to find their personal Manitou or guardian spirit who would serve as an intermediary to the Creator and guide them throughout life. These were often animals like the bear, wolf, deer or eagle who represented a talent or strength. Many private visions were simply tied to individual insights and connected one with the universal spiritual world. Even in solitude, one was never alone. The most blessed might travel to the Grandmother's world on a vision quest and obtain information about healing, hunting or the future.

At dawn every morning, a speaker would stand on a log and give thanks to the good spirits for about an hour. In addition, regular feasts, dances and ceremonies strengthened the Shawnee connection with Our Grandmother and their environment. Important cyclic events included spring and fall dances marking planting and harvest, when the Creator was thanked for renewal and bounty. The summer Green Corn Dance that celebrated the ripening of the first crops was one of their most significant observances. At that time, the guilty could be absolved of their crimes.

Like many Indigenous peoples across the continent, the Shawnee honored the four cardinal directions, the four seasons and four elements (earth, water, air and fire).

The Shawnee tradition of laws governed marriage, sex, prayer, the importance of continuing their traditions, the services provided by animals and how each should be treated, and stressed the need for humility and sacrifice. Shawnees shared a holistic, cosmic view of the Universe: their people were part of the Earth and they lived in harmony with it.

Chapter 3: Opposing Parties

Sell a country! Why not sell the air, the Great Sea, as well as the Earth? Did not the Great Spirit make them all for the use of his children?
– Tecumseh to Governor Harrison, August 20, 1810

Tecumseh and the Prophet's mother Methotasa and father Pucksinwah were born in Alabama, where the Shawnees had been living with the Creek community. It was a time of great upheaval and change, and they returned to Ohio in a mass migration around 1759.

The Treaty of Fort Stanwix between the Iroquois and British was signed in 1768, opening up Kentucky, including Shawnee hunting grounds, to settlement. Tecumseh was born on March 9 of the same year near Chillicothe, Ohio, and the family noted a very bright greenish-white meteor streak across the sky that evening. Tecumseh's name means "shooting star," "blazing comet," or "panther in the sky," invoking a Shawnee myth of a powerful spirit in the south seeking a place to rest.

Like his father, Tecumseh was a war chief, and principal war chiefs were generally from the panther clan, as the panther is a symbol of strength and courage. Pucksinwah died on October 10, 1774 in the fateful Battle of Point Pleasant. This attack on Virginia colonists led by Shawnee Chief Cornstalk is sometimes called the first battle of the American Revolution.

Tecumseh became a leader at the age of 22. He was charismatic, always respected, and a wonderful speaker. One writer said that he was "born to command," with tremendous

6 Tecumseh: Benson J. Lossing's engraving

energy, decisiveness and cheerfulness. His adversary William Henry Harrison went so far as to say that he was "...one of those uncommon geniuses who spring up occasionally to produce revolutions and overturn the established order of things." (Drake, p. 142)

Tecumseh and his brother Lalawethika both participated in the August 20, 1794 Battle of Fallen Timbers, along with a confederation of Indigenous peoples. Their older brother Sauwaseekou was killed in this engagement, another decisive loss for the Confederacy that resulted in Chiefs Blue Jacket and Little Turtle signing over much of Ohio to the Americans.

Tecumseh strove to unite the Indigenous Nations of the Great Lakes, Ohio Valley and beyond so they'd have more power to negotiate with white settlers. He promoted a Pan-Indian Federation in the early 1800s.

Tecumseh's younger brother, Lalawethika ("Lal-la-e-tsee-ka," translated as "noisemaker," "the rattle" or even "loudmouth,") who later became Tenskwatawa the Shawnee Prophet, was born around January 31, 1771 near Chillicothe, Ohio (see Appendix 1 for the horoscopes of the brothers). He was a triplet, and one of the infants died soon after birth. The Shawnee medicine man and prophet Penaghashea (Change of Feathers) may have suggested that some of the infants be killed as multiple births were unusual and could be a grave omen.

Twins are significant in many Indigenous myths, legends and stories, and provide life lessons. The Maya's oldest known book, the *Popol Vuh* featured hero twins and complementary opposites who overcame darkness and restored light. The mythical, monster-slayer twins Flesh and Spirit are common to the folklore of the Great Lakes region. Creek legendary twins also represent a yin and yang of differences in character; their dualities were connected through shared energy.

Algonquin stories of twins seem similar, and relate to free will:
...the one brother who chooses creativity and truth and the other who chooses destruction and lying. It is a teaching of acceptance and non-duality, since to kill the spiteful one would wound the heart of the good brother who is filled with compassion for him. We learn instead to heal the harmful one of his terrible ways as best we can. (Pritchard, p. 19)

Many accounts simply state that Lalawethika was a twin, and some have spoken of Tecumseh and Lalawethika as twins, possibly as a way to strike a resonance of meaning. Though they were probably born three years apart, the parallel is apt as they were different in many ways. Tecumseh was a warrior and natural-born leader who commanded respect throughout his life. The Prophet was a visionary who'd been disturbed in his early years. While he created a tremendous following, he was controversial, with many questioning his actions and motives, and his public renown did not last.

Unskilled in youth, Lalawethika blinded one of his eyes with an arrow around age ten. He later followed Penaghashea to become a medicine man, but didn't support his family well and may have already became an alcoholic in his twenties. He was angry and could be aggressive with women, abusive toward his wife, and was said to steal for liquor. But he had visions. In one he learned he could not be killed; in another, he was brought to the Creator and shown all of his flaws.

Penaghashea passed in 1805, perhaps during an influenza epidemic that winter. Shortly after he died, as Lalawethika sat before the fire to light his pipe, he collapsed. Not breathing, the family thought him dead. When he regained consciousness, he shared a revelation: he had met the Creator and was told to warn the Indigenous world. His vision showed two paths: one that led to health and happiness and the other to continued misery and poverty.

The Shawnee should be independent and self-sufficient as before. They needed to revive their traditions, reject the vices of the whites and give up drinking and stealing (Lalawethika changed his own path and did both himself). Some of his suggestions were more radical: Indigenous people should return to their own dress and leave white spouses and children. They must quit the fur trade as it created a dependence on Europeans and an imbalance in Nature. They shouldn't raise or eat white domestic animals like chicken, pigs or cattle.

While Shawnee children were usually named for natural spirits or energies by an elder, they'd also change names after major life developments such as a significant wound, illness or personal transformation. Lalawethika changed his name to Tenskwatawa ("Ten-squat'-a-way"), which means "The Open Door." He later became known as simply the Prophet. Physically unattractive with his dysfunctional eye, he was reportedly also an eloquent speaker who could be both articulate and moving, and many were attracted to his message.

The Prophet banned the personal medicine bags that were spiritually powerful but could be abused. He even abolished the long-standing female councils. Once they had reformed, he believed the Creator would destroy the Americans. He claimed to be able to predict the future; some accounts say he had a bowl with miraculous powers and a belt that made the wearer invulnerable.

Tenskwatawa sparked a re-vitalization movement, especially among younger warriors who were often frustrated with their current status. Many Kickapoos, Lenapes and others supported him, but the movement divided Shawnees. The Prophet wanted all Indigenous peoples to be spiritually and racially united. Together they'd have the influence to oppose illegitimate land deals and President Jefferson's policy of converting them to white ways.

7 Tenskwatawa by Henry Inman c. 1830

But the Indigenous population was already dwarfed by the white Americans who had rapidly outnumbered them. By that time, those in the Northwest Territory were confined to limited lands in northwest Ohio and northeast Indiana, an area that could not support their subsistence hunting and gathering.

In early 1806, Tenskwatawa gained more power as he helped the Lenape and Wyandots identify several witches, a number of whom had become acculturated to the whites, advocated cooperation or sold land to them. Indigenous justice could be cruel, and some were executed. As word spread, more disciples joined the movement from various Nations in Wisconsin, Michigan and Illinois. That spring, the Prophet moved his growing village to western Ohio on the American side of the line established by the restrictive Treaty of Greenville in 1795.

American Territorial Governor William Henry Harrison became concerned with the Prophet's increasing influence. He sent the Lenape a critical message in April of 1806, echoing the biblical Book of Joshua in saying,

Who is this pretended prophet who dares to speak in the name of the Great Creator? Wretched delusion! ...Demand of him some proofs at least of the Messenger of the Deity... If God has really employed him he has doubtless authorized him to perform some miracles, that he may be known and received as a prophet... Ask him to cause the Sun to stand still – the Moon to alter its courses – the rivers to cease to flow – or the dead to rise from their graves. If he does these things, you may then believe that he has been sent from God. (Jortner, p. 6)

Tenskwatawa soon received a report of Harrison's message from his Lenape friends. And in one of the more remarkable synchronicities in American history, a total solar eclipse crossed the Northwest Territory a few months later. In early June, the Prophet had announced its coming to his followers. Then, on Monday, June 16, 1806, he apparently darkened the Sun and brought it back to light again. Skeptics who had doubted his power were now convinced that he was truly in touch with the Creator. And if nothing else, the event established that he was knowledgeable and shrewd enough to counter Harrison's accusations. Tenskwatawa and his followers thereafter became a grave threat to Harrison's dream of dominating the Northwest Territory.

In most accounts, it's presumed that the Prophet did not forecast the eclipse himself, but obtained information from white astronomers roving the area, or a white almanac. Although he didn't read or speak English, he was certainly resourceful enough to acquire the information, though Harrison, himself, seemed ignorant of any forecast by American scientists. But the Prophet was highly attuned to the natural world and there are many hints suggesting that he, himself, may in fact have had astronomical and astrological knowledge.

Tenskwatawa continued to attract more support from various groups as far away as Minnesota. Many Wyandot, Kickapoo, Potawatomi, Ojibway, Ottawa, Menominee and Winnebago joined him in Greenville. Shawnee accommodationist chiefs like Black Hoof in Wapakoneta were upset that the Prophet and his young warriors were undermining their authority. They had grown tired of the long struggle against the Americans and only wanted hostilities to end.

Tecumseh and the elder Shawnee war chief and statesman Blue Jacket joined the Prophet and revived the idea of an Indigenous Confederacy like the one Pontiac had organized to rebel against the British in the 1760s. They agreed that American expansion was causing many of their current problems, and only wanted to continue their own way of life.

Tecumseh sought to end what many considered land stealing. He understood that joining together to oppose it would give them more power, just as the U.S. and Algonquins had the combined strength of individual states or Nations. He determined to travel in an effort to gain the support and cooperation of other

Indigenous groups, arguing that their view was sanctioned by the Great Spirit since the Prophet had gained so much support for his visions.

Governor Harrison repeatedly reported to the government that the Prophet was a British agent. But at this point, the brothers and their adherents simply preferred to keep their options open. Many followers were young warriors who did not want to cede more land to the Americans or adopt their unbalanced way of life. Tenskwatawa's people were asserting their rights to land they had never sold, and hoped for a compromise with the whites. In the spring of 1808 the Prophet and his group moved 150 miles west, settling in Indiana on the banks of the Tippecanoe River near the Wabash, and establishing Prophetstown. The Americans regarded this settlement as a great threat, and solidified their view in the 1809 Treaty of Fort Wayne that stated that all Indigenous people must leave the area.

William Henry Harrison eventually became the ninth president of the United States and was the first to die in office. A wealthy and privileged man, he was born on a plantation in Virginia, where his family had lived for over a century. William's father was the Governor of Virginia and had been one of the signers of the Declaration of Independence. Harrison, himself, would later be related to president George Washington by marriage.

William was born on February 9, 1773. As a youth he was apprenticed to two different doctors, but did not fare well in the medical field. At eighteen, he became an Army aide, perhaps after a failed relationship. Heavy drinking was typical in the military at the time, and at one point Harrison was punished with 24 hours in jail for lashing a civilian while intoxicated. He served under the brutal "Mad" General Anthony Wayne in his vicious campaigns against various Nations in Ohio. Wayne had led the Americans against the Indigenous Confederacy in the Battle of Fallen Timbers (in which Tecumseh and the Prophet had participated), leading to the Treaty of Greenville in 1795, granting most of Ohio to the U.S.

In 1799 when he was only 26 years old, Harrison was elected a territorial delegate to Congress from the Northwest Territory. He represented all lands between the Great Lakes, Ohio River and Mississippi that were ceded to the U.S. after the Revolutionary War, a vast area including much of what is now more than five states. The Indigenous peoples, British, French and Spanish were all considered threats to the area.

Harrison was eventually named Governor of the Indiana Territory by President John Adams and served from 1800 to 1812, a position he likely received due to his family connections. He became a young man with an extraordinary amount of power who was intent on gaining more. He served as head of the militia, and there was essentially no legislature (in 1806, its members were only Harrison and three friendly judges). Harrison manipulated elections, one of which Congress declared invalid, but this didn't stop him. He prohibited Black, Indigenous or mixed-race individuals from testifying in court. The territory had been free, and Harrison reinstated slavery and lived in his own plantation-style family mansion.

When the legislature formally passed anti-slavery laws in 1808, Harrison vetoed them. Abolition-ists and locals opposed his autocratic actions, but his promise to expand white settlement in the area was extremely popular. Expansion was the one thing most colonists, as well as President Jefferson, could all agree upon. Many simply believed the Americans were entitled to the land. A significant part of Harrison's job was negotiating land deals with local groups, and he handled all treaties west of the Appalachians for years.

8 William Henry Harrison, Moses Dawson 1824

From 1803 to 1809, he and Governor William Hull of Michigan made numerous treaties with Indigenous groups for what is now most of Illinois, half of Indiana, much of Michigan and Wisconsin. Many of these transactions are now considered fraudulent, though some were the result of military engagements. With each victory, the U.S. military drove out the inhabitants, burned their towns and erected forts.

Harrison ruthlessly played one group off of another, buying from those with weaker claims to a particular area, bullying some chiefs and bribing others to sell. Some of his remarkable successes were obtaining seven million acres through the Treaty of St. Louis in 1804 and over 2.5 million in the Treaty of Fort Wayne in 1809.

Not all Indigenous Nations had agreed, but all were pushed further west.

When the U.S. split Illinois from the Indiana territory in 1809, reducing Harrison's influence, he felt a greater urgency to drive out the Indigenous people. His goal was to become the governor of a state, and the more Americans who settled in Indiana, the sooner it would attain statehood.

Elder Shawnee chiefs like Black Hoof (Catecahassa) and Blue Jacket (Weyapiersenwah) had aggressively resisted the white encroachment on their lands and participated in many battles for years, at times gaining ground. But after decades of bloodshed and with no end in sight, they had both signed the Treaty of Greenville in 1795. Time had passed, they were still at war and they decided to culturally adapt, agreeing to the whites' farming methods and accepting American annuities. In 1809 Black Hoof brought a group of 500 Shawnees to Wapakoneta in the far northwest of Ohio, where they had agreed to retreat.

Tecumseh, accompanied by 75 warriors, met with Harrison and two companies of militia in the summer of 1810. Tecumseh explained that the land was common property to several Nations, and that it couldn't be sold without the consent of all. He asked that the Americans step back from encroaching on their territory.

The large group of the Prophet's followers needed ammunition, food and other supplies to oppose the Americans, as the area no longer supported them. In November, Tecumseh journeyed to Canada and the British for aid. England wanted their Indigenous allies to serve as a buffer with the Americans and considered the idea of a border state between the U.S. and Canada.

While Harrison continued advancing his career, President Madison and the government were clear that he should not deploy troops, and ordered that he refrain from surveying the area. Americans, too, needed peace. The Prophet and Tecumseh also insisted that colonists keep out of their hunting grounds and not survey the land in preparation for settlement, as they had so speedily done in other areas before. So Harrison sent in surveyors! The Shawnee forces intercepted them and some postponed their work or left. By the spring of 1811, a lawsuit against Harrison's coerced treaties was working its way through the Indiana territorial court.

Harrison had called for war in his dispatches and reports to the government for several months, repeating that he expected the

Shawnee Confederacy to attack at any moment, and accusing them of plotting his murder. He attempted to convince his superiors that it was all part of a British scheme against the Americans. Newspapers of the time echoed his rhetoric about Indigenous savagery and lawlessness. In the summer of 1811 Harrison was given the go-ahead to defend himself if attacked or seriously threatened, but was once again advised to preserve the peace.

In August, Tecumseh met with Harrison again and reiterated their desire for peace but their need for the whites to respect older boundary lines. He advised the Americans that he was journeying west and south to meet with other Nations to garner more support for his Pan-Indian Confederation. Harrison took advantage of his absence to move into the Prophet's area and disrupt his efforts.

9 Artist depiction of the Battle of Tippecanoe

His plan to march up the Wabash was approved by the government. He issued an ultimatum to the group to remove themselves from the disputed territories.

Harrison took about 1,000 men to drive out the Prophet and his followers. By the end of October, they had completed a fort nearby, and marched toward the Shawnee base on the Tippecanoe River known as Prophetstown. Scouts saw them on November 6 when they were about a mile away, and Tenskwatawa sent word that he wanted to negotiate a compromise and avoid violence. Harrison agreed to a meeting the following day and made camp with his troops.

While Harrison had acted provocatively, the battle itself may have begun by mistake. Confederacy guards were on regular patrol and prepared to fight due to the proximity of the American troops. Harrison woke at around 4:15 a.m., startled by a sentry's warning shots. American soldiers panicked and shot two warriors, and the battle began. The Prophet arrived at a nearby hill to chant prayers for protection and victory. But as dawn approached a few hours later, his followers were running out of ammunition and retreated, many abandoning the town as well.

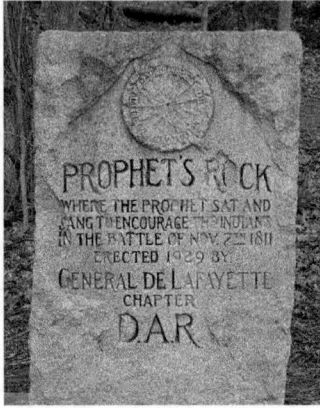

10 *Prophet's Rock Memorial, Battle Ground, Indiana*

Harrison pursued them with his men, brutally killing those in camp, including women and children. They confiscated food and burned Prophetstown and its winter stores of corn and beans, and set fire to the wigwams so none could return. As was often the case, the whites had outnumbered the Shawnee Confederacy by two or three to one, and had lost about twice as many men. Most commentators consider the battle as something of a draw, with both sides losing men and taking prisoners.

But the battle of Tippecanoe was in some ways a failure for both sides: many combatants were injured and killed in the costly expedition. Harrison was nearly court-martialed in Washington, and there was public criticism of his actions in the northeast part of the country. Prophetstown had been destroyed and Tenskwatawa lost some of his support. The conflict had become more complicated.

Tecumseh and the Prophet went on to join Great Britain and Canada to fight the Americans in the War of 1812, where Harrison commanded the Northwest Army. Tecumseh was killed in the Battle of the Thames on October 5, 1813 after reportedly having a premonition of his death the night before. His body was so mutilated by Harrison's troops that no one could identify him. The Pan-Indian resistance movement in the Northwest Territory was effectively over.

11 *Battle of the Thames, U.S. Capitol rotunda*

With the war's end in December of 1814, the Shawnees were forced to accept land cessions that the brothers had opposed. The U.S. now controlled where they could go. The Prophet remained in Canada, and others joined Black Hoof in the Mekoche town of Wapokaneta in northwest Ohio. But the farming that the U.S. had prescribed was by now completely disrupted, and in 1817, tribal leaders relinquished most of their Ohio land.

The United States eventually allowed the Prophet to return to help persuade others to emigrate to Kansas as part of their relocation of all Indigenous peoples. Tenskwatawa brought about 250 to Kansas in 1826. The Indian Removal Act of 1830 formalized the United States' policy of ethnic cleansing, and forced all Nations to move to government designated lands west of the Mississippi.

Despite William Henry Harrison's efforts to allow slavery, Ohio had entered the Union as a free state in 1803. As the Ohio River bordered slave states to the south, early migrants to former Shawnee towns like Chillicothe included free Blacks. The Underground Railroad aided escaping slaves coming north, who crossed the river to freedom.

Around 1832, the American lawyer and artist George Catlin painted Tenskwatawa's portrait. While he had worn some European-style clothing in an earlier picture by James Otto Lewis, he was now dressed in traditional garb. He held what the artist called his "medicine fire," a rod with feathers (perhaps a prayer stick) in one hand and sacred beads in the other, with strings of wampum necklaces around his neck. He was almost 60 and the artist found him "silent and melancholy." (Edmunds, p. 187)

12 Tenskwatawa: George Catlin, 1832

The Prophet died in November, 1836 at age 65 in Kansas City, Kansas.

Harrison went on to be elected a Congressman and Senator. He ran for president in 1836 and was later elected in the "zero year" of 1840. His campaign slogan, "Tippecanoe and Tyler Too," referred back some 30 years to the battle against the Prophet's forces, capitalizing on a campaign that he had never really won. Harrison, then 68 and the oldest president to date, delivered the longest Inaugural address in history in freezing weather without a hat, coat or gloves. Vulnerable to

13 William H. Harrison, Albert Gallatin Hoit, 1840

indigestion, it's currently thought he succumbed to gastroenteritis and pneumonia a month later, becoming the first in a long line of presidential fatalities connected with the Shawnee brothers in legend.

PART II: THE MYSTERY

Chapter 4: Sacred Space and Time

What's on the earth is in the sky; and what's in the sky is on the earth.
– Stanley Looking Horse, Lakota.

History has justifiably characterized William Henry Harrison as playing a pivotal role in the destruction of the Indigenous resistance movement in the Northwest Territory, though Christian values nevertheless judged his actions as brutal and unfair. There was good reason for the Shawnees to resent Harrison and the United States for taking their land and livelihood. Retribution was certainly understandable. But could they possibly place a general curse on an entire country and generations of American leaders? Probably not. And "bad magic" would create an imbalance in the natural order.

The Shawnees, like most Indigenous peoples, honored the natural world. Humans had an integral role to play within it. Being part of Nature meant understanding and respecting it, and taking the time to truly know and celebrate all of Earth's cycles. They honored the spiritual world, their inner lives and the many unseen energies around them. Medicine people were trained by experienced practitioners and worked closely with individuals who needed healing. Tenskwatawa was a medicine man, but as he also experienced visions, he became a shaman, too, someone able to directly encounter higher metaphysical realms.

Because the Shawnees considered themselves part of a living environment, spiritual ceremonies and rituals strengthened them. They thanked the Manitou and Our Grandmother for their help and called on their cooperative relationships with the natural forces that surrounded them. The shared energies reinforced their relationship and ensured cooperation. One was obliged to be humble and respect all other creatures for the part they played in the grand scheme of things.

Their close kinship with the natural world made living in balance with other spirits and energies vitally important. The Moon was the Shawnee's Grandmother. Tecumseh had stated that, "The Sun is my Father, the Earth is my Mother." (Smith, p. 125) In transcribed speeches, he addressed Harrison and his fellows as "Brother," and referred to the U.S. President as the "Great Father." These titles could sometimes be diplomatic, but more importantly, provided an acknowledgement of their sacred connections and inter-related destinies. All were gifts of the Creator, to be recognized with thanks and sometimes payment.

As in the ancient western world, humans' intimate connections with the gods, their petitions, prayers and offerings could have an influence on one's destiny The Hebrews, Greeks, and Romans all made offerings of animals or food to ensure positive outcomes. Ancient Mesopotamians sometimes installed a substitute king during eclipses to protect the real king from any celestial penalty. (Once the danger was past, the imposter was executed.)

The people of the Ohio Valley had the utmost respect for Nature, as it sustained their lives. Members of the community would all be involved in what we might today see as magic: calling on natural powers in ritual and ceremony to ensure a good harvest or luck in hunting or battle. These exchanges of energy fulfilled reciprocal obligations and maintained harmony. They may have used various colors, feathers and plants or totems to symbolize animals, spirits or forces of Nature in order to contact the powers they were invoking. The winds might represent action, or a stone, endurance. Each animal had its own kind of magic. The eagle, bear, buffalo, wolf and horse were older relatives who taught life lessons, and many people could easily access their energies. Songs, drumming, deer hoof rattles and dances added to the rituals. Masks could symbolize a disease or evil spirit in rituals or ward off negative energies.

Ceremonies often incorporated articles from medicine bundles, which were hide bags containing various magical items needed for the proper execution of rituals. Symbols such as a circle were used to represent the cycle of the seasons, the path of life or the connection with Nature. Medicine people or calendar priests determined the timing of important seasonal celebrations based on solar or lunar cycles.

Honoring tradition and respecting the knowledge of the elders was vitally important. But as many groups held taboos against sharing stories and information, those in the outside world cannot know all about them. Tobacco, for example, indigenous to the Great Lakes area, was the first plant given to the people by the Creator. Indigenous tobacco differed from modern commercial tobacco, was not inhaled when smoked, and was not used for personal gratification. Smoking was a form of prayer.

Tobacco had special significance and was used as an offering both every day and in special ceremonies, always with positive thoughts and feelings. Tobacco was held in the left hand, closest to the heart. Its use signaled an exchange of energy, and common ceremonies included communication with the spirit world, carrying thanks or prayers to the Creator, the Manitou, spirits of plants and animals, or medicinal use.

Shawnees tossed tobacco into a fire during major ceremonies. The smoke alerted Our Grandmother that a message was coming and drew the prayers to her.

Tobacco could be mixed with sage, cedar, red willow bark or sweet grass as an ingredient in sacred bundles or sacred fires, was burned to clear energy from homes, and used in healing. It could also be offered as a gift, or to request help from another, strengthening friendships. The dried leaves were put down at the beginning of a trip or when moving into a new place, at the start of a birth, and in naming, marriage or death ceremonies in order to solicit blessings for these events.

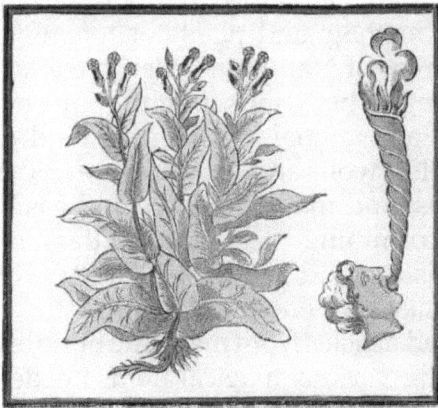

14 *Indigenous tobacco and smoking: Lobel, 1570*

An offering of tobacco before crossing a dangerous river helped ensure a safe passage and appease potentially malevolent deities. In hunting, fishing, harvesting or taking anything from the Earth, tobacco was used to ask permission and forgiveness and to formally honor the other creatures for giving up their lives. Planting tobacco was also tied to the seasons and some groups planted before the first full Moon of spring. The timing and procedures for harvesting were also important, and included rituals and ceremonies.

Nature empowered both individuals and the community, and human efforts sustained harmony. Hunting and killing more than was needed for food, committing murder, or unnecessarily destroying plants or other creatures showed disrespect for the laws of Nature and ultimately created an energy imbalance. The Prophet saw the hunting and trading of animal skins as disruptive of natural laws because lives were taken and the meat and other valuable body parts often wasted, upsetting the natural order.

Motshee Monitoo was the one evil spirit or "mean creature" recognized by the Shawnee (Kinietz and Voegelin, p. 41), and it could enter into people or animals. Indigenous groups felt witches used natural energies improperly. Unclean matter like dog feces, rot and pollution would lead to disease or illness.

Europeans, too, abused the environment, and many Indigenous people viewed Europeans as insatiable monsters who destroyed the natural world through greed and gluttony. Europeans often perceived the environment exactly as they viewed the Indigenous peoples: as wild, untamed and even savage. Their materialist perspective led them to acquire land and exploit its resources for their own personal gain. This created imbalance and, like the Greek hubris, showed arrogance toward the Creator's gifts, in direct contrast with the Indigenous belief in the sacredness of the Earth and the harmonious interrelationships between Nature and its creatures.

While something like a curse was not unheard of in the Shawnee world, their philosophy and belief system would frown upon it. Though we don't know much about Shawnee cosmology, Tenskwatawa's connection with both an eclipse prediction and a cyclic 20-year so-called "curse" suggests astrology and its repeated patterns. But little has been published about Indigenous astrology in what is now North America.

What can we find that would support the possibility of an astrological tradition for the Shawnees? We know that the Indigenous cultures to the south had full-blown astrologies that were integrated into their daily experience, religious beliefs and ceremonial practices.

The Maya were one of the most highly developed cultures that we know of in the west, and a major influence in the history of Central America. With a significant astrological tradition, they thrived from approximately 1,800 BCE to around the 12th century, with their civilization at its peak in the 7th century. When the Spanish conquered the New World in the 1500s, they suppressed what they considered to be their heathen ideas. This may have been understandable as some were practicing ritualized human sacrifice. But Spanish priests also burned most of their books and manuscripts, so few of their records survive.

Maya people in Guatemala and Mexico today continue to practice regular ceremonies to maintain their relationship with the land and their calendar, and to keep the Earth in balance. These rituals may ask for rain, thank the spirits for a good harvest or celebrate the New Year, sometimes with offerings. Four altar stones represent the cardinal directions, with one in the center marking the connection between the Earth and sky.

The Maya had a unique system of astrology and organized their lives around the calendar and celestial movements. They maintained observatories, and a few of their eclipse prediction tables and almanacs have been preserved. Their astrology influenced later cultures like the Aztecs in Mexico. (The astrology commonly practiced in the United States today is imported from Europe, the Middle East and India.)

One of the basic Maya units was 20, and there were 20 signs in the Maya calendar, one for each of their days, not unlike our twelve zodiac signs. In addition to the 20 day-signs, another essential unit for the Maya was called a katun, a period of 20 years of 360 days each (exactly 7,200 days), close to the Jupiter-Saturn conjunction cycle. The katun periods were significant, and the Maya had cyclical prophecies based on them. At the end of each katun they erected stelae, engraved stone towers that still stand in various places, to mark historical events and new political regimes. The much publicized Maya "doomsday" of 2012 was the end of the last katun, considered to be the darkness before the dawn of a new cycle.

Maddeningly, we know little about Maya astrology. Though it is intriguing that important 20-year periods also appear to be significant in the U.S. presidency.

Some later Maya manuscripts, called books of Chilam Balam, were saved. Chilam Balam might be the best known Maya shaman or prophet, and he lived at the time of the Spanish conquest. The name Balam means jaguar, which was one of the day-sign names, and also symbolized the Maya priesthood. Balams for the Maya were four protective spirits who moved through the night (shooting stars were seen as the cigar stubs they threw away). In the beginning of the 16th century, Chilam Balam had predicted that bearded men from the east would arrive and introduce a new religion. The people expected the return of one of their gods, Quetzalcoatl, and his priests, but instead the Spanish arrived at Yucatan and subsequently destroyed much of it.

The rescued books of Chilam Balam were written after the Spanish conquest, using the Spanish script and the Maya language. They're books of prophecy, and several have been translated and are differentiated by the location where they were written. They note the types of events expected in each 20-year period of the katuns.

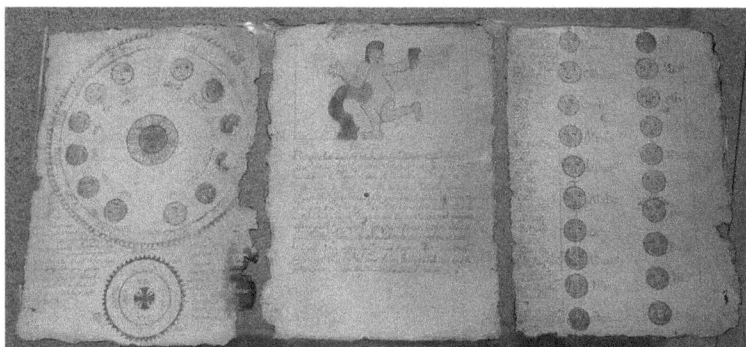

15 Book of Chilam Balam of Ixil

History was cyclic and would repeat itself: similar events and themes would recur when a katun returned, providing continuity by linking the past and the present with the future. Like many of our older western astrology almanacs and guides, these books included some history and often forecast dire events like a plague of locusts, fires and death. And they're also a little obscure and difficult to understand. Some include drawings for each katun with the year number. The *Chilam Balam of Chumayel* for example, literally listed and illustrated the zero years of 1680, 1700, 1720, and so on, alongside corresponding forecasts. (There had been notable calendar reforms in the early 16th century and various cities had different dates for the beginning of their cycles.)

In the book of prophecy from Chumayel, the first katun, 11 Ahau, is correlated with 1540, when the foreigners arrived in their land (the accompanying drawing of the Lord of the Year included the European year). The prophecy states in part that, "There shall be sufficient poison and also ropes to hang their lords [or fathers]." (Roys, p. 148) And, "Prepare yourselves to endure the burden of misery which is to come among your villages... It shall burn on earth, there shall be a white circle in the sky, in that katun in time to come..." (Roys p. 149)

A white circle is mentioned twice in the description of this katun, and may refer to an annular eclipse anticipated in the next 20 years. There were two annular eclipses visible from Yucatan, on February 14, 1542 and July 10, 1553. Both were

Fig. 34—The lord of the katun. (Chumayel MS.)

16 Katun 5 Ahau (1600) Roys' Chilam Balam

somewhat off the central path of the eclipse and might not have provided the full ring of solar fire expected, but would have nevertheless been influential astrologically, as all eclipses are. (Since the books of Chilam Balam are historical chronicles, they may have been drawn from earlier centuries when more evident eclipses occurred.)

17 Photo of an annular eclipse, 10/3/05

The next katun, 9 Ahau, is labelled 1560, when the Spanish began imposing Christianity on the people. 1580 brought katun 7 Ahau (the key numbers move backwards in time), when "Heaven and earth are truly lost to them... Then the head-chiefs of the towns, the rulers of the towns, the prophets of the towns, the priests of the Maya men are hanged. Understanding is lost; wisdom is lost." (Roys, p. 151)

The fourth katun is called 5 Ahau and is correlated with 1600. The text prophesizes challenges for the ruler, official deceptions (even treachery), avarice, hangings, pestilence and low birth rates. Battles between warrior chiefs may be metaphorically indicated by animals like the kinkajou and jaguar.

The katun prophecies regularly anticipated changes in leadership, challenges to authority and wars. The Maya believed in an "Ahau principle," which posited that their kings were conceived supernaturally and had divine intelligence and power (somewhat similar to western kings who were often thought to rule by divine right). The word Ahau in Maya means king, lord, Sun or light, essentially a prominent leader. For the Maya, the king derived power from Nature and specifically from the sky deities. The planets legitimized or authenticated their rulers: "To be Maya was to be part of the patterns of history formed by the actions of kings within the framework of sacred space and time." (Schele and Friedel, p. 215)

A king named Yax Pak, whose name translates to "New Sun on the Horizon," lived in Honduras in the 8th century. We know about his reign from inscriptions on ruins, monuments and stelae, stating when he came to power and mentioning important celebrations and wars. Archaeoastronomers and anthropologists have found that many of these memorialized events were tied to the movement of Venus, and for Yax Pak, Venus was connected to his power and authority. The monuments always provide the dates when the stelae were dedicated, and the dates, when analyzed, show important movements or turning points in the cycle of Venus. The motion of Venus was seen as mirroring events on earth. Temple windows may site Venus at its maximum south or at its stationary point, for example, and buildings and even entire plazas may have been built with celestial orientation and used to observe the planets.

The cosmology of the Aztecs in Mexico from the 12th to 16th centuries was similar to that of the Maya before them. They had a cyclic view of time and followed a divinatory calendar of feast days that astrologer-priests would also interpret for births, marriages, journeys and the elections of chiefs.

When Hernán Cortés and his entourage arrived at the capital of Tenochtitlán in 1521, they witnessed priests at the Great Temple slicing the hearts of sacrificial victims out of their chests in ritual human sacrifice. This was done at certain dates in the calendar to reinforce the Sun's continued presence. Often the victims were prisoners of war. We can see these practices as extreme examples of Indigenous people's communal acceptance of the essential order of things and their reciprocal relationships with Nature, sharing a tangible demonstration of the difference between winners and losers. As in the food chain, some must die so that others may live. The ancient Aztecs explored the boundaries between life and death, and in an odd way, also honored the courage and heroism of the vanquished.

18 Aztec capital Tenochtitlan model, Mexico City

Ritual bloodletting was another example of reciprocity. The gods had created humans by sacrificing parts of their own bodies, and the rulers were participating in a circle of life, so to speak, by offering their own blood (or those of victims) back to them.

We ultimately know little about how the Aztecs or Maya considered the planets, and we know even less about North American Indigenous astrology. But the bits and pieces that are documented suggest some similar beliefs and traditions.

Many Indigenous people of the north observed the sky for ceremonial, religious and agricultural purposes, and used celestial movements to order their lives. Their myths connected them with the heavens. Solar cycles divided the seasonal year and the lunar calendar included named months. These allowed them to hunt, gather and farm at the proper times, and provided context for ceremonies. Some used landmarks, light and shadow in the surrounding environment to predict sunrise and sunset at the solstices. Stars oriented them when travelling and some groups noted the rising of the Pleiades or the stars in the constellation of Orion to fix the beginning of the year. Most held the cardinal directions as sacred, and many based their architecture or city layout on astronomical alignments. They recorded the years and their events, meteor showers and other phenomena on calendar sticks, rock drawings, beadwork and animal skins.

19 *Medicine Wheel, Bighorn National Forest*

In what is now North America, we know that the Hopi studied the Sun in its cyclic movement against various natural features on the horizon. Pawnee lodges in Kansas were observatories; they appear to have watched the Sun and Moon in their cycles as the Maya did. Skidi Pawnee people in Nebraska dedicated shrines to some stars, drew star charts, and their organization of stars actually corresponded with social rank.

We can even see some similarities with the Aztecs and Maya in communities further north and east. If we consider that an 18th century trader had dubbed the Shawnees "the greatest travelers in America," and that the remains of the ancient ceremonial centers of the Ohio and Mississippi River Valleys show evidence of vast trading networks, we can begin to understand how easily a diffusion, sharing, or transfer of ideas and customs may have taken place.

We have difficulty studying the past of North America because the Indigenous people lacked the bricks and stone used by their neighbors to the south. Their earth and wood structures did not withstand the passage of time as well. But we know they studied the sky. Priests or shamans tracked the Sun and Moon to determine planting and ceremonial times, and leaders followed the stars' movements during travel. Knowledge and traditions would be carried by elderly practitioners and passed on to the next generation.

Like ancient Babylonian ziggurats and Mayan temples, the architectural mounds that were left on Turtle Island provided places to not only observe the sky. Perhaps more importantly, they brought the priests and community closer to the celestial gods.

20 Mississippian mound at Owl Creek, Mississippi

There were an estimated 200,000 ceremonial mounds in the U.S. at one time, only a tiny portion of which remain. Creek and Cherokee who lived near the mounds in the southeast part of the continent around 1790 have been linked with the Teuchitlán tradition of western Mexico. (Some of these people may have been described in Hernando de Soto's chronicles of his expedition to America in 1540.) Mound sites in Alabama are some of the larger Indigenous complexes in the U.S. Today, the Choctaw of Mississippi see mounds as ancestral community lands. Their predecessors may have been much more skilled than many assume. When their neighbors the Creeks gave up over a million acres of land in northeast Georgia in 1773, a principal chief established to all that their surveying methods were far more accurate than the white surveyor's compass. (Richard Thornton reported on natural historian William Bartram's account of this story.)

As Creek historian Jean Chaudhuri explains,

The Creeks were at the center of the mound builder's culture in the south, southeast, and Midwestern United States. Their oral history abounds with stories of mounds of various shapes – round, rectangular, oval, flat-topped, conical, and even serpentine. In their oral [history] Creeks were extensive travelers, not merely for trading purposes but also for ritual and natural pilgrimages. They traveled by boat in the Gulf of Mexico and took regular journeys north through the Mississippi Valley into the Midwest and Ohio regions. Again, given the confederated nature of Creek society, they generally had good relationships with such tribes as the Shawnees in the north, which persisted through the rebellions against the Americans in the time of Tecumseh, whose mother apparently was a Creek. (Chaudhuri, p. 6)

Tecumseh and Tenskwatawa's parents had migrated to Ohio from Creek lands before the brothers were born. Tenskwatawa and Black Hoof both confirmed that their ancestors or other Indigenous people in Ohio originally built the wooden and earthen structures as a defense. The Ohio River Valley has one of the highest concentrations of ancient mounds on the continent. They served as social, business and ceremonial centers and some may have originally been built as much as 5,000 years ago.

21 Mound City, Chillicothe, Ohio

Earth and wood monuments in Newark Ohio and elsewhere had probably been used to sight lunar standstills, when the Moon's orbit reaches its northern and southern-most points, much as the Maya used their stone temples. The Sun and Moon could also be sighted against nearby hills. Earthwork complexes in the area contain immense, precisely-drawn geometric shapes with astronomical alignments. These sites were built by thriving cultures with the knowledge and ability to construct large, long-standing public works projects that attracted thousands.

The Cahokia mound complex east of St. Louis was the largest in the U.S., consisting of over 100 mounds in platform and circular shapes with connecting waterways and causeways over seven square miles. At least 20,000 may have resided there in the 11th century, though the city was abandoned by 1600. Great causeways, plazas, mounds and neighboring homes were all oriented to summer solstice sunrise and southern maximum moonrise.

22 Monk's Mound, Cahokia, East St. Louis, Illinois

The largest mound still in existence is Monks Mound in what is now southwest Illinois, a terraced, truncated pyramid with a platform top at the center of its complex. It was 100 feet high and nearly 1,000 feet long (imagine the height of a 10-story building and length of three football fields end-to-end). The mound had a large wooden ceremonial building at its summit and faced a grand plaza framed by smaller platforms and burial mounds. Half a mile to the west are the remains of five timber-post circles. One of these, now known as American Woodhenge, has been reconstructed; it marks the equinoxes and solstices.

The Newark earthworks complex built by the Hopewell in central Ohio included eight rectangular mounds and a 20-acre circle (equivalent to more than 50 hockey rinks) connected with a 60-acre octagon by a set of 14-foot high walls. Three 175-foot wide, walled-in walks (wider than a football field) extended to other mound and circle sites. The somewhat larger Great Fairgrounds Circle was enclosed by an eight-foot wall and a five-foot deep moat. Many believe the Newark site is connected to the High Bank Works in Chillicothe, about 60 miles to the southwest, as it nearly duplicates the circle and octagon pattern.

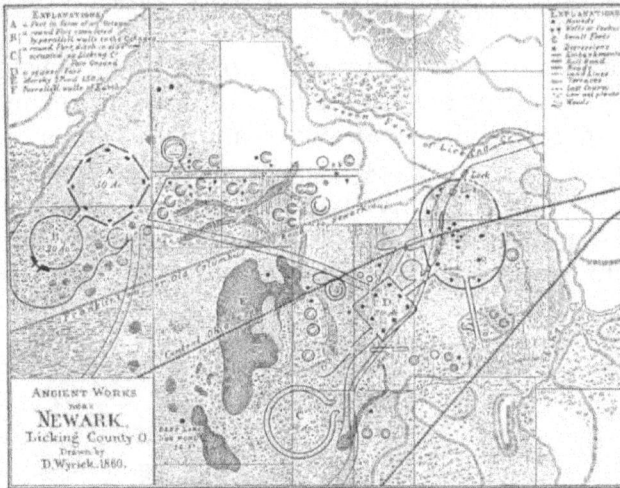

23 Newark, Ohio earthworks: 19th century map

Archaeologists have established that the Octagon and its connected Observatory Circle were built to track the 18.6-year lunar cycle with its northern and southern moonrises and sets, and could have predicted lunar eclipses. Shaman-astronomers would have supervised the construction of these intricate structures.

The straight, 100-foot wide Great Hopewell Road from Newark, Ohio to Chillicothe ran for nearly 60 miles. Researchers have connected the parallel walls and roads of the Hopewell people with the sacred white roads of the Maya in the Yucatan, which represented the Milky Way and the afterlife of the soul.

The Great Serpent Mound in the Shawnee heartland of south central Ohio is over 20 feet wide and runs for a quarter of a mile, shaped like an undulating serpent who seems to be swallowing an oval object. Called an effigy mound, it's one of many that represent animals or figures. Its most accurate alignment is through the head and oval to the summer solstice sunset. But its various curves are also aligned with the solstice and equinox sunrises or sunsets and to several cyclic lunar positions.

As some Indigenous histories see eclipses as being caused by a giant serpent or other creature who swallows the Sun, the Serpent Mound may represent a solar eclipse. Tenskwatawa confirmed that the Shawnees prayed to the four serpents who occupied the four cardinal points. Shawnees also honored a Grandfather serpent who inhabited the lakes.

Creek chronicler Jean Chaudhuri confirms the astronomical importance of the mounds in oral tradition, saying, "...the basic cosmology symbolized by the mound as a platform to the cosmos gave them [the Creeks and ancient mound builders] a common cultural nucleus." (Chaudhuri, p. 135) They provided a place for people to gather for shared religious ceremonies, rituals and other events of importance to the community.

The Creeks were centuries-old associates of the Shawnee, who had migrated from Alabama back to Ohio in the 18th century. Their histories are connected.

Many of the mounds served as observatories for the Creeks. High, flat areas with various arrangements of long poles provided the necessary elaborate sets of empirical readings for answering the basic astronomical questions... they were interested in the 'true' or polar north, south, east, and west; these directions provided important paths or sets of values. Even now, the four logs of

24 Serpent Mound, Peebles, Ohio

the ceremonial fire (which is related to the sun) must be laid according to the four cardinal directions. The four arbors in contemporary ceremonial grounds are also lined up according to the four cardinal directions. After abandoning the mounds, single poles and their shadows and also the North Star aided in fixing the directions. (Chaudhuri, p. 7)

Resonances of similar practices can be seen elsewhere. Contemporary Maya also continue their most important ritual, the fire ceremony, offered to the spirits of the day-signs and their ancestors, to request fertility and abundance. An altar in the shape of the day-sign relating to Venus, symbolized by a circle inscribed with a cross, represents the four directions, and offerings are piled on it. The day-keepers start and tend the fire and chant the sacred day names, and participants may contribute their offerings of tobacco and flowers.

Aztecs believed that at the end of each of their centuries, life would disappear if they didn't renew a sacred fire on the Hill of the Star in the former Tenochtitlán (now Mexico City). The New

25 Maya solstice ceremony at Iximche ruins, 12/21/12

Fire Ceremony was held every 52 years to ensure another cycle of the Sun. Priests led a procession of townspeople to the foot of the hill. The priests climbed it and set a new fire in the altar on top when the Pleiades cluster was overhead to ensure peace and prosperity. Lesser priests then brought some of the fire to other temples in the city and adjoining towns, where they were met with songs and bell-ringing. (The ceremony had once been more gruesome. In 1507, Spanish conquistadors witnessed priests kindling a fire in the chest of a sacrificial victim, while the townspeople cut their ears and threw drops of their own blood toward the sacrifice.)

The Mississippian mound builders (of the Mississippi River Valley and its tributaries) are considered the most advanced culture in what is now North America, and reached their peak around 1300 CE. They've been linked with the highly sophisticated Mesoamerican cultures further south. They, too, worshipped the Sun. As fire symbolized the Sun on Earth, villagers kept perpetual sacred fires and celebrated the power of fire in rituals and ceremonies. Chiefs and their associates resided in large houses atop the earthen mounds. They believed in the active interaction of humans with the spirit worlds of the Earth and sky in order to create more stable and peaceful lives. Their extensive trading networks and ritualized warfare practices share some similarities with their neighbors to the north and south.

Algonquins and Iroquois recognized the pointer-stars to Polaris (our Ursa Major or Great Bear constellation) as a bear or hunters chasing a bear, as do Inuits of the Arctic. The bear effigy mound in northeastern Iowa also reflects the sky. It's believed that fires were burned in these mounds where the heart or head would've been located, an echo of the Aztecs who kindled their new fires in the chests of sacrificial victims after their hearts had been removed.

The Creeks from the south also continued to celebrate a long tradition of sacred fire:

The communal fire, with its elements of earth, air, and water was kept going in the center of the roundhouse all year long, symbolic of the continuity of Creek spiritual life... while each community or talwa or town square also had its own fire. The fire of the smaller town squares would be symbolically kept alive between meetings by using the coals and embers in companion fires in homes and then using them to assist in reigniting the central fire of the square throughout the years... The sacred fire that symbolically includes the energy from Grandfather Sun must be fed, traditionally with a deer tongue. (Chaudhuri, p. 100)

The sacrifice of the deer tongue reminds us of Maya ritual blood-letting ceremonies, when a royal might draw a thorned rope through their tongue to draw blood. Indigenous cultures believed fire was a gift of the Creator; in stark contrast, western mythology depicts Prometheus stealing fire from the gods and being punished as a result.

Shawnees always maintained a sacred fire as well, carrying it with

26 *Chiapas royal bloodletting ceremony*

them on their seasonal travels. It represented continuity, and was safely stored in a lodge and suspended from the roof, said to be everlasting and something like a stone. Fire represented their devotion and the eternal life of the spirit. The Prophet believed they would eventually return with the fire to the Shawnee River to judge the credibility of the white race.

Indigenous warriors were highly esteemed in their society and many ceremonies and traditions relate to war and battle. Battle followed mental, emotional and spiritual preparations and represented the ultimate exchange of energy. The warriors themselves spent four days in purification rituals with medicinal roots and subsistence food to clear their bodies and spirits. They were trained to be stoic. Whether in actual combat or as captives, all parties sought to assert their power in both the physical and metaphysical worlds and test their control of their rational and emotional minds.

The night before battle, Shawnee warriors celebrated a war dance with drumming, song and fight enactments, feasted on deer meat and drank root teas for strength. A principal war chief of the Panther clan would lead them to battle, and the chief warrior of the Wolf clan would escort them home. As we have seen with Tenskwatawa and Tippecanoe, a medicine man also accompanied the men to battle. He might chant incantations and reinforce prayers that they'd be invisible to their enemies or evade them.

As warriors returned from a successful engagement, the group would celebrate with feasting and dancing, and recount recent events and those of other battles. Prisoners brought back would be tied to posts and reviewed by a female chief (or great war woman), who'd ritually thank the war party; they would often become servants or be adopted into the group.

The heart was an important metaphor and heart symbolism metaphysically ties the Shawnees to the Creator and their homelands. As Tenskwatawa related the Shawnee creation story, the Master of Life "would give them a piece of his heart, which was good and would mix it with the hearts which they had, so that a part of their hearts at least should be good." (Kinietz and Voegelin, p. 2)

Not only people but also places were intrinsically connected to the Creator. The Prophet had also said of their creation, "That the earth had not yet a heart as all men and animals had and that he would put them, the Shawnees, at Shawnee river for the heart of the Earth." (Kinietz and Voegelin, p. 56)

The long-lived Shawnee chief Black Hoof reiterated this account. He had probably once lived in Alabama himself, and we can see a similar emphasis in Creek traditions:

The Creeks have been fascinated by the heart since time immemorial, because it represented much of a person's spirit... Creek stories also refer to earlier ceremonial offerings, elevated on mounds, and of youthful hearts, perhaps sacrificial, thanking the sun for its energy. In order to diffuse the energies of the enemy, the hearts of captured or dead enemies were sometimes taken and destroyed. (Chaudhuri, p. 123)

If this sounds grisly to contemporary minds, consider that Christians metaphorically eat their savior's flesh and drink his blood, and are therefore metaphysically going even further in a ritual ceremony to share or absorb the courage of Christ. One way Moravian missionaries (one of the oldest Protestant denominations) explained Jesus to the Shawnees and Lenapes was as a long-suffering warrior captive.

The heart is also strongly associated with the Sun in western astrology.

These few examples show that some ceremonial and ritual traditions reminiscent of what we know about the sophisticated cultures to the south had also been practiced on Turtle Island for centuries. But the mounds had been abandoned before the Shawnees returned to the Ohio Valley and colonists began arriving. The local customs were completely alien to the American colonists and most did not understand anything about them, leading to many misunderstandings.

Chapter 5: Curses, Omens and Prophecies

When the legends die, the dreams end. There is no more greatness.
– Tecumseh

Curses are different than omens and prophecies, but they all add metaphysical meaning to events around us through a focus on the future. "Tecumseh's Curse" implies a broad, centuries-long malediction against generations of an entire country. Is such a thing even possible?

The Prophet had condemned witches when he came to power. Whether his actions had a political or spiritual purpose or both, the Shawnee recognized that there were some who misused the energies of Nature for negative reasons or their own gain. Plants like the mapleleaf viburnum (a low shrub with maple-like leaves, white flowers and berries) could provide protection against curses and black magic. But anything hinting at the paranormal was sure to disturb American colonists.

Indigenous curses are an odd part of the legend and lore of the United States. The 19th century American press regularly published their accusations of abusive treatment by whites, and the need for retaliation was often included. These stories were morality tales for charitable Christian believers who felt the Turtle Islanders should have been treated better. They also served to reinforce Americans' sense of being victors, while ironically also ennobling the Indigenous groups, who many whites still thought of as heathens or even devils. The press coverage of the Prophet and his followers in the early 1800s routinely referred to them as "savages" believed to be in league with the English.

Since many Indigenous leaders were wonderful orators, some of their speeches were given to white school children to memorize for public speaking lessons, and many of the supposed transcripts became fictionalized and exaggerated. The tendency toward sensationalizing these stories in popular American media also seems commonplace.

Logan, a Cayuga named for a white man, had long called for peace. He married a Shawnee woman and later fought under the war chief Cornstalk and with Tecumseh's father Pucksinwah in the infamous Battle of Point Pleasant in 1774. There, members of seven Nations had failed to repel white incursions on the West Virginia side of the Ohio River. Logan's sense of reciprocity and justice was grossly affronted after the murder of his family. His famous address, read at the meeting for peace terms, may reflect his original thoughts:

Such was my love for the whites, that... I had even thought to have lived with you, but for the injuries of one man. Colonel Cresap, the last spring, in cold blood, and unprovoked, murdered all the relations of Logan, not sparing even my women and children... This called on me for revenge. I have sought it: I have killed many. I have fully glutted my vengeance. For my country, I rejoice at the beams of peace. But... who is there to mourn for Logan? Not one. (Barber, p. 385)

The concept of revenge for Logan would have included the lawful taking of life in battle that was approved by the larger group. The quote sounds like what may have been Logan's realistic thoughts and feelings. Thomas Jefferson tells us in his *Notes on the State of Virginia* that the translation of Logan's words was immediately published, circulated, reprinted and used for student exercises. (He recounted his research in an appendix that included correspondence from 1779-1798.) But there are obvious differences between this excerpt and what later became stereotyped Indigenous speech and over-blown rhetoric.

27 Chief Logan the Orator statue, West Virginia

Chief Cornstalk (Keightugh-gua or Colesquo), who led the Indigenous coalition at Point Pleasant, was a Chillicothe Shawnee. The loss at Point Pleasant drove the Shawnees and their neighbors north of the Ohio River border. But Cornstalk subsequently worked for peace. Like Tecumseh, he earned great praise from whites, while still referred to as "savage" in an 1850 account:

Cornstalk possessed all the elements of savage greatness, oratory, statesmanship and heroism, with beauty of person and strength of frame. In appearance he was majestic, in manners easy and winning. Of his oratory, Colonel Benjamin Wilson, Senr., an officer in Dunmore's army, in 1774... says — 'I have heard the first orators in Virginia, Patrick Henry, Richard Henry Lee, but never have I heard one whose powers of delivery surpassed those of Cornstalk on that occasion.' Of his statesmanship and bravery there is ample evidence. (Foote, p. 534)

In late 1777, Cornstalk, his son, and a Lenape named Red Hawk visited a white fort to warn of a coming Indigenous attack, and were taken hostage. Rogue American soldiers eventually killed them in revenge for others' misdeeds. Cornstalk's dying words appeared in print in 2012, 235 years after the fact, and were subsequently repeated in other publications. They seem to have been dramatized for effect in the stereotypical accusation-vengeance format in use for over a century:

I was the border man's friend. Many times I have saved him and his people from harm. I never warred with you, but only to protect our wigwams and lands. I refused to join your paleface enemies with the red coats. I came to the fort as your friend and you murdered me. You have murdered by my side, my young son.... For this, may the curse of the Great Spirit rest upon this land. May it be blighted by nature. May it even be blighted by its hopes. May the strength of its peoples be paralyzed by the stain of our blood. (de Vos, p. 59)

28 Chief Cornstalk from an 1892 drawing

While the idea of an imbalance leading to difficulties for the whites seems appropriate, a curse on the land itself from a peace-making, respected warrior like Cornstalk doesn't ring true. Despite vulgarizations in horror novels and films of the 1970s and '80s, for Indigenous groups, Nature, the land and burial grounds were sacred. Perhaps the following account of Cornstalk's words, reported a little closer to the actual events and reflecting Indigenous traditions, more accurately captures what he said.

When I was a young man and went to war, I thought that might be the last time, and I would return no more. Now I am here among you; you may kill me if you please; I can die but once; and it is all one to me, now or another time. (Howe, p. 366, 1849)

Most agreed the triple murder was an outrage. Cornstalk was buried near a fort at Point Pleasant, but his remains were later moved and a 12-foot monument erected in his honor in a West Virginia park in the 1950s. Nearby, an 86-foot tall obelisk dedicated to the Americans killed in the Battle of Point Pleasant had been completed in 1909, after a delay caused by an installation crane that was said to have been damaged by freak lightning. According to local lore, another lightning strike damaged the monument twelve years later. Paranormal enthusiasts suggest that it's evidence of a curse and Cornstalk's displeasure with his own smaller monument.

Some have called the area between southeast Ohio and northwest West Virginia "one of the most haunted areas of the country." (*AmericanHauntingsInk.com*) Air crashes, explosions, toxic contamination, a bridge collapse, fires and floods have plagued the area and led to many deaths. Numerous sightings of UFOs as well as huge, birdlike creatures have also been reported and were popularized in the fictionalized 2002 film, *The Mothman Prophecies* with Richard Gere (the book on which it was based contained no prophecies, Indigenous or otherwise).

West Virginia actively promotes tourism to reputedly haunted places like the Mothman Museum in Point Pleasant, Lake Shawnee Amusement Park (a long-abandoned park outside of Princeton where deaths of children have occurred) and the 1875 West Virginia Penitentiary in Moundsville (near the largest ancient Adena burial mound on the continent).

29 *Cornstalk monument, Point Pleasant, Virginia*

Is Cornstalk's spirit still seeking revenge? Or are these examples of irrational fear and stereotyping of metaphysical practices and courageous individuals? No historian has ever identified a source for the supposed Shawnee curse on the American presidents, yet one has proliferated in contemporary popular culture. Many of these accounts are obviously fictionalized, with dialogue sounding like transcripts from Hollywood B movies. Sometimes Tecumseh inflicts the curse:

Before one winter shall pass, the chance will yet come to build our nation and drive the Americans from our land. If this should fail, then a curse shall be upon the great chief of the Americans, if they shall ever pick Harrison to lead them… His days in power shall be cut short. And for every 20 winters following, the days in power of the great chief which they shall select shall be cut short. Our people shall not be the instrument to shorten their time. Either the Great Spirit shall shorten their days or their own people shall shoot them. (Connery and others)

More commonly, it's the Prophet who utters the dire pronouncements, as in this example:

Harrison will not win this year to be the great chief. But he may win next time. If he does… He will die in office… You think that I have lost my powers. I who caused the Sun to darken and red men to give up firewater. But I tell you Harrison will die. And after him every great chief chosen every twenty years thereafter will die. And when each one dies, let everyone remember the death of our people. (Poling, p. 12 and others.)

We've seen the parallels with 20-year cycles in Maya astrology, a significant system that we know little about. Nevertheless, the recent accounts don't sound much like curses (invocations to inflict harm). Rather, they may instead be considered prophecy, or, in more common language, forecasts or predictions, which could potentially be astrological.

In February of 2001, astrologer Ken Irving recalled an interesting story in the pages of *American Astrology* magazine, where he shared:

...a conversation some years ago with a Kickapoo (one of the tribes defeated at Tippecanoe) who very seriously stated that there not only was a curse... but that every twenty years his tribe and others would hold a powwow to reinforce it... we were struck by the connection of the Kickapoo with the origin of the supposed Tenskwatawa curse: the land at Tippecanoe Creek was owned by the Kickapoo and the Potawatomi, who had allowed Tecumseh and his brother to start a settlement there... (Irving, p. 45)

The Kickapoo in Ohio were long-time neighbors and allies of the Shawnees, and many of them had supported the Prophet. But unfortunately the facts are sketchy and don't lead us to a definite conclusion. A curse is hard to prove, especially in light of the common Indigenous penchant for reserve in religious and cultural matters. The Kickapoo gatherings may have been organized rituals to regain balance. And the communal establishment of balance in the natural world is not something supported by modern American values.

A 21st century story concerned a Creek curse on the Talladega Superspeedway in Lincoln, Alabama. After the Indian Removal Act of 1830, the Creeks and other southeastern Nations were forced to relocate to Oklahoma on the Trail of Tears. As a medicine man left the land, he was said to curse the whites. The

30 R. Thrower, Talledega, Anniston AL Star, 10/23/09

speedway was built in 1969, and the various catastrophes that drivers experienced over the years gave the story momentum. So in 2019, officials brought in the Poarch Creek medicine man and ordained Southern Baptist minister Robert Thrower. Thrower performed a ceremony to restore balance to the land, one not usually made public. He offered four native plants (red cedar, tobacco, everlasting and wild sage) to the four winds and prayed for the drivers' protection and that the curse be gone. He added, "This thing about a curse, a lot of times that's people's perceptions." (Demmons, 2009)

Most legitimate histories of Tecumseh and Tenskwatawa, whether sympathetic or not, mention the dramatic eclipse forecast. None of them ever includes a 20-year curse. As we don't have a historical source, the curse is probably folklore or speculation of paranormal events. But it is striking that Tecumseh and Tenskwatawa are consistently connected with both an eclipse prediction and a cyclic prophecy. This suggests that they, themselves, may have been familiar with a sky watching tradition or known something about astronomy and astrology themselves.

Omens, in contrast, are natural events that may be considered signs with meaning, or that signify events to come.

A bright comet had been sighted by astronomers in the spring of 1811, and was visible for 260 days (nearly ten months or a full Maya Tzolkin count), a tremendous length of time and one of the longest known periods of visibility prior to Comet Hale-Bopp's appearance in the 1990s. But it wasn't until September of 1811 that its curved and unusually long, forked tail approached 10° across, longer than an outstretched fist. Great comets like this one come along once in a generation, and were much more notable before modern light pollution lessened their impact. Novelist Leo Tolstoy captured the awe and wonder felt by many who viewed comets before the days of light pollution in his book *War and Peace*:

Above the dirty, ill-lit streets, above the black roofs… an immense expanse of dark starry sky presented itself to his eyes. Almost in the center of it, above the Prechistenka Boulevard, surrounded and sprinkled on all sides by stars but distinguished from them all by its nearness to the earth, its white light, and its long uplifted tail, shone the enormous and brilliant comet of 1812 [sic] – the comet which was said to portend all kinds of woes and the end of the world.

In [the wealthy heir] Pierre, however, that comet with its long luminous tail aroused no feeling of fear. On the contrary he gazed joyfully, his eyes moist with tears, at this bright comet which, having traveled in its orbit with inconceivable velocity through immeasurable

*space, seemed suddenly – like an arrow piercing the earth – to remain
fixed in a chosen spot, vigorously holding its tail erect, shining and
displaying its white light amid countless other scintillating stars.*

In Europe, the comet of 1811 was called Napoleon's comet. The
emperor had been born a week after the first sighting of the great
comet of 1769 and believed it protected him. He may have seen it
as a sign of victory; many feel it emboldened his disastrous
invasion of Russia in the spring of 1812 (though the comet itself
had substantially faded by January of that year).

31 Comet of 1811, Jean-Michel Faidit

Comets had been seen as ill omens for millennia because their
appearance was unexpected, in stark contrast to the regular
movements of the planets, Sun and Moon. Those with long tails
were expected to augur the deaths of important people, and have
been linked to the demise of Julius Caesar, Constantine the Great,
Attila and Muhammad. Comets were also believed to be
harbingers of the strange, unusual and drastic. Even catastrophic
events like war, invasions, revolution, plague, extreme weather,
crop failures and other disasters (like the destruction of Sodom
and Gomorrah and the Battle of Hastings in 1066) have been
linked to comets.

Ten years before Cortés arrived in Yucatan, a comet appeared.
Moctezuma's astrologers couldn't interpret the omen
satisfactorily. But the wise Nezahualpilli and his court viewed it
as a grave omen, and it may have been associated with his
prediction of the arrival of newcomers and the destiny of the

kingdom. (Some had expected the cyclic return of the god Quetzalcoatl from the east.)

Comets also have a long association with the births of leaders, and supposedly heralded such diverse individuals as Krishna, Abraham, Buddha, Lao-Tze, Asclepius and even President Franklin D. Roosevelt. When highlighted in an astrological horoscope, they may indicate prominent or unusual people (perhaps Mark Twain was one of them, as he was born during the appearance of Halley's comet in 1835 and famously forecast his exit in 1910 when it returned).

As Tecumseh travelled south in the fall of 1811 to urge other Indigenous groups to unite against the Americans, the comet blazed brightly in the sky. Many would have taken it as a sign. To the Shawnee and many other Nations, the Sun, Moon and stars are animate beings who convey important messages from the Master of Life.

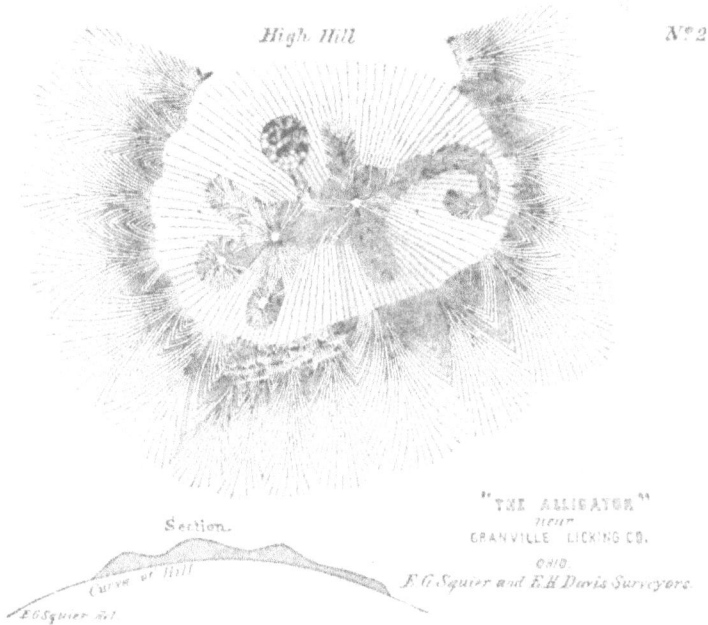

32 Alligator Effigy Mound in Granville, Ohio, 1891

Falling stars or meteors like the one that marked Tecumseh's birth were associated in Shawnee legend with a panther jumping from one mountain to another. Some researchers speculate that the alligator effigy earthwork in Ohio represents a panther.

The Incas' descendants, the Quechuas, continue to believe that seeing a panther is a lucky omen. For the Shawnee and Nations like the Ojibway, Creek, Chickasaw and Seminole, as well as the Pueblo of New Mexico, the panther was a noted clan animal, a leader and warrior of the animal kingdom, symbolic of powerful hunters.

When the comet was visible in September, it appeared south of the pointer stars in the Big Dipper, or constellation of the Great Bear. The Iroquois similarly associated this star group with three hunters pursuing a bear.

Tecumseh was named for a meteor, and he and the Prophet were both of the panther clan. So he may have especially been seen as a messenger associated with the celestial visitor, with the comet itself a sign signaling his coming. His biographer, John Sugden, states that Tecumseh, himself, suggested the connection. As he met with various groups, the comet was at its brightest, making the association an obvious one.

The comet was visible in the night sky when the most violent series of earthquakes in U.S. history struck the central Mississippi Valley. From December of 1811 through the following March, thousands of quakes shook the land, centered in southeast Missouri near the junction of the Ohio and Mississippi Rivers. Residents felt the effects of the New Madrid quakes as far away as Boston, Montreal, Washington, D.C., Michigan and Louisiana. Some have estimated the first one, on December 16, 1811, at 8.1 on the Richter scale. Major aftershocks included those on January 23, 1812 at around 7.8 and on February 7 at a whopping 8.8 (only about 15 earthquakes in recorded history have been larger).

The tremendous quakes were accompanied by a rumbling like thunder or explosives. Quartz crystal lights flashed from the ground, and the sky was darkened by smog and dust. Trees were toppled and the Mississippi River inundated the land. Two temporary waterfalls were created, and the Mississippi's current even reversed itself for a time. A 135-acre sand boil (more than five times the size of New York's Yankee Stadium) rose up in Missouri. A lake was created in Tennessee. In the coming months, crevices and fissures running north to south cracked open the Earth. However, fatalities and property damage were not that high as the area was not densely populated.

Animals anticipate the onset of earthquakes and often become nervous and excited or behave in an unusual manner. Snakes in the ground will come out of hibernation. A contemporary guideline for forecasting quakes suggests checking local bulletin boards, as increasing numbers of pets typically go missing before their onset. Certainly a people attuned to Nature would be aware of these not-so-subtle signs and could expect this type of event shortly in advance. Since most Indigenous people valued the metaphysical world, they knew that Nature spoke in metaphors. So they would also view the quakes as ominous signs. Earthquakes, like eclipses, comets and other natural phenomena, all provided important messages.

The breaking of the Earth could symbolize the divisions between the Turtle Islanders and the whites (especially as the Indigenous people would be officially consigned to the western side of the Mississippi in less than twenty years' time). Many felt earthquakes showed the Creator's anger at both the whites' abuse of the land as well as the locals for adopting white ways, underscoring the disruption of their traditions and the lack of harmony in their current way of life.

Some Creeks and Cherokees believed that the tremendous underground snakes who kept order were writhing from a lack of balance above. Their predecessors, the Mississippians, had held similar ideas.

The Lenape and Wyandot neighbors of the Shawnees in the Ohio Valley saw quakes as a result of the Great Turtle shifting his weight and moving the Island. But they could also serve as warnings that rituals weren't being properly practiced, or of other disruptive behavior. In these cases, people had the power to petition the spirits to intervene to re-establish order and balance.

By the end of December, rumors spread that Tecumseh had caused the earthquakes, stamping his foot in anger. In early 1812, newspapers reported that some believed the Prophet had caused the quakes to destroy the whites. If he, himself, didn't originate the idea, it was certainly another coincident sign of the urgency of their situation. But most didn't need to imagine that a particular person caused the Earth to break open. The message was clear: there was spiritual trouble in the land and action was needed to correct it.

Numerous Indigenous people across the continent advocated a return to their traditional ways and counseled abandoning white influences. But by the early 19th century, the situation was complicated. Game had become scarce in many regions and the land no longer supported hunting and gathering. Many were already dependent on trading with whites and were enmeshed with them personally, financially and politically. There were often internal disagreements and even conflict over what actions to take, as the Shawnees themselves had experienced. Radical splinter groups used excessive violence in the hope of driving out the whites. Others prayed for compromise.

Some communities publicized a prophet's visions to gather support for their views, and at times their claims were grossly exaggerated. But legitimate prophecies involving earthquakes among Indigenous peoples are not that unusual. (Both Tecumseh's father Pucksinwah and brother Chicksicka were said to have intuited future events, including their own deaths; Eckert, Note 569, p. 759.) Earthquake forecasts usually included messages.

While observing the 1811 comet after the first quake, the Cherokee chief Skaquaw (the Swan) had a vision of two children sharing a message from the Great Spirit: the quakes were a sign to leave the area. Their lives were out of balance and the whites would be destroyed. The group relocated and escaped further damage from later earthquakes.

Similarly, in later years, the Wanapum prophet Smohalla (Dreamer) had already gained great respect in Washington State for his ability to forecast salmon runs, find fertile fields and foretell eclipses, insisting that his information was from the spirit world. Like Tenskwatawa, he'd advocated a return to the ways of their ancestors. In 1872, Smohalla predicted an earthquake for the area that materialized in the North Cascades quake on December 14, which may have reached 7.0. The next year, Kolaskin, a Sanpoil prophet also in the Washington area, forecast a major disaster, which was followed by the 7.3 Oregon-California quake of November 23, 1873.

Before he died on September 20, 1932, the Paiute prophet Wovoka in Nevada said that an earthquake would show that he'd entered heaven. On December 20, a 7.2 quake shook the area. (As a younger man, Wovoka's vision during an 1889 solar eclipse inspired the Ghost Dance movement.) In a 1959 Spirit Lodge ceremony, the Cree in Montana were chastised for abandoning their traditional ways, and told that an earthquake would remind them of it. A month later, in August, the strongest earthquake yet to hit the area, at 7.2, killed 28, created a lake, and set off major landslides.

33 *Paiute shaman Wovoka*

Did Tecumseh have anything to do with the 1811 earthquakes? He'd left Harrison after their August 4, 1811 meeting, as he and his entourage turned south to meet with tribal chiefs and enlist further support for his nationwide Pan-Indian resistance movement. The group visited with Creek and Chickasaw chiefs in Alabama, the Choctaw and Natchez in Mississippi and Seminoles in Florida. They continued to the Beloxies and Alabamas, then turned north and west, crossing the Mississippi River to address the Osages in Missouri in December. As they moved beyond the Des Moines River on their return trip, the Shawnees stopped with the Iowas, Sacs and Sioux in Wisconsin, crossed Illinois territory and visited the Kickapoo, Potawatomi, Obijway and Ottawa before returning to Ohio in January of 1812. (Tecumseh's movements have been painstakingly documented by biographer John Sugden.)

Most of the Nations they encountered were concerned with their own local problems, with many in the south even more enmeshed with Americans than those in the Northwest Territory. But Tecumseh inspired some to join them in fighting the Americans in the north. Some communities, like the Choctaw and Cherokee, who had warred with the Shawnees or their allies in the past, were not inclined to do more than politely listen to Tecumseh's talk.

There are many reports of Tecumseh's addresses, and most cover similar ground. He spoke about how the Nations needed to unite to repulse the insatiable and unbalanced Americans. Tecumseh was prophetic as he insisted that like the Shawnees, all Indigenous groups would soon be forced off their land. While there are no contemporaneous records of his speeches, the best one we have comes from John Dunn Hunter, a young white man who'd been adopted by the Kickapoo as a toddler, had grown up with the Kansas, and was living with the Osages when he heard Tecumseh speak. Like many, Hunter was inspired by Tecumseh's words and manner and moved by his eloquence. He admitted that he couldn't possibly capture the charisma of the orator or the impact of his words, but he displayed a remarkable memory in his book. In 1824 he recalled that the Shawnee chief had said,

Brothers, my people wish for peace; the red men all wish for peace; but where the white people are, there is no peace for them, except it be on the bosom of our mother.

Brothers, the white men despise and cheat the Indians; they abuse and insult them; they do not think the red men sufficiently good to live. The red men have borne many and great injuries; they ought to suffer them

no longer. My people will not; they are determined on vengeance; they have taken up the tomahawk; they will make it fat with blood; they will drink the blood of the white people...

Brothers, if you do not unite with us, they will first destroy us, and then you will fall an easy prey to them. They have destroyed many nations of red men, because they were not united, because they were not friends to each other.

Brothers, the white people send runners amongst us; they wish to make us enemies, that they may sweep over and desolate our hunting grounds, like devastating winds, or rushing waters.

Brothers, who are the white people that we should fear them? They cannot run fast, and are good marks to shoot at: they are only men; our fathers have killed many of them: we are not squaws, and we will stain the earth red with their blood.

Brothers, the Great Spirit is angry with our enemies; he speaks in thunder, and the earth swallows up villages, and drinks up the Mississippi. The great waters will cover their lowlands; their corn cannot grow; and the Great Spirit will sweep those who escape to the hills from the earth with his terrible breath.

Brothers, we must be united; we must smoke the same pipe; we must fight each other's battles; and, more than all, we must love the Great Spirit: he is for us; he will destroy our enemies, and make all his red children happy. (Hunter, p. 30-31)

Many have suggested that Tecumseh predicted the earthquakes in his speech, when it's likely the first had already struck by the time he reached the Osages. Given how things stood, he would certainly not have been that surprised by them. As the band continued on their journey, the quakes could be felt north and west, and Tecumseh used them as an omen for the diverse Nations to unite and drive out the Americans.

It's easy to see how the story of Tecumseh's travels became linked with the earthquake. Certainly there was a powerful synchronicity of the comet, the quakes, and Tecumseh's movements. The signs had meaning and were closely associated with Tecumseh's efforts to resist the Americans.

Dr. Lyman Draper was a Wisconsin librarian who worked on a U.S.

34 Historian Lyman Draper, 1881 portrait

history of 1750 to 1815 (his year of birth). Beginning in 1838, he wrote to many witnesses of past events. His correspondence shows how Tecumseh's travels became legendary and further linked with the earthquakes. Most writers reported to Draper decades after the quakes.

In a letter to Draper of November 30, 1881, G.W. Stedman shared an account of Tecumseh's speech relayed to him by a Creek chief, which quoted the Shawnee leader as saying,

I am now about ready to take up arms against the United States, and when I strike them a blow, you will know it, as I will shake the whole earth. The ground will give way from under the white man's feet, and he will mire down. I will be on firm ground... (Eckert, Note 602, p. 764)

Another of Draper's correspondents, George Washington Campbell summed up reports from a Creek and Cherokee who had both heard Tecumseh speak:

War NOW! War FOREVER!... My prophets shall tarry with you. They will stand between you and the bullets of your enemies. When the white men approach you, the yawning Earth shall swallow them up. Soon you shall see my arm of fire streaked across the sky. I will stamp my foot and the very Earth shall shake. (Eckert, Note 604, page 764-5)

The above is more radical and violent than what we expect from Tecumseh. While he was a war chief, he was a diplomat as well. In his transcribed remarks to William Henry Harrison at Vincennes before the group travelled south, he was clear and reasonable:

Brother, this land that was sold, and the goods that were given for it, was only done by a few. In the future we are prepared to punish those who propose to sell land to the Americans. If you continue to purchase them, it will make war among the different tribes, and, at last I do not know what will be the consequences among the white people.

Brother, I wish you would take pity on the red people and do as I have requested. If you will not give up the land and do cross the boundary of our present settlement, it will be very hard and produce great trouble between us. (Smith, p. 125)

Thomas Loraine McKenney, a Superintendent of Indian Affairs, also provided an account of Tecumseh in 1838, reporting that he had been unsuccessful in gaining the support of the Seminoles and some others to unite. After Tecumseh reached Tuckabatchee in mid-September and found the principal Creek Chief, Big Warrior, headman of his mother's home town, unsupportive, McKenney related that Tecumseh replied,

You do not believe the Great Spirit has sent me. You shall know. I leave Tuckabatchee directly – and shall go straight to Detroit. When I

arrive there, I will stamp on the ground with my foot, and shake down every house in Tuckabatchee. (Drake, pp. 144-145)

As many of the Creeks, Osages and Cherokees were not receptive to Tecumseh's message, his words to them were later embellished to become a curse. According to McKenney, the quakes began on the date of his arrival. He added that, "We received the following from the lips of the Indians, when we were at Tuckabatchee, in 1827 [16 years after the event], and near the residence of the Big Warrior. The anecdote, may, therefore, be relied on." (Drake, pp. 144-145)

Another correspondent of Dr. Draper's, George Stiggins, born of a European father and a Creek mother, reported in the 1830s or '40s that in response to Big Warrior, Tecumseh claimed "great super-natural power," promising to climb a mountain and stamp his foot three times to "make the whole earth tremble" weeks before the first quake. (Hancock, p. 55)

However McKenney himself had also said of Tecumseh that,

He detested the white man, but it was with a kind of benevolent hatred, based on an ardent love for his own race, and which rather aimed at the elevation of the one rather than the destruction of the other... Though his whole career was one struggle of adverse circumstances, he was never discouraged, but sustained himself with a presence of mind, and an equability of temper which showed the real greatness of his character. (McKenney, p. 46)

Those who have written about Tecumseh are united in their praise of his character. While he may have exaggerated his support and the extent of his role as leader of an Indigenous Confederacy to William Henry Harrison and others, and was always said to have been a moving speaker, he's never depicted as being small-minded, egotistical or vindictive as some of the earthquake "curse" reports suggest.

Discrepancies of fact and tone can be attributed to a natural tendency for writers to elaborate or dramatize facts and events (as in the children's game of telephone). But in analyzing the reports, we should also consider how both Indigenous and western chroniclers recalled these events, how they remembered history and how much their world views differed. As Creek historian Jean Chaudhuri explained, whites were described by them,

...not in reference to color but to the common denominators of radically different European ways and the conceptions of the isolated self, of private property, and of linear time... Anglo historians are compelled by chronology and the written word commingled with conjecture and recorded hearsay. The Creek disciplined elders were governed more by

major spatial events and the disciplined perceptions of the keepers of oral traditions... The Muscogee Creek way of life included key metaphors that were contained in the legends... These key legends were then extended by owalas, intuitive logicians or prophets, who would point toward the implications of the legends for the future. (Chaudhuri, p. 64)

Stories provided history as well as life lessons, and perhaps also anticipated future events. We might say today that Tecumseh was closely associated with both the comet and the earthquakes. He may not have caused them, but there was a synchronicity, with one event enhancing the meaning of the others, as we see in the metaphors of astrology. But we still haven't discovered the source of a 20-year curse. That may be another legend or story. But if we can't identify its beginning, its recent history is well documented.

Robert S. Pohl has reconstructed the history of the presidential curse in mainstream American print publications. In 1934, Robert LeRoy Ripley listed the five previous presidents elected in zero years who had died in office, ending with question marks beside the 1940 election date, soon to be filled by Franklin D. Roosevelt. (*Ripley's Big Book Believe it or Not!*, p. 296) A later edition added Roosevelt's death and a blank next to 1960. (Pohl, p. 56-59)

Skeptic Timothy Redmond cited two subsequent references to a curse. John Hix, in his syndicated column "Strange as it Seems" in 1940 had said,

The man who attains the executive chair for the next four years faces the jinx of a 100-year-old 'curse,' for death in office has come to every President elected at 20-year intervals since 1840. (*Oakland Tribune* 11/5/40, p. 18)

When another 20 years had passed, journalist Ed Koterba said,

The next President of the United States will face an eerie curse that for more than a century has hung over every chief executive elected in a year ending with zero. ("Pennsylvania Avenue Ponderings," *Hammond Times*, 2/25/60, p. 25)

And in 1980, columnist Lloyd Shearer recapped the tale again:

Legend has it that the Prophet, who was the Shawnee shaman, or medicine man, thereupon invoked a curse upon Harrison and his government. The curse was that all future U.S. presidents, starting with Harrison, who were elected in a year whose last digit was zero would die in office. ("Curse or Coincidence?" *Parade*, 9/28/80)

In effect, these non-astrological writers had made accurate predictions based on a recurring cycle. (Forecasting that seven presidents elected in zero years would die is a 1 in 128 probability.) One wonders how they all felt as they watched it unfold!

Chapter 6: Shamans and the Moon

When we see the changes of day and night, the sun and the moon, the stars in the sky, and the changing seasons upon the earth... anyone MUST realize that it is the work of someone more powerful than man.
– Chased-by-Bears, Santee-Yanktonai Sioux

The historically acknowledged part of the Shawnee legend is Tenskwatawa's prediction of a total solar eclipse. Many writers have argued that this was impossible, a clever ruse, since the Prophet's people lacked the written language skills necessary to the expertise to predict an eclipse. The near-universal supposition is instead that Tenskwatawa resorted to the use of a white almanac or obtained information from roving American astronomers, though evidence for these conclusions has not been presented. The judgment is probably the result of cultural arrogance (a sense of intellectual elitism, similar to that used by astronomers against astrologers today), along with ignorance of Indigenous traditions and practices. Could Tenskwatawa have predicted an eclipse?

Eclipses have a bad reputation in astrological lore. Some say they bring emotional instability, discontent and even disaster. Ancient Babylonian cuneiform tablets shout warnings of the death of kings and the destruction of temples under their auspices. Sixth century BCE Chinese classics see the phenomenon as ugly and abnormal. Bible commentators have linked not only the death of Christ, but also the great flood to eclipses. Shakespeare had both Gloucester in King Lear and Othello attribute their domestic mishaps to the influence of the dreaded eclipse. And Joan Quigley, Nancy Reagan's astrologer, persuaded the President to delay announcing his second term candidacy until January of 1984: there were two eclipses the previous November.

Most of us regularly survive at least four eclipses a year, but catastrophic prophecies continue. One can understand why: for all our modern understanding, there's still something spooky about the Sun being darkened and the temperature dropping in the middle of the day, or the Moon turning blood red, a primeval drama in the midst of the information age.

Whether dangerous or not, eclipses remain potent astrological energies that mark memorable events and turning points. A total solar eclipse in Central New York signaled the end of incessant warfare and the beginning of the Iroquois Confederacy as it darkened the sky for over 3½ minutes on August 22, 1142, according to oral history and modern astronomy calculations. The Great Peacemaker (the prophet Deganawida) along with Jigonhsasee (an influential female mediator) and Hiawatha (the well-known orator) were instrumental in joining the first five Nations of the Confederacy together under the Great Law of Peace Agreement (viewed by many as a model for American democracy).

The Maya were great astronomers and astrologers who used patterns of whole numbers in their work. The Maya Dresden Codex from 12th century Yucatan appears to be an almanac that lists all of the partial and total solar eclipses in the 8th century, most of which would not have been visible in the area. We find the same in astrological ephemerides today. While the path of a visible eclipse can be meaningful astrologically, the influence of an eclipse is not limited to its actual path.

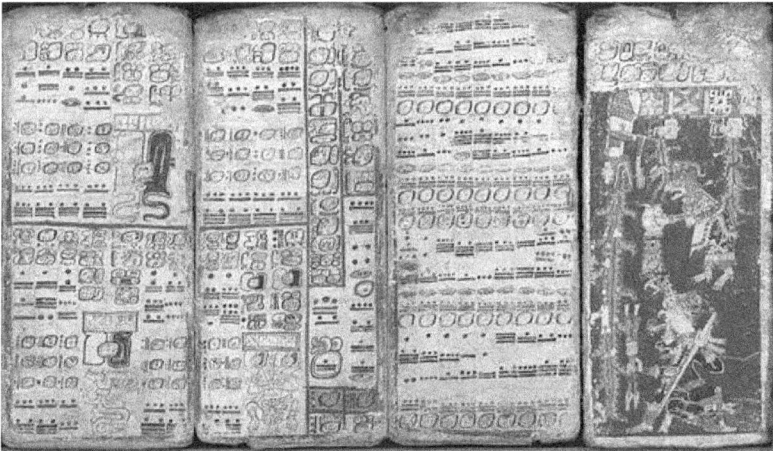

35 Dresden Codex including eclipse tables

Scientists have argued that long-term record-keeping was necessary for the sophisticated scheme of the Maya. But writing and record-keeping were certainly part of many other Indigenous cultures.

The Incas in the Andes used collections of colorful knotted strings, or quipus, through the 17th century; they served as ledgers to record data such as taxes, the ritual calendar, astronomical events and census records. Many were destroyed, but scholars continue to work on deciphering them.

In a similar manner on Turtle Island, wampum necklaces, strings or woven belts of marine shell beads served as documents to record and confirm history, a titled office, discussions, speeches, agreements or treaties. They were used as passports, invitations, warnings, declarations or announcements. A chief could read "Chief Beads." Belts to record important transactions were stored in council houses.

Black strings, beads, fabric, ribbons or feathers on wampum might alert recipients to a serious topic. Red indicated urgency; purple could signal news of sorrow or death; green the topics of life or parenthood. The

36 *Inca quipu*

length and number of strands might also be significant.

The Seven Fires prophecy wampum belt of the Algonquin Nation of Quebec has been preserved for over 400 years. In purple with white diamond patterns, each diamond represents one "fire" in history. Its teachings have been passed down through generations of elders.

Various groups also used hieroglyphic writing on bark, prepared skins or wood. The boundaries of hunting grounds could be written on a chief's robes or skins kept in public lodges. Remarkable events were also recorded on skins, while maps and

37 *Iroquois-Algonquin belt for 17th century treaty*

travel instructions were written on trees.

Biographers R. David Edmunds and John Sugden document many instances when Tenskwatawa sent wampum belts with messages to other peoples and even the whites (at times in secret), with both the British and

Americans sometimes responding in a similar manner. The Prophet told ethnographer C.C. Trowbridge that the belts were used on many occasions by the Shawnees.

Antoine Grignon (1829-1913), a French Winnebago interpretter and trader from Wisconsin and Minnesota, recalled inspirational speeches made by elders like Decorah, a Winnebago chief and orator, whose cane was carved with hieroglyphics. Handed down through his family, the cane was a record of the group's history that he could read. The history and traditions of the Winnebago were also shared through the generations by "word passers," young people who were drilled in past events to provide the next generation with a living history.

38 Six Nations Chiefs and Horatio Hale, 9/14/1871

The Prophet and Black Hoof's separate recounting of the Shawnee creation story and other important events in their history were very similar: both obviously received an oral tradition. Similarly, Creek culture emphasized memory development, repetition, feedback and practice. The most talented students would keep the history. Cayuga Chief Jake Thomas continued the Iroquois tradition in the 20th century, ritually reciting their Great Law of Peace at the Confederacy's council fire every five years, an oration that took three or four eight-hour days to complete. He also crafted Condolence Council canes, mnemonic devices that commemorated the founding of the Confederacy and provided a pictographic record of the titles of the 50 hereditary chiefs. Tenskwatawa made "story sticks" about the size of a ruler with pictographs for his warriors, that included prayers to the Sun, Moon, Earth and fire, and perhaps more immediate news and instructions. Also known as talking sticks, medicine sticks or sacred slabs, they recorded information, much as wampum beads could do. The type of wood, grooves, color of beads, feathers and hide tassels that were attached could all communicate meaning to those in the know. Notches in a stick might count the time to a planned gathering, celebration or battle.

George Catlin, the artist who painted Tenskwatawa and other Indigenous people, also depicted a Kickapoo shaman with his prayer stick. Creek counting sticks provided by the calendar priests and chiefs indicated the timing of community events, planting schedules and more.

Record-keeping was not an issue.

Shamans typically maintained a calendar and timed public ceremonies and planting. They mapped the heavens into constellations and followed the changes of the Moon, studying

39 Kickapoo elder and prayer stick, George Catlin 1830

the stars on cold nights when the light of the constellations was most brilliant. Winnebago Antoine Grignon remembered the elder Big Fire, who he called "a noted astronomer." (Grignon, p. 133) Algonquian calendar sticks kept track of the Moons and solstices. The lunar ceremonial calendar, beginning with the spring new Moon, established order with timed feasts and tributes, connected communities with their past, and gave homage to the ancestors.

The Moon takes a little more than 27 days to return to the same place against the backdrop of the stars (a sidereal month), but there are 29.5 days from new Moon to new Moon. There are also twelve or thirteen new Moons in a solar year. A common Indigenous tool was a turtle shell used as a calendar. The thirteen larger plates in the center of the shell and 28 plates surrounding them represent whole-number figures that remind us of the Moon's annual and monthly cycles. 13 Moons x 28 days = 364 plus a day of rest, with adjustments. It's a lovely metaphor for the similar "as above, so below" idea attributed to Hermes Trismegistus' ancient Greek text. The calendars are also a reminder that all things are connected, as the Great Turtle holds the Island on its back. (The Maya thirteen-day week and thirteen katun prophecy cycle also reflected a lunar cycle.)

In the Shawnee creation story, a Chillicothe had proved his power by "shooting the Sun" and causing an eclipse that darkened the Earth. (Kinietz and Voegelin, p. 8) The Sun was later restored by medicine. For the Shawnee, a solar eclipse is called a "Black Sun," and was a sign of great change and even war to come. (Kinietz and Voegelin, p. 37) Tenskwatawa himself may have also performed the shooting the Sun ritual in 1806, singing it back to brightness like the Ojibway of Lake Superior, who would shoot flaming arrows into the sky to symbolically replenish the Sun during an eclipse.

Tecumseh and Tenskwatawa's clan was associated with the panther, the American equivalent of the jaguar or ocelot, one of the Mexican calendar signs. The jaguar stood for shamans. (The word panther is a common term for several big cats.) Chilam Balam was the jaguar priest of the Maya, and the Shawnee Prophet was also a jaguar shaman.

Munro S. Edmonson, an American anthropologist who translated and commented on the *Chilam Balam of Tizimin*, evokes the partnership of the Shawnee brothers when he talks about the Maya:

The highest ranking priesthood was that of the Jaguar, who governed the entire city for one katun… he was seconded by his spokesman (Chilam) and together they manifested the complementarity (and friction) of variously named dualistic gods. (Edmonson, p. 25, Note 426)

Christopher Columbus famously turned to his almanac to forecast a total lunar eclipse in order to manipulate the Arawak of Jamaica in 1504. Mark Twain had his 1889 protagonist in *A Connecticut Yankee in King Arthur's Court* predict an eclipse in order to escape execution. Commentators feel that Twain was inspired by the Columbus story, but as his fictional eclipse was solar and he grew up in the Midwest, it seems more likely that he was inspired by the Shawnee Prophet's experience.

A lunar eclipse, visible across wide swaths of territory, occurs when the full Moon is shadowed by the Earth, which may turn it a deep red when both are precisely aligned. A solar eclipse's visibility, on the other hand, is limited to narrower areas where the shadow of the Moon blocks the Sun, and can be much more dramatic when total, temporarily putting out the Sun's light. Solar eclipses are therefore more difficult to pinpoint locally. Virtually all commentators state that Tenskwatawa must have gotten his astronomical information from the whites, and refer to the presence of published almanacs, British intelligence or American astronomers in the area as possible sources. Other accounts appear to have embellished or exaggerated reports of exactly what happened.

Tenskwatawa's biographer Adam Jortner analyzes the replication of the eclipse anecdote from one biography to the next over more than a century. He begins with the fact that, "The only eyewitness accounts... were recorded well after the event." (Jortner p. 7) He is also keenly aware that most writers simply accept the accusation that the Prophet faked his eclipse-predicting abilities.

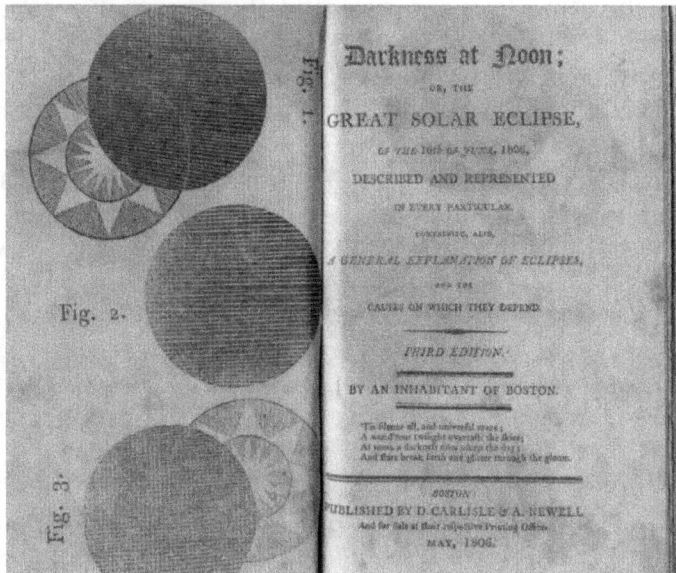

40 The Great Solar Eclipse (Carlisle & Newell, 1806)

R. David Edmunds in his 1983 biography of the Prophet states that "several teams of astronomers and other scientists" had set up observatories in Indiana, Kentucky and Illinois at the time of the eclipse, citing Glenn Tucker's 1973 book on Tecumseh. (Edmunds p. 48) Subsequent writers have accepted and reiterated this story. But Tucker's information in turn comes from an 1878 U.S. history by R.M. Devens, *Our First Century*, that mentions both the 1806 and 1869 eclipses and not the Prophet. The teams of scientists were in Springfield and Des Moines in 1869, but certainly not in 1806, when the area was still considered the frontier. The erroneous 1973 conclusion stuck.

And American expertise was not always so superior or exemplary. Edmond Halley was the first westerner to accurately predict the paths of solar eclipses in the early 18th century. But in North America at the time, scientists may not have been as accurate. Samuel Williams of Harvard University brought an expedition to Maine to study the total solar eclipse of October 27, 1780, but due to errors in his calculations, the tables, or the maps he used, he failed to catch totality.

While western scientists like to assume they have a monopoly on the truth, foreknowledge of eclipses was possible with an established tradition, faith in the elders and a close connection with the natural world, all of which many Indigenous people possessed. But solar eclipses are difficult to pinpoint in terms of location as they have a narrow path. Nevertheless, the Ojibway practiced a solar eclipse ritual, and the Shawnees incorporated it into their creation story and even had a name for it, pointing toward an important tradition.

And it is possible to forecast an eclipse from observation. Eclipses only occur when the Sun and Moon are lined up exactly. If one studies their movements regularly from a place like Woodhenge in Ohio (or a contemporary living room window), the Sun's cycles through the seasons and the monthly path of the Moon soon become apparent. Much research has supported the probability that the Moon's cycles and the extremes of its orbit could be observed from various Indigenous earthworks, and that long-standing cultural traditions were necessary to create these structures in the first place.

Places like the Newark earthworks observatory, where one could view the 18.6-year lunar standstills (when the Moon may also sometimes stray beyond the Sun's path), certainly provided the tools for shamans to forecast lunar eclipses, as Creek historian Jean Chaudhuri informs us:

Creek stargazers, astronomers, or miccos attempted to understand lunar eclipses. Fascination with and fear of eclipses were common in many traditional societies. For the Creeks, however, lunar eclipses were meaningful acts of sheer beauty... The Creeks knew that after enticements (partial eclipses) the final tryst, that is, the full lunar eclipse and its special relationship with the sun, occurred once every eighteen years and, according to oral history, special ceremonies occurred at this time... (Chaudhuri, p. 10)

We know that many Indigenous groups tracked eclipses. How difficult is it to forecast them? Can it be done without western technology or scholarship?

Eclipses follow a definite pattern. Lunar eclipses, when the face of the Moon is darkened by the shadow of the Earth and sometimes turns it a rusty or reddish color, only happen on a full Moon. And more than half of the time, once there's a lunar eclipse, another will follow on the sixth full Moon to come after it. And two-thirds of lunar eclipses will then follow one on the sixth or twelfth Moon after that. These guidelines provide an early alert of when to be on the lookout.

William H. Calvin outlines over a dozen straightforward, low-tech ways to forecast lunar eclipses in his book *How the Shaman Stole the Moon*. When the full Moon rises, it often appears very large and reflects the colors of sunset. If it rises immediately before the sun sets, it also ensures the that Sun and Moon are in the proper alignment for an eclipse. (If the Moon rises even ten minutes before the Sun sets, it will tend to rule out a lunar eclipse, as the Earth, Sun and Moon will not be exactly opposed to each other in the sky.)

Shadows cast at the time of a lunar eclipse tend to be longer. In facing the Moon on the horizon, if one's shadow from the setting Sun stretches just toward the left of the Moon, it promises a much better chance that the Earth's shadow will be cast on the Moon's face, especially for those eclipses occurring a few hours after sunset. The same shadow could also be viewed along a column or post. And two observers sighting shadows between each other and the Moon will similarly either fore-shadow or rule out an anticipated eclipse. Practice with these methods over time would sharpen the observers' skills.

For a lunar eclipse, the Sun will also rise at an equal distance from the solstice point as the

41 Cahokia winter solstice sunrise with shadow

Moon will rise that night (again, this shows they will line up opposite each other in the sky). Societies with shamans who had established these solar turning points would have been able to sight along a string of beads held at arms-length to compare the two distances, once again establishing if the bodies were properly aligned.

An elevated bank, post or tower (all of which are found in remnants of ancient Indigenous earthworks) can also be used as a back-sight to compare distances between the rising Sun and Moon with a notched stick or long necklace. A more accurate method might be to frame the Sun and Moon between a post or column and an elevated bank, the side of a cliff or other natural feature. The Creeks, long-time Shawnee associates, used a pole:

...the Creeks maintained their central information system regarding the sun. Even now, every ceremonial ground has a central pole. With one pole rather than multiple poles on mounds, one can find the polar north and then infer other directions... Additionally, by laboriously drawing the circles between morning and afternoon shadows of the same length, one can find the full length of the sun's apparent 'journey,' that is, the summer and winter solstices. (Chaudhuri, p. 7)

But observable solar eclipses, with much narrower bands of visibility, are more challenging to forecast. They only occur on new Moons, though they also follow a very definite pattern. With a similar six-month spacing, they fall about two weeks before lunar eclipse dates. If a partial lunar eclipse is seen, it's more likely that a solar eclipse will occur on a new Moon five or six months later. The Sun can also sometimes be eclipsed by two successive new Moons. A shaman would often be wrong with estimates using this method, but there are also ways to fine-tune the forecast.

The little crescent-shaped shadows of a progressing eclipse are readily seen as the eclipsed light filters through the leaves of a tree onto the ground or a wall. This seems like an obvious method for cultures living close to the Earth, who would notice them immedia-

42 Shadows in leaves reflect the eclipsed Sun

tely. Eclipse watchers today may also be familiar with the pinhole camera, which many of us used as children to avoid looking directly at the Sun. Through a card with a small hole, we can see a tiny reflection of the Moon's shadow moving across the lighted disk of the Sun on a flat surface during a partial or total solar eclipse.

A crystal or reflecting stone can also be used to project the eclipsed Sun's image into a cave or on a darkened wall. An observer alerted to the possibility of a solar eclipse would be on the look-out for these signals, which could even warn of a total solar eclipse within an hour or more, resulting in an accurate prediction. And as the visible effects of a solar or lunar eclipse may last for hours, the forecast can conceivably pay off with quite a dramatic show.

The beauty of these methods is that they don't require much to achieve. Consistent observation over time will reveal the secrets to those who make the effort to discover them. Faith in the words of the elders, of course, would shorten the learning curve quite a bit. The Shawnees revered their elders and respected tradition, so time and patience were the key requirements.

Still, how was Tenskwatawa able to forecast a total solar eclipse? Let's return to our sky watchers in the Great Lakes region and Ohio River Valley in the early 19th century. On January 26, 1804, a partial lunar eclipse was visible in most of North America. If that one happened to be overlooked, a near-total lunar eclipse was more likely to be seen six Moons later, on July 22, 1804. To anticipate another possible eclipse, our shaman would then continue checking the next new and full Moons at five and six-month intervals.

Eleven Moons later (5 + 6), on June 26, 1805, there was a partial solar eclipse in the Ohio area, with about half the Sun's disk covered. It would have been visible with a pinhole camera or through shadows in leaves. Another eclipse can sometimes occur at the following syzygy, so our calendar keeper would be alert to that possibility. And sure enough, on July 11, 1805, there was a total lunar eclipse visible throughout the U.S. This was likely quite a notable and dramatic sight, with the Moon colored a deep red. Had we missed any of the previous eclipses, an interested astrologer-priest would begin counting in five and six month intervals from this event.

The visible lunar cycle revealed nothing special in Ohio in December or the following January. But if we kept watching and counting, we would very likely anticipate the total solar eclipse of June 16, 1806. If we looked through a pinhole camera or at leaf patterns on the ground on the new Moons in anticipation of a potential celestial event, we might observe a bite being taken out of the Sun as early as four or more hours before its maximum effect, and forecast the possibility of an important eclipse ahead.

Tellingly, biographer Adam Jortner reports of the Prophet that, "On that June Monday, he remained in his tent, only emerging later to say, "Behold! Did I not prophesy correctly – see darkness is coming." (Jortner, p. 3) Tenskwatawa might have been meditating and praying inside while observing the beginnings of the eclipsed Sun projected on his wall with a reflecting stone. He would come out only after he was sure his forecast would be correct.

The June 16, 1806 eclipse cut straight across the U.S., crossing Indiana, Michigan, Lake Erie and Ohio before reaching New England. At about 11:00 in the morning, the Sun was completely darkened for nearly five minutes, making for an effect that one couldn't help but notice. Venus, Mars and perhaps even Mercury may have all been seen in totality. The temperature would have dropped, plants closed their flowers, and birds begun to groom themselves, expecting the end of a day. Fish may have jumped more eagerly for bait, as they do in the evening.

History records that the Prophet predicted a total solar eclipse. We don't know when or how, but many things might have contributed. Tenskwatawa was a trained medicine man who counseled returning to the old ways, so he must have had knowledge of them. He could have estimated the coming eclipse and confirmed it hours before totality, maximizing his announcement for effect. The Shawnee network with other Nations was vast; they easily learned about the plans and movements of Harrison and others of interest. When they needed information, they found it. If Tenskwatawa didn't foresee the 1806 eclipse himself, a supportive shaman in the area who'd learned the forecasting methods could have alerted him to the coming event.

Luck certainly played a part as well. What a marvelous cosmic coincidence that Harrison had demanded proof of the Prophet's power only months before one of the most remarkable eclipses to cross the continent in the 19th century. Tenskwatawa may not have been as sure of the eclipse as history recalls, but his correct forecast has been remembered for over 200 years.

Tenskwatawa was known for his visions, and as a medicine man and shaman, he would have been trained to enter altered states of consciousness. So it's also possible that he might simply have intuited the coming eclipse in a psychic flash of extra sensory perception.

When the Prophet was interviewed by ethnographer C. C. Trowbridge in 1824, it was 18 years after his 1806 eclipse forecast, or a full eclipse cycle later. The 18-year, 11¼-day Saros eclipse cycle is also not very far from the 20-year Jupiter-Saturn cycle that astrologers have correlated with the deaths of U.S. presidents. These two cycles both repeat in about a generation of time:

The importance of the eighteen-year cycle is corroborated by Creek stories. A generation is an eighteen-year cycle – after that, a new generation or 'spiritual regeneration' occurs. In Creek beliefs when the 'wedding' of the moon and the sun takes place every eighteen years, a new set of spirits is created which invigorates the earth under the blessings of the seven miccos of the Pleiades. It is in these eighteen-year adjustments that the creative "miracles" of new spirits and energies are infused in nature and in human societies and cycles. (Chaudhuri, p. 11)

Eclipse watching was something practiced long before any Europeans arrived at Turtle Island's shores. The Midewiwin, a mystical society of the Indigenous peoples of the Great Lakes, northeast U.S. and Canadian Maritimes, was dedicated to healing and spirituality. Their Seven Fires prophecies were recorded in a wampum belt preserved by Algonquian elders for over 400 years, and solar eclipses play a significant part in them. Two life walk cycles of 56 years each were originally granted to all, so that a period of approximately 112 years is considered to be a "fire" according to Algonquin historian Evan T. Pritchard's calculations (see Appendix 2 for more).

Meeting in what is now St. Johns, New Brunswick, Canada in 1217, eight prophets arrived to address the coming cycles. Their insights became the Seven Fires, wide-ranging prophecies that foretold the need to move west, the coming of the white race, the alienation of the Indigenous people from their heritage, and the eventual resurrection of their culture. Mi'kmaq descendant Pritchard outlines what Algonquin tradition recounts from the prophets:

They spoke of 'medicine wheels,' and hoops within hoops of what we'd call ecosystems, and hoops within hoops of what we'd call 'time'... In order to warn the people of certain moments... seven of these fires... would be the length of the era of the great prophecy that was about to begin... This was the largest of hoops, a single round of which would take 784 years to 'walk.' The important highlights would be preceded (or in some cases, followed) by solar eclipses, rings of fire visible from the Bay of Fundy's Fire Island [in Nova Scotia], and would roughly coincide with the newness or the fullness of that cycle... (Pritchard, p. 10)

"Rings of Fire" describes annular eclipses, when the new Moon's disk incompletely covers the Sun, creating the appearance of a ring of fire in the sky. The *Chilam Balam of Chumayel* similarly mentions what may also be annular eclipses. The katun prophecies twice mention "a white circle in the sky." (Roys, p. 148, 164)

The 56-year life walk period of time coincides with three returns of the Moon's Nodes, and of course the Nodes are enmeshed with eclipses. (There are 56 Aubrey holes at Stonehenge.) Eclipses were signs of things to come. Evan Pritchard estimates that the significant midpoint of the Algonquin prophecy cycle was highlighted by a solar eclipse witnessed by Captain John Smith on August 10, 1608. The Algonquians anticipated the arrival of someone the following year, within the year of signs and omens following the eclipse, when Henry Hudson arrived at New York harbor.

The projection of interrelated cycles far into the future is also a feature of both the western and the Mayan astrological traditions. The 784-year Algonquin prophecy period is rather close to the 794-year western Jupiter-Saturn Grand Mutation cycle as well as two baktuns (or 20 katuns) for the Maya (about 788 years). But how were Indigenous calendar keepers able to calculate so far into the future? The turtle shell could be used as an abacus and astronomical calculator:

...the 28 smaller plates around the perimeter of the shell of the calendar turtle, which have 13 large (month) and 28 small (day) platelets on their shells, can be used quite effectively to measure the 364 (28 x 13) + 1 day solar year, or the 56 year life walk wheel, accomplished by dividing each platelet in two. By dividing only one platelet in two (or using the turtle's neck as a space) Algonquin people also measured 29 days/nights of the lunar month, of which there were also 13, a 377 night 'lunar year,' adding seven nights at the end (to make 384). These two calendars, run simultaneously, would only coincide every 98 years, and would also be subject to periodic adjustments. Did Algonquin people make these adjustments? The seven fires cycle of 784 years, as proposed here, indicates that they did, and that they, or the prophets, had intimate knowledge of solar and lunar calculations on a par with any other culture on earth... As solar eclipses are rare, and appear almost anywhere in

earth, this author has yet to discover their method of predicting this highly unusual chain of variable eclipses. It suggests that these prophets had been part of a society that charted out the sun and moon for thousands of years. (Pritchard, p. 280, Note 8.)

From this perspective, if we once again consider the historical events in the Ohio Valley in the early 19th century, things look very different. The Lenape may have also been proponents of the Seven Fires tradition. This group had moved west to the Great Lakes area in the 18th century and were long-time supporters and associates of the Shawnee. Let's return to April of 1806: William Henry Harrison has written to the Lenape about the Prophet, saying that,

If God has really employed him he has doubtless authorized him to perform some miracles, that he may be known and received as a prophet... Ask him to cause the Sun to stand still – the Moon to alter its courses – the rivers to flow – or the dead to rise from their graves. If he does these things, you may then believe that he has been sent from God.

Many recognized Harrison's words as an attempt to undermine Tenskwatawa's mission. Midewiwin calendar priests quickly receive word of the letter. They know they will soon be in eclipse season and they laugh among themselves at the unusual coincidence. Their tradition of eclipse prediction goes back hundreds of years, and Harrison clearly doesn't understand the ways of Nature. But the situation is deadly serious as the Americans have already taken so much land that there is no longer enough left to provide for their livelihood.

The experts soon agree on important watch dates for a probable coming eclipse. One even suspects the Sun might be put out, as records show that there was a partial eclipse visible in the area 54 years before, part of a triple Saros cycle returning the eclipse shadow to a similar geographic area. (Total solar eclipses crossed Central America on April 10, 1698 and the Gulf of Mexico and Florida on May 13, 1752 as the recurring path moved northward to June 16, 1806. The total solar eclipse of July 18, 1860 could similarly be seen as partial in the Great Lakes area as its shadow crossed what is now Canada.) The information is duly relayed to the Prophet, and the rest is history.

In 1824, when Tenskwatawa was interviewed by ethnologist C.C. Trowbridge, he recounted how the Great Spirit, before sending the Shawnee to their Island, would take "12 days, which days were equal to years of the Indians." (Kinietz and Voegelin, p. 37)

The technique of metaphorically equating one period of time with another period of time is one commonly used by western astrologers today with day-per-year calculations called secondary progressions. (There were so few capable western astrologers in the U.S. at the time as to make it virtually impossible for any to have influenced the Prophet.) Many point to biblical verses as ancient testaments to similar practices in the distant past. Ezekiel 4:6 says, "I have appointed thee each day for a year." And Numbers 14:34 similarly refers to this symbolic metaphor of time: "... you shall bear your guilt forty years – a year for each day..."

From the oral tradition, the Prophet recounted that the Shawnee had traveled twelve days before coming to a river. The Great Spirit said that after their travels, they would remain at the Mississippi,

...a short time and where they would discover something coming towards them (the whites), which would make them very poor and miserable. They moved to the Mississippi where they saw the prediction verified. (Kinietz and Voegelin, p. 56)

So the Shawnees, too, had known known of the whites coming before their arrival. Tenskwatawa also shared a prophecy that had been handed down to him. It resembles the Algonquin Seven Fires prophecy in its use of fire imagery and in speaking of an end period in which they expected a reckoning. The Prophet said of the Shawnees that,

In all these travels they took with them the sacred fire, and now that they see the settlements of the whites progressing so rapidly, they look forward to a time when it will be necessary for them to endeavor to retransmit the fire to Shawnee river. Twelve men will be deputed to carry this fire, who, when they have arrived at Shawnee river, will open the fire and put to the test the power of the whites. If it be foreordained that everything is to belong to the whites, in four years the fire will become visible to all the world... Twelve days (years) after the destruction of the world by this fire the Great Spirit will cause it to be reformed & repeopled, but they don't know what description of persons will inhabit it. (Kinietz and Voegelin, p. 56)

Tenskwatawa's remarks are rather cryptic. He spoke through a translator (probably one of Tecumseh's sons). Were his words transcribed properly over 20 years before the invention of shorthand? We do not know exactly what the fire represents. Unfortunately, we also don't know what Tenskwatawa meant by his symbolism of twelve days or years, or what period of time he might have been suggesting; it was probably not literal.

Shawnees had also been members of the Midewiwin Grand Medicine Society of the Great Lakes area as early as the 17th century, and this group included active and eager eclipse watchers. Their Seven Fires prophecy cycle of 784 years is unusually close to the western Jupiter-Saturn conjunction Grand Mutation cycle (of about 794 years). Like Mayan time periods, this historic round probably contains many different interlocking cycles within it, the "hoops within hoops" of time that Algonquin historian Evan T. Pritchard

43 *Tecumseh portrait may depict his son Paukeesaa*

wrote about. One of them must have been the nineteen-year cycle of the Moon's Nodes so intimately connected with eclipses, since the prophecies utilized eclipses as signposts.

The combination of sky watching, cyclic tracking, projecting celestial events into the future and relating their movement to life on Earth has a name: we call it astrology. Some of the Midewiwin must have been astrologers as well as priests.

Tenskwatawa was most likely either a member of the Midewiwin lodge himself or had close connections to it. His prediction of the eclipse was part of an ancient practice. His vision and prophetic insight occurred near the middle of the Sixth Fire (approximately 1776 to 1888), which the prophets and elders described as representing a time when the new generation could be disconnected from their past and life would become imbalanced. The Prophet's vision of a need to return to traditional ways was consistent with the centuries-old prophecy, and he and many others worked to reconnect with their age-old customs and practices at this time.

The Jupiter-Saturn conjunctions every 20 years could be noted from generation to generation, anticipated and observed during a lifetime. As any experienced astrologer would know, they define an accessible period in history, another one of the hoops of time that may have ultimately determined the much longer prophecy period. Dedicated sky watchers in the Northwest Territory, like those from many diverse cultures around the world, would certainly have been aware of the Jupiter-Saturn conjunction cycles. Only legends tell us that Tenskwatawa forecast danger to the United States presidents every 20 years. We have no proof, except for what we can glean from the pages of history.

Western society has elevated the linear mind above all else, and considers that we in the present have advanced well beyond those of previous eras. As a result, much of what is past in the timeline is considered inadequate or primitive. There is no room in this belief system for the ideas of cyclic time, spiritual insight or prophecy, all of which Indigenous peoples embraced. Astrologers, too, understand these important values and depend upon recognizing forces that cannot be measured or proven by experiment. As Shakespeare's Hamlet attests, "There are more things in Heaven and Earth... than are dreamt of in your philosophy."

Part III: THE ASTROLOGY

Chapter 7: Jupiter, Saturn and the United States

A very great vision is needed and the man who has it must follow it as the eagle seeks the deepest blue of the sky.
– Crazy Horse, Oglala Sioux

The presidential deaths have often been attributed to Jupiter-Saturn conjunctions, which occur with regularity about every 20 years. Georgio de Santillana and Herta von Dechend in their 1972 book, *Hamlet's Mill*, discussed these conjunctions, their relationship to myths around the world, and how myths may communicate astronomical information. In Shakespeare's play, the young prince Hamlet is the youthful Jupiter figure and his uncle Claudius, who killed Hamlet's father, married his mother and took control of the kingdom, would be represented by Saturn. By the end of the play Hamlet does kill Claudius but is killed himself as well. The situation is righted and a new regime follows.

In Greek myth Chronos (also known as Saturn) received a warning that one of his children would overthrow him. So every time a child was born, he'd eat them. Chronos' wife Rhea was incensed when she discovered what was happening. When the next baby was born (who happened to be Zeus, the Greek name for our Roman Jupiter), Rhea wrapped a large stone in baby clothes and Chronos ate the stone instead. Jupiter escaped to become the king of the gods, usurping Chronos' position. So once again the symbolism shows a change in leadership.

In *Hamlet's Mill*, the Jupiter-Saturn succession in leadership acts as the minute hand to precession. Another book, *The Secret of the Incas* by William Sullivan, takes the premise of *Hamlet's Mill* and applies it to the succession of leadership in Inca myths.

As archetypical characters, Tecumseh and Tenskwatawa and their histories are somewhat reminiscent of the biblical Moses and Aaron. Tecumseh was the public spokesman and Tenskwatawa had a connection with the Creator. Their saga began with a vision, and they then stepped out of their usual roles in life to seek justice and defend their oppressed people. Unfortunately, theirs was a "let my people stay" story, and the Shawnees were driven out of their homelands and forced to cross the Mississippi River into something of a wilderness.

But mythology isn't astrology. Myths provide meaningful stories by resonating with the cultures that create them. In astrology, the metaphors, myths or analogies symbolize actual events that manifest in our lives and the world around us.

Why do Jupiter and Saturn astrologically relate to rulers? Jupiter is associated with expansion and growth and has resonance with the legal system, religious figures and royalty. Saturn is very different; it relates to safety, contraction and destruction. But Saturn also represents authority figures, the "old guard" and established leaders. When Jupiter conjoins Saturn, there's a sense of a "clash of the Titans." This occurs with regularity approximately every 19.86 years. (The Jupiter-Saturn synodic cycle is slightly less than 20 years, so it doesn't exactly line up with the zero year elections.)

Jupiter and Saturn are traditionally known as the "great chronocrators," meaning markers of time. The ancients looked to them for insight into the larger changes in civilization and culture, as they were the outer-most visible planets. The time of their conjunction in the sky was significant, and those born with the placement in their horoscopes might also have unusual destinies.

Prominent astrologers throughout history have studied this cycle. The ancient Persian astrologer Gjamasp al Hakim may have already written his *Judgments of the Grand Conjunctions of the Planets* by 520 BCE, and this work was translated and read for centuries thereafter. The Jewish Persian astrologer Mashallah studied the conjunctions in Baghdad in the 8th century, as did the Muslim Persian astrologer Abu Mashar a century later. In 12th century Spain, the Jewish philosopher and astrologer Abraham ibn Ezra translated Mashallah and wrote more about the Jupiter-Saturn conjunctions himself.

In the 15th century the Sephardic Jewish philosopher Isaac Abarbanel concluded that a Jupiter-Saturn conjunction preceded the births of Moses and Jesus, and the famous astronomer and astrologer Johann Kepler took his lead. Kepler had been observing the triple conjunction of Mars, Jupiter and Saturn in 1603 and agreed that the great conjunction was a feature of the horoscope of Jesus Christ in 6 BCE. In this scenario, Jesus is the king of Heaven (Jupiter) and Herod the Saturn authority figure. (With both planets at the time in the sign of Pisces, the fishes, a fish was an early symbol of the Christians.) The Prophet Muhammad was similarly believed to have been born with a Jupiter-Saturn conjunction in the sign of Scorpio in his birth chart.

Other important historical figures like Galileo, Nostradamus, Isaac Newton, Mary Baker Eddy and Ida B. Wells all lived out the conjunction in their birth charts. U.S. Presidents Thomas Jefferson, Martin van Buren, Ulysses S. Grant and Franklin Delano Roosevelt were born with it as well.

Astrologer Marjorie Orr has identified modern cultural icons whose lives were marked by heavy impacts from the conjunctions. Queen Victoria died in 1901 when Jupiter was conjunct Saturn in Capricorn, and her husband Prince Albert had died with Jupiter conjunct Saturn in Virgo in 1861. John Lennon was born on the conjunction in 1940, the Beatles were created in 1960, and Lennon was killed in 1980, all Jupiter-Saturn zero years. Princess Diana was born in 1961 near the end of a Jupiter-Saturn conjunction and was married to Prince Charles in 1981 during another.

The Maya succession of leaders was also linked to astrological history. A famous bas-relief sculpture called the Tablet of the Cross at Palenque (in what is now Chiapas in Mexico) depicts an old, shriveled king, perhaps even in his burial garments, giving his blessing to his young, vital son. The sculpture commemorates the 75th anniversary of King Shield Pacal, as well as the anniversary of the reign of his son Chan Balam.

As usual, a date is included, probably chosen astrologically for the dedication of the sculpture, and in our western horoscope chart for July 20, 690 C.E. we can see a Jupiter-Saturn conjunction. The date metaphorically connects the leaders with the sky gods and even their origins, though it appears that the Maya may have also associated the Jupiter-Saturn conjunction with a transfer of power. Similarly, the Yaxchilan,

44 Tablet of the Cross at Palenque

Mexico, king named Shield Jaguar commemorated the 80th anniversary of his father Bird Jaguar III and his own 28th anniversary in a doorway lintel bas relief dated October 23, 709. The Jupiter-Saturn conjunction on this date was in Cancer in our western chart.

Our base ten numbering system inherited from the ancient Hindu-Arabic causes us to appraise things in blocks of ten. References to decades easily evoke the characteristics of the times: the exuberant 1920s, the depressed 1930s, the troubled '40s, the family-centric '50s, the radical '60s, the weird '70s, the materialistic '80s and so on.

But the zero-year presidential elections don't happen every decade. Because of the four-year term of office and our decimal calendar system, the two cycles only mesh every 20 years. The cyclic deaths of leaders do not appear to happen with the same regularity in other parts of the world.

Name	Pt	Long.	Hs	Decl.
Sun	☉	00°♌13'01"	6	+20°14'
Moon	☽	24°♏11'02'	9	−20°33'
Mercury	☿	21°♋38 ℞	5	+17°49'
Venus	♀	16°♊46	4	+20°38'
Mars	♂	09°♏18	9	−16°45'
Jupiter	♃	11°♏25	9	−14°34'
Saturn	♄	15°♏31	9	−14°39'
Uranus	♅	22°♊19	4	+23°33'
Neptune	♆	04°♒27 ℞	12	−19°30'
Pluto	♇	00°♋42	5	+22°47'
North Node	☊	12°♐51	10	−22°30'
South Node	☋	12°♊51	4	+22°30'
Ascendant	As	24°♒51'00"	1	−13°19'
Midheaven	Mc	03°♐30'38"	10	−21°00'

Chart
Palenque Anniversary
Natal Chart
Jul 20 0690, Wed
8:00 pm LMT +6:07:52
Palenque, Mexico
17°N31' 091°W58'
Geocentric
Tropical
Placidus
True Node
Rating: X
Date Milbrath p. 298–99

45 Horoscope: Palenque Anniversary

In the Yucatan Peninsula, the Mayan Chilam Balam 20-year prophecies generally forecast one unfortunate time after another, but certainly the original writers, as well as those who transcribed them for posterity, were experiencing a great era of transition and change, when their beliefs and lifestyle were threatened.

The Maya had identified a significant 20-year cycle. Can we similarly characterize 20-year periods? We think of 20 years as a generational cycle: the time it takes for one generation to reach adulthood. The Silent Generation, the Baby Boomers and Millennials may not exactly align with 20-year intervals, but fashion, music, culture, weather, economics and politics all have repetitive cycles that many have analyzed in terms of 20-year trends. It does take about 20 years for a nostalgic look back to earlier times, as the long-running television shows *Happy Days*, *The Wonder Years* and *That '70s Show* aptly demonstrated.

Our time-keeping system of days, months and years is based upon the cycles of the Sun, Earth and Moon. The sacred Mesoamerican system of 20-day Tzolkin, approximately 20-year (7,200-day) katuns and ever longer periods went even further in its elegant and elaborate intermeshing of cycles of eclipses, Venus and other planets.

In addition to periodic Jupiter-Saturn conjunctions, similar astrological cycles also contribute to the importance of generational periods. The Saros eclipse cycle of 18 years, 11¼ days, Moon phase Metonic cycle of 19 years, Lunar Node cycle of approximately 18.6 years and Uranus' 21-year quarter cycles all add their influences to this period of time.

The placement of the Nodes is always significant in any birth or inception chart because the eclipses that surround them always fall near the degrees of the Nodes. The Nodes also appear to be important to the zero-year presidencies. But as their cycle is shorter, they move back through the zodiac by a sign (short of a few degrees) every 20 years. In reviewing their regular movements, we can immediately see how their zodiac signs point toward repeated themes. They often activate the presidents' charts as well as key points in the U.S. horoscope, as we will see.

The Sun in hard aspect to Uranus repeats in a number of the zero-year presidential inaugurations. Transiting Saturn's aspects to Uranus also occur with regularity and resonate with some of the presidential deaths. Saturn squared Uranus in 1860 and opposed it in 1920. They conjoined in 1942, squared in 2000 and opposed one another again in 2008. These tend to be periods of great conflict or change, but they don't all coincide with the 20-

year cycle. In addition, the hard aspects between Saturn and Uranus at the time of a presidential election or inauguration often signal a change-over in the political party in the White House.

While the Jupiter-Saturn conjunction cycles represent generational influences, trends and developments, they are also part of much larger periods of time of growth and change. Jupiter-Saturn conjunctions manifest in the same element of fire, earth, air or water (called trigons or Lesser Mutations) for about 200 years before beginning to change to the next element, where they remain for another 200 years (called the Great Mutation cycle). All four elements are represented over about 800 years. Jupiter-Saturn conjunctions were in fire signs (Aries, Leo and Sagittarius) from 1603 to 1782, during the age of European exploration and the conquest and settlement of the Americas. This time included the so-called intellectual "Enlightenment," the Revolutionary War, and the ratification of the U.S. Articles of Confederation.

Indigenous peoples inhabiting Turtle Island at the time also represented fire. They lived as part of the environment, held important spiritual traditions, and shared things of practical use. Material goods were valued mainly for their ability to symbolize principles, thoughts or feelings. The western astrological fire signs began giving way to earth signs in 1802.

In keeping with the Jupiter-Saturn conjunctions in earth signs in the 19th and 20th centuries, the Europeans in America perpetuated a focus on physical matter like land, material possessions and the study of science. Money, property, work, goals and achievements were also highlighted. The earth signs may also resonate with the physical self (since the actual bodies of the presidents were attacked).

Evangeline Adams, financial astrologer W.D. Gann and leading English astrologer C.E.O Carter all used a Gemini rising horoscope with Mars conjunct the Ascendant for the U.S. (This chart is probably at least somewhat symbolic, and many astrologers have excellent results with different U.S. horoscopes.) While Gemini rising charts have faded in popularity, they were commonly used in the 20th century, particularly those with Uranus conjunct the Ascendant. Robert Carl Jansky in 1979 said that this is the chart "that a majority of astrologers have come to recognize as the correct one." (p. 75) Donna Cunningham similarly stated in 1982 that, "Most astrologers use the traditional chart calculated for July 4, 1776 at 2:13:32 AM in Philadelphia" (p. 29), virtually the same horoscope Jansky referred to. And

Washington D.C. astrologer Barbara Watters also referenced a U.S. Gemini rising chart in her 1973 book (p. 208).

In Adams' horoscope for the U.S., Capricorn is on the eighth house cusp and Aquarius is on the ninth and tenth, all traditionally ruled by Saturn. Most of Pisces is in the tenth, Pisces rules the eleventh, and Sagittarius falls on the seventh house cusp. So almost all of the top half of the chart (above the horizon) is traditionally ruled by Jupiter and Saturn. Saturn falls in the fifth house and closely squares the Sun. This is a notable affliction that may specifically relate to authority figures since Saturn indicates status and rules the Midheaven, and the Sun is a general significator for a leader. Jupiter in Cancer also squares Saturn in Libra by sign, accentuating the natural differences between them. There are several sensitive degree areas in the horoscope of the United States. The square between Saturn and the Sun falls in the middle degrees of cardinal signs, a dynamic combination when activated. Saturn also trines Uranus, a pairing that can bring periodic ups and downs and distinct phases to the country's experience, with upheavals in the nation's sense of stability from time to time.

Ascendant ruler Mercury is placed in late Cancer and opposes Pluto in Capricorn, accenting the late cardinal signs. This is an intense pattern that may precipitate disputes related to security or even survival. As Mercury falls in the financial second house, the opposition to Pluto also suggests trade conflicts, economic disparity and the possibility of extreme market and economic swings.

The Lunar Nodes in early Leo and Aquarius have no classical aspects except a sextile and trine from Uranus in Gemini. As Uranus falls in the twelfth house, traditionally relating to concealed threats, the combination may lend a fated quality to sudden or unforeseen news and events.

The mid to late fixed signs also stand out, since the Moon is in the ninth house at 18½ Aquarius and the Midheaven and fourth house cusp (the bottom of the chart, Imum Coeli or IC) are in late degrees of Aquarius and Leo.

The Ascendant at 20½ Gemini and Mars rising at 21 Gemini, with both squaring Neptune at 22½ Virgo create another sensitive area in mutable signs. These squares might produce misunderstandings, a tendency to fall prey to deception, or the inability to perceive what might be obvious. (The "American Dream" is an idea to think about in this context.) There could be conflicts between assertiveness and tolerance or discussion and action that may lead the country toward unhealthy connections, a lack of focus, passive-aggressiveness, or acting rashly under precon-ceived ideas.

The U.S. July 4 horoscope does not have much essential dignity, though Jupiter in Cancer and Saturn in Libra are both in the signs of their exaltation, maybe another reason for the impact of the Jupiter-Saturn conjunction cycles on the country.

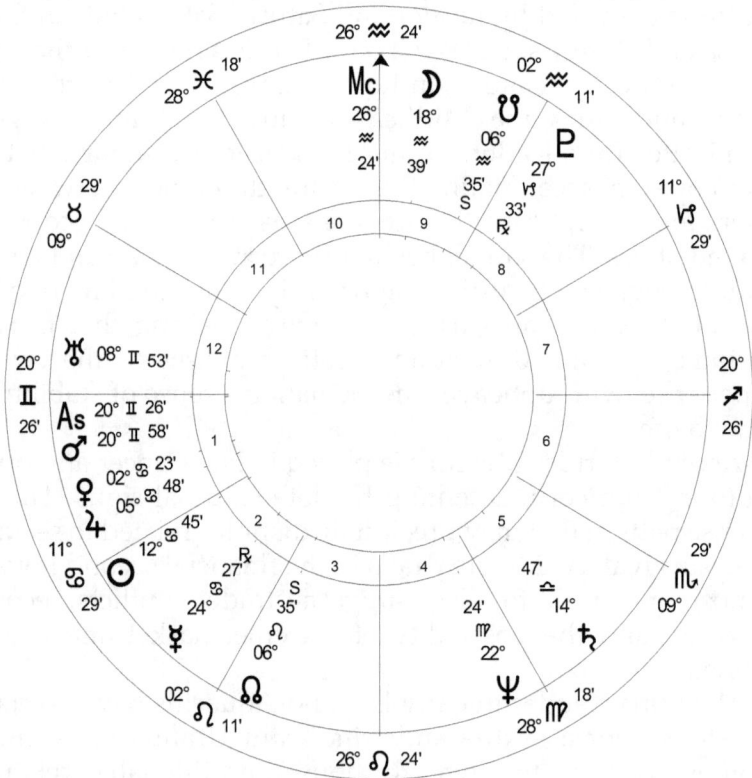

Name	Pt	Long.	Hs	Decl.
Sun	☉	12°♋45'43"	2	+22°51'
Moon	☽	18°≈39'48"	9	−16°17'
Mercury	☿	24°♋27 ℞	2	+17°34'
Venus	♀	02°♋23	1	+23°31'
Mars	♂	20°♊58	1	+23°32'
Jupiter	♃	05°♋48	1	+23°16'
Saturn	♄	14°♎47	5	−03°30'
Uranus	♅	08°♊53	12	+21°44'
Neptune	♆	22°♍24	4	+04°09'
Pluto	♇	27°♑33 ℞	8	−23°43'
North Node	☊	06°♌35	3	+18°38'
South Node	☋	06°≈35	9	−18°38'
Ascendant	As	20°♊26'38"	1	+23°07'
Midheaven	Mc	26°≈24'01"	10	−12°43'

Chart
United States
Natal Chart
Jul 4 1776 NS, Thu
3:03 am LMT +5:00:39
Philadelphia, PA
39°N57'08" 075°W09'51"
Geocentric
Tropical
Placidus
True Node
Rating: DD
After E. Adams, W.D. Gann

46 Horoscope: U.S., Adams' Gemini rising chart

Planets in exaltation express themselves with greater strength, as the quality of the sign allows them fuller expression. But a planet in exaltation can sometimes be too strong, and its influence is not always balanced. Astrologer Zoltan Mason felt that exaltation could indicate too much change or activity surrounding the planet. However we choose to interpret it, these essential dignities are significant.

Jupiter is also highlighted as it falls in the country's first house, conjoining both Venus and the Sun. With all in Cancer, they promise security and a prominent image. Bold Jupiterian themes are characteristic. The United States is known as a large country where people think big and do things on a grand scale. Many can attain their dreams of education, and freedom of speech is a prized value. Since Jupiter rules the seventh house relating to others, as well as the eleventh of community, it has given the U.S. great diversity. But its influence has also resulted in divisiveness and the pervasive racial issues that the country has always experienced. An "us versus them" attitude was evident in the subjugation of Indigenous peoples, the enslavement of Blacks, the ensuing Civil War, the existence of white supremacists, and the continued need for civil rights activism.

While the U.S. Sun conjunct Jupiter emphasizes the tremendous diversity of people, places and ideals that the country has always enjoyed, the Sun's closer square to Saturn in Libra indicates that the greater challenge for the country is equality. Since Libra is the sign of the scales, it would follow that maintaining a sense of balance in lifestyle and relationships is key.

Mars is conjunct the Ascendant in this Gemini rising U.S. horoscope. It trines the Moon, which could relate to violence as well as the country's fascination with firearms. Mars is ruled by Mercury in Cancer opposed to Pluto, at times resulting in deadly consequences. And with Mars square Neptune, a link can also be seen between gun violence and substance abuse or the possibility of mental and emotional instability (since Neptune in Virgo is also ruled by Mercury opposite Pluto).

The U.S. chart also has unusual configurations in declination, an astronomical measurement that parallels the celestial equator, separate from the commonly used measurement in longitude (degrees of the zodiac). The United States has five planets (the Sun, Venus, Mars, Jupiter and Uranus) as well as the Ascendant, all parallel in north declination within less than 2 degrees, with Pluto then contraparallel most of them. This is a highly focused grouping with explosive overtones. (The closest pairing, Venus parallel Mars, is within a minute of arc, and both contraparallel Pluto within 11 minutes.) The focus on north declination emphasizes the outside, material world, natural abilities and even power, corresponding somewhat to the earth signs. Venus, Mars and Pluto all placed out-of-bounds in declination (beyond the Sun's path of 27° 27'), also create an unusual need for security, especially as they fall in the achievement-oriented signs of Cancer and Capricorn.

There has always been an emphasis on property ownership in the U.S., and those who want to achieve their goals often have the ability to work their way up. But the downside of this combination results in acquisitiveness and self-interest, those with wealth and power isolating themselves from others, and an elite moneyed class enjoying greater opportunities. Our consumption-focused society and the alarming rate of obesity today (an estimated 40% of adults and nearly 20% of children as of this writing) are also natural byproducts of the out-of-bounds influence in Cancer.

Jupiter falling in the middle of this significant pattern in declination also highlights the Jupiterian issues evident in longitude. Multiculturalism is a given in a country created by pushing out Indigenous people, importing slaves and settling immigrants.

Saturn's only aspect in declination is a contraparallel to Neptune. This could lead to the ideals of compassion offset by hard reality, inspiration and dreams as a necessary part of government, or the need to balance the arts with business. But ineffective leadership, neglect of duties and the possibility of corruption reflect Saturn-Neptune themes as well. (Since the planets fall in the fourth and fifth houses in the Gemini rising chart, they may more specifically relate to property, speculation or creativity.) As general significators, the combination of Saturn and Neptune might also result in the loss (Neptune) of a chief executive (Saturn), and the two planets are combined in some of the presidents' horoscopes as well. In personal charts, they may indicate an individual's life direction or even destiny being caught up with events, trends and generational influences outside of their own control.

Another influence in the U.S. horoscope that may be more obvious in declination than in longitude is Uranus' parallel with the Sun. This aspect, at a little over a degree, is intensified by the four other planets and the Ascendant in the grouping, and indicates radical changes and startling developments from time to time in the country's history, some of which might be violent. Of course, as the chart is based on the Declaration of Independence, the country itself began in a similarly tempestuous way.

Birth charts form the basis of much western astrology. Astrologers do well in interpreting natal horoscopes and advising about the types of events and experiences that a person can expect in their lifetime. And while there are many varied techniques and practices, it's always a more complicated task to forecast events in the future or anticipate when a life-changing development is likely to arise. Pinpointing when local, national or worldwide trends will develop is even more complex.

If we imagine the vast numbers of people in the world, their individual relationships, goals and issues, all constantly acting, interacting and reacting, we can gain some perspective on how intricately interwoven reality is, and how we are all affected, to one degree or another, by planetary trends. We've all experienced periods of time when events in our lives feel inevitable, and forecasting astrologers can often identify the planetary triggers and timing points. It's a more daunting task to predict in advance the extent to which they will affect a person's life or exactly how they will manifest.

In addition, each town, city and country has its own birth chart (often responding to more than one horoscope that mark major initiatives, changes or reorganizations). These are generally not as easy to interpret as a personal chart, and forecasting from them becomes more challenging, too.

Like nested layers, facets of a jewel or perspectives in a hologram, all are part of a vast organic whole. This explains why different analysts reach diverse conclusions about any particular matter, and why experts and commentators in politics, economics and many other areas often disagree and fail to anticipate correct outcomes. We are trapped in time, but astrology provides a more objective view.

Planetary cycles have been studied for millennia, and they are ultimately different than working with birth charts. Repetitive cycles show overall trends and recurring patterns to review and anticipate, and they return with expected regularity. While their interpretations, too, may be difficult to project into the future, and their timing and details may not always be exact, they provide a guideline. We should not expect astrology, as a symbolic system, to be precise in describing future events in all their details. Kepler referred to a "mean" in writing about the mutations of Jupiter conjunct Saturn from one element to another. (Boner, p. 215) Or, as historian Evan T. Pritchard stated, the 56-year Algonquin life walk cycle is "an approximation, as the universe is constantly in flux." (p. 9)

The United States' Uranus in Gemini cycle, for example, has become well-known. First observed by homeopathic physician Luke D. Broughton, and explained in his 1898 book *Elements of Astrology*, Uranus transited Gemini from 1607 to 1614 for the Jamestown colony's founding (the first permanent English settlement in North America) and at Henry Hudson's arrival in New York in 1609 (another starting point of later colonization). It returned to Gemini during the years 1691 to 1698 during the Salem witchcraft trials and French and Indian Wars, and was an astrological dynamic during the American Revolution (1775-1782) and the Civil War (1858-1866). Though the dates don't always line up exactly, U.S. history would not be complete without these epochal events, some of which occurred before there was an American horoscope. So it was relatively easy in the 1920s for Evangeline Adams to forecast another war for the U.S. from 1942 to 1944 when Uranus was again in the sign of Gemini, along with Saturn. Financial astrologer Louise McWhirter in her 1938 book reiterated that the same period signaled "war, depression, government change, social upheaval and a financial panic" to come for the U.S. (p. 91)

For each of the presidents, we could analyze their birth charts, checking to see if they had a propensity toward violent attacks, and identifying periods of possible danger. But determining death is so extraordinarily difficult as to have become taboo since the early 20th century. (As Al H. Morrison said, although we can identify the exits in the highway of life, it doesn't mean that the individual will necessarily take them.) Some with expertise in traditional or more contemporary techniques might go further. But the charts that follow are considered within the context of the zero-year, Jupiter-Saturn pattern. The larger planetary cycles are more impersonal, and in a sense, removed from the individual. (As Robert Ripley noted in his 1934 article on the presidential cycles with "???" next to the year 1940.) We don't need a birth chart to use the cycle.

Astrologers in the past have described the Jupiter-Saturn link to the deaths of U.S. presidents in office. In 1917, astrologer John Hazelrigg called attention to

...the striking effects of the Saturn-Jupiter conjunctions at intervals of 20 years... These now occur in the earthly triplicity... and near each recurrence the Nation has been grief-stricken through death of its Chief Magistrate, four having passed out during the term of office under the reign of these conjoined arbiters... The deduction is obvious as to the next conjunction, which occurs in April, 1921. (Hazelrigg, p. 124)

In 1973, Washington, D.C. astrologer Barbara Watters wrote that,

Since Jupiter and Saturn express two opposite principles, equally strong and equally necessary to life, their conjunctions, which occur every 20 years, are extremely important in mundane astrology. They indicate a reversal of trend in mundane affairs because the Jupiter influence expands blindly in a given direction until it suddenly meets Saturn, which stops its forward march like an insurmountable stone wall. That is why charts drawn for those conjunctions are called Mutations, as their changes reflect the changes on earth...The Great Mutation of 1842 occurred in the 9th degree of Capricorn, falling in the eighth house (death) of our [Uranus rising] national chart. Since then every president elected or inaugurated in the year of the Lesser Mutation has died in office. These deaths symbolize changes in the internal structure of American affairs and in our status as a world power. They are often connected with the end or beginning of wars as well as with more subtle changes. (Watters p. 50)

We might even say that the cycle is part of the manifest destiny of the United States.

If a president is elected in a zero year at the time of a Jupiter-Saturn conjunction, or if the conjunction falls during the term of office, the president has often died in office. Most astrologers feel this cycle relates specifically to Jupiter and Saturn in the earth signs Taurus, Virgo and Capricorn. In Evangeline Adams' U.S. chart, the only earth sign is Pluto in Capricorn in the eighth house, which could also be associated with death, since the planet and sign emphasize age, survival and harsh reality, and the eighth house emphasizes the line between the material and metaphysical worlds as well as the potential for danger.

The president doesn't necessarily die during his first term, and Franklin D. Roosevelt is a good example. He was elected four times, beginning in 1932. The zero year of 1940 was his third term in office and he served the full term throughout much of World War II. Roosevelt died shortly after he began his fourth term. And the president isn't necessarily assassinated, sometimes death is due to natural causes, as we see in this example. Similarly, Abraham Lincoln was elected in 1860 but wasn't assassinated until 1865. (These two Aquarius presidents were both deeply immersed in war during Uranus' transit of Gemini during their last years of service.)

Since 1845, elections in the United States are held every four years on the first Tuesday in November, and they regularly fall in years ending in zero. Inaugurations follow in the early months of the next year. Twelve presidents were elected in zero years since the Jupiter-Saturn conjunctions were established in earth signs in 1840 (including Joe Biden's election when Jupiter and Saturn were still in Capricorn) and there are some interesting similarities. Eight of them had the Sun in Aquarius or Scorpio (five were Aquarius, perhaps reflecting the Aquarius Moon in the U.S. horoscope). Eight of the twelve (⅔) also had Moons in earth signs, interesting because the death in office pattern relates to Jupiter and Saturn in earth signs.

The influence of the Jupiter-Saturn conjunctions builds over months and even years of time. While most sources reference the dates of exact conjunctions, which generally have a stronger influence, it's important to remember that the entire phase or period marked by these regular conjunctions will imprint people and world affairs. The proximity of the two planets to one another is a consideration, and because of the patterns of their orbits, in some years the influence of the conjunction lasts for a longer time than in others. For example, from March of 1901 to January of 1902, Jupiter and Saturn in Capricorn were conjunct within less than 7° and parallel within about a degree (and usually closer). From May of 1940 to April of 1941, Jupiter and Saturn in Taurus were conjunct within less than 7° and parallel within 2° (and usually closer in both measurement systems).

The Jupiter-Saturn conjunctions establish the tenor of the times, though their impact will be different for various individuals as they move through their course in the sky. Like an eclipse, the degree of the conjunction may also be highlighted and activated by other planets and aspects at a later date.

Presidential terms are sensitized to this long-term astrological pairing. Since Jupiter and Saturn can relate to leadership and authority, the U.S. presidential elections coinciding with the conjunctions are particularly marked by their influence. And, as we have seen, the United States horoscope (for July 4, 1776, the date that continues to be officially celebrated by the country) also shows challenges surrounding leadership and authority, symbolized by Jupiter and Saturn. These energies reiterate similar themes in different ways and set the groundwork for what follows.

Astrologers draw horoscopes for an inauguration or coronation in order to describe what to expect from the term of office begun at that date and time. These charts provide something of a snapshot or overview of the coming years. Inception horoscopes can give us insight into what we may anticipate from the matter started, and both political elections and inaugurations can be considered types of inceptions or events marking the beginning of a new phase. With a Jupiter-Saturn conjunction in this type of chart, one of the issues will be leadership, with the possibility of notable events, a change of course, or reversal of trend.

Astrologers generally consider a president's terms of service in their first inauguration chart. Logically speaking, at the time of the first election, we don't know if there will be another term. The second inauguration chart may more specifically relate to events in a president's second term.

Chapter 8: The Presidents

Sing your death song and die like a hero going home.
– Tecumseh

Lack of accurate birth times for several of the presidents born in the 19th and early 20th centuries may limit our ability to analyze their horoscopes. But birth dates alone or those with estimated times will allow us to see the basics and examine patterns in the leaders' charts. And while we have accurate birth times for more recent inauguration horoscopes, as well as good estimates for earlier ones, they, too, are not always exact.

Presidential inaugurals follow a similar pattern. In the 19th century, the presidents often gave their addresses first, and took the oath of office after that, almost always around mid-day. In the 20th century, the oaths generally came first. In 1933, the 20th Amendment to the Constitution changed the inauguration date from March 4 to January 20, transforming the resonance of the Sun and presidency from mid-Pisces (closely trine the U.S. Sun) to the first degree of Aquarius (conjunct the U.S. South Node). The time was also set for the new president to officially take office at noon. When I have found the time of the oath, usually a few minutes later, I use it, as presidents cannot officially act until they take the oath. As a number of the inauguration times are somewhat estimated, I more consistently look to the Sun as a generic symbol of the leader, rather than the Midheaven. (See the chart Notes for more detailed sources of birth and inauguration times.)

The first president involved in the Jupiter-Saturn earth-sign pattern was Thomas Jefferson, who is rarely mentioned as part of the cycle. He was elected in 1800, took the oath of office on March 4, 1801, and the Jupiter-Saturn conjunction in Virgo occurred during his term in 1802. This was the first Jupiter-Saturn conjunction in an earth sign, and since the conjunction was only beginning to mutate into earth signs (it was not yet established in earth signs), he was not affected. Jefferson also had the conjunction in his birth chart with Saturn in Leo and Jupiter in Virgo, and his inauguration at nearly 58 years old was near his Jupiter and Saturn returns. (See page 151 for his inauguration chart, and Appendix 3 for a list of inauguration dates, Jupiter-Saturn conjunctions and the dates of presidential deaths.)

Still, Jupiter and Saturn's influence in earth signs can be seen in the Louisiana Purchase, which nearly doubled the size of the country by adding lands west of the Mississippi. The enthusiasm for expansion exemplified by the Lewis and Clark expedition relates more to fire. (Saturn was still in Leo at the inauguration and Jupiter was also in Leo during much of 1801.)

Jefferson was not connected with the Shawnee brothers. But while he showed an interest in Indigenous culture and history, he believed the Turtle Islanders should adopt European lifestyles and beliefs well before his presidency, and he supported their removal west of the Mississippi. As a former two-term governor of Virginia, he often thought Indigenous resistance resulted from plots with the British, stating in the Declaration of Independence that King George III had "endeavored to bring on the inhabitants of our frontiers, the merciless Indian savages, whose warfare is an undistinguished destruction of all ages, sexes, and conditions."

Jefferson didn't die in office.

For the Indigenous peoples, the earth signs presented limitations and boundaries. Their land continued to be aggressively seized by the Americans. (Jesuits and other missionaries had zealously pushed the Christian religion on them in the previous two fire-sign centuries.)

James Monroe was a lifetime politician, who was the first to ascend to the presidency after the Battle of the Thames (where Tecumseh was killed). Re-elected in a landslide in the zero year of 1820, he established the "era of good feelings." Jupiter conjunct Saturn was in Aries: the combination had returned to fire signs for one final time before it would continue exclusively in earth. Monroe was inaugurated on March 5, 1821 and the conjunction was exact in June.

Reflecting the end of the fire-sign influence, Monroe is best remembered for broad initiatives that set legal policy. The Monroe Doctrine recognized the South American republics and announced the independence of the Americas from European influence. The Missouri Compromise was enacted in 1820 and allowed slavery in Missouri, a state west of the Mississippi River, but disallowed it in Maine. Spain transferred Florida to the U.S. in 1821, and the Seminole communities were subsequently confined to the center of Florida, but allowed to remain in the area for the time being.

Going forward, the Jupiter-Saturn conjunctions became established in earth signs and would continue steadily in earth for nearly two hundred years.

William Henry Harrison was the first president to die in office, and at 68, he was also the oldest chief executive to date. He was elected in 1840 by touting his role in driving the Shawnees and other groups out of the Northwest Territory. Some have suggested that his history of conflict with Tecumseh, Tenskwatawa, the Shawnee coalition and numerous other Nations set him up for retribution and an Indigenous curse.

Harrison was the first to travel by train to Washington and he met with crowds, gave speeches and attended receptions at many stops along the way. He arrived in Washington in a snowstorm. For his oath of office, the new president rode in on a white charger, along with officers and soldiers who had fought with him. He disdained a coat and hat on the chilly March 4 inauguration day (maybe in an attempt to prove himself still vigorous) and spoke for an hour and forty minutes, still the longest inaugural address in history. It was thought to be a long, boring talk even after Daniel Webster helped him edit it.

Harrison caught a bad cold that turned into pneumonia, and he was bedridden for a month. During this time he was treated with cupping, blistering and bleeding. When these measures didn't work, he was given brandy, laxatives, mercury and opium and finally an Indigenous remedy called snakeroot (which they had used to draw venom from a bite). Snakes are associated with violence and revenge in several cultures, so snakeroot's use has ironic overtones. Harrison died on April 4, only a month after taking office.

Tecumseh had been killed in the Battle of the Thames in 1813. Nearly 28 years had passed, and Saturn was approaching the same place in Capricorn where it had been then. Some feel that the cycles of Saturn have karmic resonance, and if so, it seems appropriate here.

Harrison was elected in 1840, and the conjunction in Capricorn wasn't exact until January of 1842, though Harrison had already died in office before then. At the time of his election, inauguration and death, Jupiter and Saturn were still over 10 degrees apart in longitude (signs of the zodiac). If we want to widen the Jupiter-Saturn orb, Harrison's death fits the pattern, but most astrologers don't use such a large orb for this conjunction. Some astrological writers have even said that Harrison's death was a coincidence. But the two planets were very closely parallel in declination (within minutes) at the 1841 inauguration and Harrison's death.

Over the years, many astrologers have written about the presidential death cycle. It doesn't work in what would be considered a strictly regular pattern. Astrology is a complex study that is certainly neither linear nor a science, and it would be both simplistic and unrealistic to literally expect deaths spaced exactly 20 years apart. Despite the repetitive nature of Jupiter conjunct Saturn, there are numerous other planets, aspects and other celestial influences to consider. But astrologers haven't generally looked beyond the conjunctions in longitude (measurement in degrees on the ecliptic or the circle of zodiac signs).

Parallels of declination (measurement in degrees parallel to the celestial equator) have become more popular in the last 30 years, with more astrologers understanding and using them. Declination has been studied since the days of Hipparchus around 150 BCE. This measurement is often thought to be more significant than longitude, as aspects in declination last for longer periods of time and have a more pervasive, underlying influence. A conjunction in a horoscope chart suggests that two or more planets are placed together in the sky, but observers will immediately notice that they're often not very close, even when in the exact same degree. The planets need to be both conjunct and parallel, a noticeably stronger aspect, for them to actually be seen right next to one another. Whether they are conjunctions in longitude or parallels in declination, each measurement ultimately represents a visual alignment. Jupiter and Saturn will never actually overlap visually, at least not for thousands of years; that would be called an occultation, and happens during eclipses. (The Moon occults the Sun during a solar eclipse, and the Earth occults the Moon in a lunar eclipse.)

Jupiter and Saturn both have rather regular orbits, and when they conjoin in longitude they will always be close in declination as well. (They are often both exactly conjunct and parallel within about a month.) The two planets may first be more closely parallel, then more closely conjunct as they go through their preordained dance in the sky. Other planets do not have the same regularity, and this may be one reason why the combination of Jupiter and Saturn is so important astrologically.

Parallels of declination move much more slowly and are therefore generally longer-lasting than conjunctions. (Their influence may be similar to conjunctions. Contraparallels, when planets are on opposite sides—north or south—of the celestial equator, have been compared with oppositions.) But due to the differences in Jupiter and Saturn's orbits, periodic retrograde motion, and the fact that Jupiter moves out-of-bounds (beyond the limit of the Sun's path of the ecliptic) from time to time, the two planets don't always move in lock-step.

William Henry Harrison's case is different than the other presidential years. Jupiter and Saturn were both parallel in declination (and less than a degree apart) during all of 1841. However both were in Sagittarius for a good part of that year, including the time of the election. The two planets were within orb of conjoining in earth-sign Capricorn by December of 1841, after Harrison had passed. They exactly conjoined in longitude in January of 1842. Throughout that year, they were within orb of a conjunction in longitude (less than about 8 degrees) and parallel in declination (less than 1½ degrees), including three more exact parallels that year.

Similarly, Jupiter and Saturn were exactly parallel on January 3, 1960, a day after John F. Kennedy announced he would seek the presidential nomination. The pattern repeated over a year later, six weeks after he was inaugurated. William McKinley's inaugural Jupiter and Saturn were exactly parallel a month after his election. The aspect repeated over a year later and was exact less than a month after he was shot. The power of the parallel aspect between Jupiter and Saturn puts Harrison squarely in the pattern of presidential deaths in office. The conjunction, whether in longitude or declination, need not occur before the president takes office.

Harrison's seven planets in earth signs include the Moon, Saturn and Neptune in Virgo; Mercury, Venus and Pluto in Capricorn; and Uranus in Taurus. With most part of a grand trine pattern, he seems a natural to usher in the Jupiter-Saturn conjunctions in earth. These placements show his relentless insistence upon land acquisition for both himself and the country. (Evangeline Adams equated Uranus in Taurus with empire-builders such as Napoleon, Cecil Rhodes and Wilhelm II; like Harrison, the acquisition of power or land seemed an imperative for each of them).

Harrison's dignified Jupiter in Pisces opposing a Saturn-Neptune conjunction shows his lack of restraint and the inclination to look the other way. He either misunderstood or fudged the facts with superiors in order to attain his goals. Those with Saturn conjunct Neptune may bring their dreams down to earth, but this combination could also indicate a negative attitude or uncomfortable psychic impressions. The idea of a curse surrounding Harrison stems from this pattern, and the president metaphorically shares a similar destiny with the U. S. and its close Saturn-Neptune parallel.

We lack a well-timed horoscope, but Mars in Cancer opposing Mercury, Venus and Pluto in Capricorn could indicate tremendous personal desires, a cruel streak, or the experience of violence.

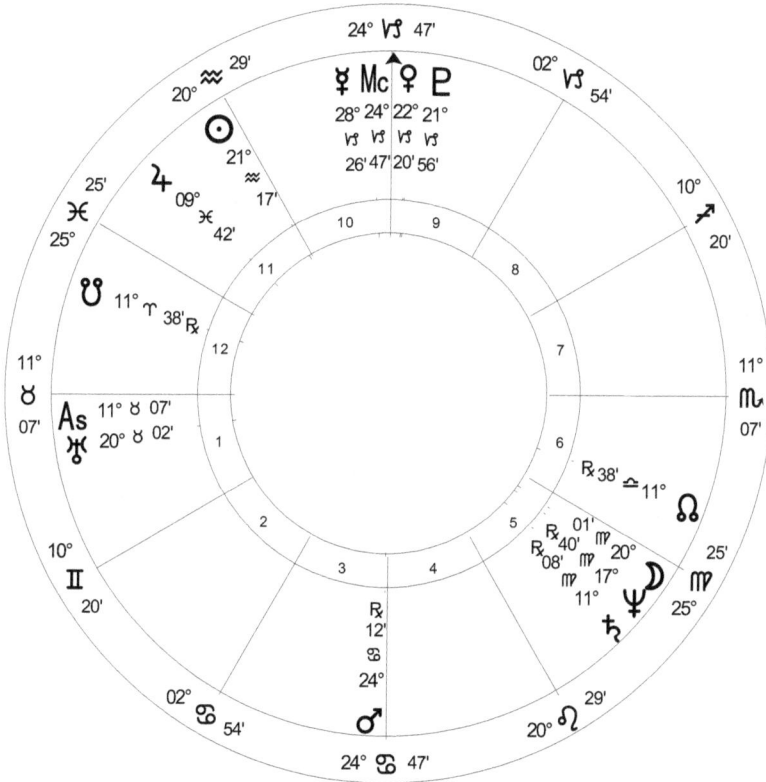

Name	Pt	Long.	Hs	Decl.
Sun	☉	21°≈17'42"	11	−14°25'
Moon	☽	20°♏01'58"	5	+02°12'
Mercury	☿	28°♑26	10	−21°18'
Venus	♀	22°♑20	9	−21°30'
Mars	♂	24°♋12 ℞	3	+25°29'
Jupiter	♃	09°♓42	11	−08°52'
Saturn	♄	11°♏08 ℞	5	+09°16'
Uranus	♅	20°♉02	1	+17°31'
Neptune	♆	17°♏40 ℞	5	+05°54'
Pluto	♇	21°♑56	9	−22°49'
North Node	☊	11°♎38 ℞	6	−04°36'
South Node	☋	11°♈38 ℞	12	+04°36'
Ascendant	As	11°♉07'15"	1	+15°11'
Midheaven	Mc	24°♑47'52"	10	−21°11'

Chart
William Henry Harrison
Natal Chart
Feb 9 1773 NS, Tue
10:26:53 am LMT +5:08:16
Charles City, VA
37°N21' 077°W04'
Geocentric
Tropical
Placidus
True Node
Rating: C
Isaac Starkman rectification

47 Horoscope: William Henry Harrison

Harrison's out-of-bounds Mars (beyond the ecliptic degrees of 23 N/S 27) highlights Martian issues in his life, and his success was through the military and armed actions.

The 1841 inauguration chart clearly shows unusual circumstances surrounding the president. The Sun in the ninth house conjoins Uranus (reiterating the Sun-Uranus parallel in the U.S. horoscope), and both also square Jupiter. The Jupiter square Uranus also turns the U.S. Mars square Neptune into a mutable grand cross, provoking uncommon or unforeseen events.

The North Node conjunct Neptune in Aquarius in the eighth house falls on the U.S. Moon and activates its grand trine in air, which may indicate the possibility of loss or circumstances out of everyone's control. And the U.S. Mercury-Pluto opposition falls across the inauguration Ascendant-Descendant axis. In addition, the inauguration Sun parallel Pluto shows the potential for danger to the head of state.

Eclipses fell on both Harrison's Sun and the U.S. Moon (as they were closely conjunct), signifying the possibility of important changes to come. Before the election, a lunar eclipse in Aquarius on August 13, 1840 formed a T-square with Harrison's natal Sun square Uranus and the U.S. Moon. A month before the inauguration and three days before the president's birthday, a lunar eclipse on February 6, 1841 with the Sun conjunct transiting Neptune in Aquarius similarly activated the same pattern.

Another president was also elected in 1840: Harrison's running mate, John Tyler, who served almost the full four-year term as president. And while he survived, there was a notable instance of bloodshed during his term of office.

Tyler's administration promoted expansion of the Navy, and when a new warship, the U.S.S. Princeton, was completed, the President, cabinet officials and 400 guests took a promotional cruise up the Potomac River on February 28, 1844. A new cannon, the "Peacemaker," was fired to demonstrate its power, after which the elite guests retired below deck for lunch and refreshments. Some clamored for another cannon shot, which proved deadly. The cannon, later found to be faulty, exploded, and shrapnel killed six, including the Secretary of State and Secretary of the Navy. Seventeen others were injured.

Tyler was halfway up the steps to the deck when the explosion occurred, but was unharmed. And he gained a bride: a young woman less than half his age who'd previously spurned the widower's overtures soon changed her mind when her father was among those killed (see Chart Notes for his data).

William Henry Harrison's inauguration horoscope included Jupiter in fire-sign Sagittarius and Saturn in earth-sign Capricorn, suitable for the transition to earth. We can see resonances of broad, dynamic fire-sign initiatives as well as practical, down-to-earth developments during the term and in the years to come.

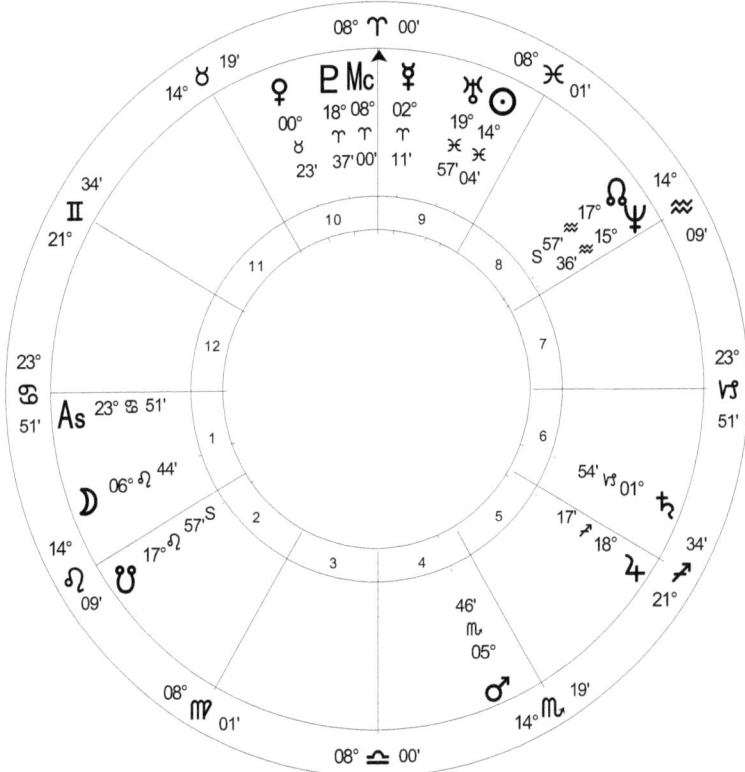

Name	Pt	Long.	Hs	Decl.
Sun	☉	14°♓04'28"	9	−06°16'
Moon	☽	06°♌44'18"	1	+19°35'
Mercury	☿	02°♈11	9	+02°36'
Venus	♀	00°♉23	10	+13°50'
Mars	♂	05°♏46	4	−11°11'
Jupiter	♃	18°♐17	5	−22°15'
Saturn	♄	01°♑54	6	−22°23'
Uranus	♅	19°♓57	9	−04°39'
Neptune	♆	15°♒36	8	−16°18'
Pluto	♇	18°♈37	10	−08°18'
North Node	☊	17°♒57	8	−15°27'
South Node	☋	17°♌57	2	+15°27'
Ascendant	As	23°♋51'19"	1	+21°21'
Midheaven	Mc	08°♈00'25"	10	+03°10'

Chart
Harrison Inauguration
Natal Chart
Mar 4 1841 NS, Thu
1:40 pm LMT +5:08:09
Washington, DC
38°N53'42" 077°W02'12"
Geocentric
Tropical
Placidus
True Node
Rating: A
Boller, Pres Inaugurations

48 Horoscope: Harrison Inauguration

Harrison and Tyler had been elected during a recession. There was bank restructuring and trade limitations in the coming years, in keeping with the restrictive influence of Capricorn, but wide-ranging actions (relating to fire signs) were also taken. Labor unions were recognized, the first telegraph line was completed and a treaty with Great Britain regularized borders. The U.S. also expanded further, annexing Texas and California following the Mexican war (1846 to 1848). Like Texas, Florida was admitted to the union as a slave state.

Zachary Taylor, the twelfth president, was the only one not elected in a zero year to die in office (see Chart Notes for his data). He had Saturn square Neptune in his birth chart and succumbed to gastroenteritis on July 9, 1850. Transiting Jupiter and Saturn were nearly exactly parallel and also quincunx one another at his death. Taylor was a plantation owner, career army officer and general who had served under William Henry Harrison, defending Fort Harrison against Tecumseh's coalition during the War of 1812. He later fought the Seminoles in Florida and earned victories in the Mexican-American war.

Indigenous people didn't ordinarily share their prophecies with whites. However when Munsee leaders (a sub-group of the Lenape) wrote to Taylor a few weeks after he took office to entreat him to make good on American promises, they also mentioned the following:

Previous to your arrival into our vast Continent, our Ancient Prophets and wise men had a Vision and Revelation in regard to your coming, though they did not understand fully the meaning of it, whether it was to be the Almighty himself or our fellow men, this was a matter of deep consideration for a while with our forefathers until you did arrive. (Pritchard, p. 11)

Like the Aztecs and Shawnees, they had anticipated visitors to their shores.

Abraham Lincoln was elected in 1860. As he arrived at his first inaugural, a reporter noted that he looked pale, fatigued and anxious. He survived his first term during the Civil War and was assassinated by John Wilkes Booth in Ford's Theater on April 14, 1865, a month after his second inauguration. (Three of the seven presidential deaths occurred in April and two in September.)

Lincoln's Saturn and Neptune conjoin his Midheaven, showing his remarkable position, but also indicating complicated circumstances and a potential fall. The seventh house ruler, the Sun in its detriment in Aquarius, representing open enemies, comes right to him (falling in his first house) and trines Mars in its detriment in the eighth house in Libra, a suggestion of potential violence from others. The twelfth house of hidden enemies holds the Moon (also in detriment) with its square to Mars, showing the secret plot against him. The Moon in Capricorn, ruled by Saturn conjunct Neptune at the top of his chart, symbolizes its impact on his life and career (especially as the ruler of the first is also Saturn).

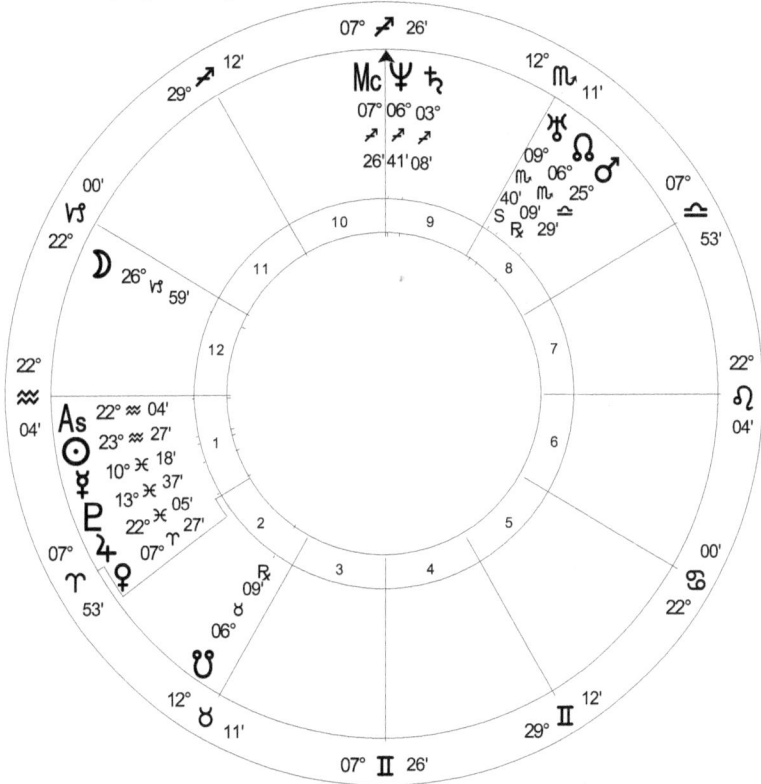

Name	Pt	Long.	Hs	Decl.
Sun	☉	23°≈27'27"	1	−13°42'
Moon	☽	26°♑59'33"	12	−15°54'
Mercury	☿	10°♓18	1	−07°42'
Venus	♀	07°♈27	1	+03°10'
Mars	♂	25°♎29	8	−07°24'
Jupiter	♃	22°♓05	1	−04°09'
Saturn	♄	03°♐08	9	−18°50'
Uranus	♅	09°♏40	8	−14°17'
Neptune	♆	06°♐41	9	−19°51'
Pluto	♇	13°♓37	1	−19°25'
North Node	☊	06°♏09 ℞	8	−13°35'
South Node	☋	06°♉09 ℞	2	+13°35'
Ascendant	As	22°≈04'20"	1	−14°10'
Midheaven	Mc	07°♐26'44"	10	−21°34'

Chart
Abraham Lincoln
Natal Chart
Feb 12 1809 NS, Sun
6:54 am LMT +5:42:58
Hodgenville, Kentucky
37°N34'26" 085°W44'24"
Geocentric
Tropical
Placidus
True Node
Rating: B
Sandburg: Abraham Lincoln p 22

49 Horoscope: Abraham Lincoln

Lincoln had a bad dream the night before the shooting, and reportedly told his cabinet that something similar had happened before the Battle of Bull Run, an early and decisive loss for the Union. With all of his planets but Venus in southern declination and Mercury conjunct Pluto in Pisces, he was probably quite intuitive or even psychic.

Homeopathic physician and astrologer Dr. Luke D. Broughton in his *Monthly Planet Reader* of April 1865 had forecast that, "Some noted General or a person in high office dies or is removed about the 17th or 18th." (Broughton, p. 70 Note) Dr. Broughton may have considered transiting Jupiter stationing in late Sagittarius in April as it trined Uranus in Gemini and sextiled Saturn. Mars in Cancer also conjoined the U.S. Sun and squared its Saturn, while transiting Saturn in late Libra trined the U.S. Midheaven at the same time.

In declination, transiting Venus and Mars were both out-of-bounds (25+N) and transiting out-of-bounds (OOB) Uranus paralleled the U.S. Sun, Venus and Mars while contraparalleling Pluto. Lincoln's death on April 15 was only a week after Confederate General Lee's surrender at Appomattox.

The 1861 inauguration South Node and Ascendant conjoin U.S. chart ruler Mercury, suggesting the possibility of loss or unpleasant news to come. Mars conjunct Pluto in Taurus in the tenth house points toward tough circumstances, and inaugural Uranus has returned to its natal place in Gemini. Since the presidential terms continued to start on March 4, the Sun would always be placed near 14 Pisces. Uranus' cycle is about 84 years long, and a quarter of that is 21 years, bringing it close to hard aspects to the March 4 Sun every 20 years. Harrison's 1841 inauguration had the Sun conjunct Uranus, and in 1861 the Sun in Pisces squared Uranus, once again suggesting unusual circumstances for the country and its leader.

As in Harrison's example, Jupiter and Saturn were both conjunct and parallel in earth-sign Virgo well after the inauguration, in the fall of 1861. The conjunction at 18 Virgo 22 on October 21, 1861 conjoined U.S. Neptune and squared its Ascendant and Mars. It also opposed Lincoln's Jupiter, co-ruler of his first house (himself) and ruler of his Midheaven and eleventh house (his standing in the community).

Eclipses involving Mars may relate to violence if the radix charts they activate have that predisposition. Before the election, a total solar eclipse in Cancer opposite Mars in Capricorn on July

18, 1860 fell right on the U.S. Mercury-Pluto opposition. Three days before Lincoln was shot, a lunar eclipse on April 11, 1865 with the Moon conjunct Saturn in Libra conjoined his eighth house Mars. The eclipse Venus, Mars and Uranus were all out-of-bounds in declination and variously paralleled the U.S. out-of-bounds Venus, Mars and Jupiter, and contraparalleled U.S. Pluto.

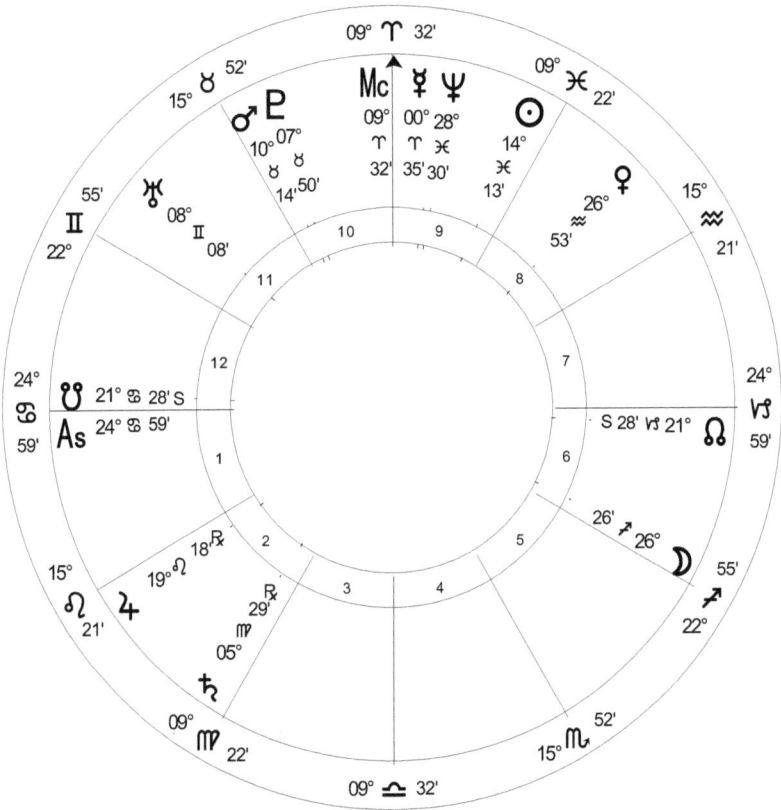

Name	Pt	Long.	Hs	Decl.
Sun	☉	14°♓13'24"	9	−06°12'
Moon	☽	26°♐26'47"	6	−25°34'
Mercury	☿	00°♈35	9	+02°44'
Venus	♀	26°♒53	8	−13°37'
Mars	♂	10°♉14	10	+15°30'
Jupiter	♃	19°♌18 ℞	2	+16°06'
Saturn	♄	05°♍29 ℞	2	+11°18'
Uranus	♅	08°♊08	11	+21°39'
Neptune	♆	28°♓30	9	−01°47'
Pluto	♇	07°♉50	10	−00°59'
North Node	☊	21°♑28	6	−21°44'
South Node	☋	21°♋28	12	+21°44'
Ascendant	As	24°♋59'56"	1	+21°08'
Midheaven	Mc	09°♈32'06"	10	+03°46'

Chart
Lincoln Inauguration
Natal Chart
Mar 4 1861 NS, Mon
1:45 pm LMT +5:08:09
Washington, DC
38°N53'42" 077°W02'12"
Geocentric
Tropical
Placidus
True Node
Rating: A
Estimate based on description

50 Horoscope: Lincoln Inauguration

The government imposed tariffs and sold bonds and land to fund the war. The following years found the end of slavery in the U.S., as the southern states lost their influence in the Reconstruction period. Land was granted to railroads and a system of national banks was established. Manufacturing and industry increased in value.

James Garfield was elected in November of 1880 and served less than a year. He was shot and wounded by disgruntled office seeker Charles Guiteau on July 2, 1881 at a railroad station where he was to meet his wife and family for a tour of the eastern states. He died over two months later.

We have a relatively accurate time of birth for Garfield. His Jupiter closely conjoins his South Node, and Uranus, conjoining Jupiter on its other side, squares Mars, indications of the possibility of sudden events of a potentially violent nature at some point in his life. Pluto in Aries in the seventh house is inconjunct Mars and opposes Venus in his first house, which could bring intense, obsessive people or even those bent on doing him harm into his experience. His Jupiter and Nodes align with the United States' Moon, so he shares any impacts on these points with the country.

Garfield has an exact Venus-Saturn semi-sextile in his birth chart, and Venus-Saturn connections are common in the horoscopes of the zero-year presidents. Lincoln had a trine (Harrison's was wide), Franklin Roosevelt a square, John F. Kennedy a novile (40°) along with a parallel in declination, and Ronald Reagan a sextile. (Even Thomas Jefferson had a trine and James Monroe a semi-sextile.) Perhaps these show something about their ambitions or responsibilities, as well as the unusual limitations of their lives and administrations.

Jupiter and Saturn were conjoined in Taurus in 1881 (Garfield was inaugurated with the planets both conjunct and parallel while still in Aries). In the inauguration chart, the Pisces Sun opposed Uranus, once again reiterating the theme of unanticipated events impacting on the country's leader. With Saturn in its fall in Aries in the tenth house of leadership conjoining Jupiter and Venus, there might be unpleasant issues for the chief executive. The Moon square Mars in fixed signs creates a T-square with the U.S. North Node, adding to the potential for violence. The inauguration South Node conjunct the U.S. Ascendant and Mars also create a potentially dangerous combination. Inauguration Jupiter and Saturn squared the U.S. Mercury-Pluto opposition.

Aspects in declination reiterate many of these themes but draw a more definitive picture. Jupiter, Saturn, Uranus and Pluto are all tightly parallel in North declination, as well as contraparallel the Sun in the south (Pluto within 10′): the upheaval faced by the president (whether represented by the Sun or Saturn) is clear.

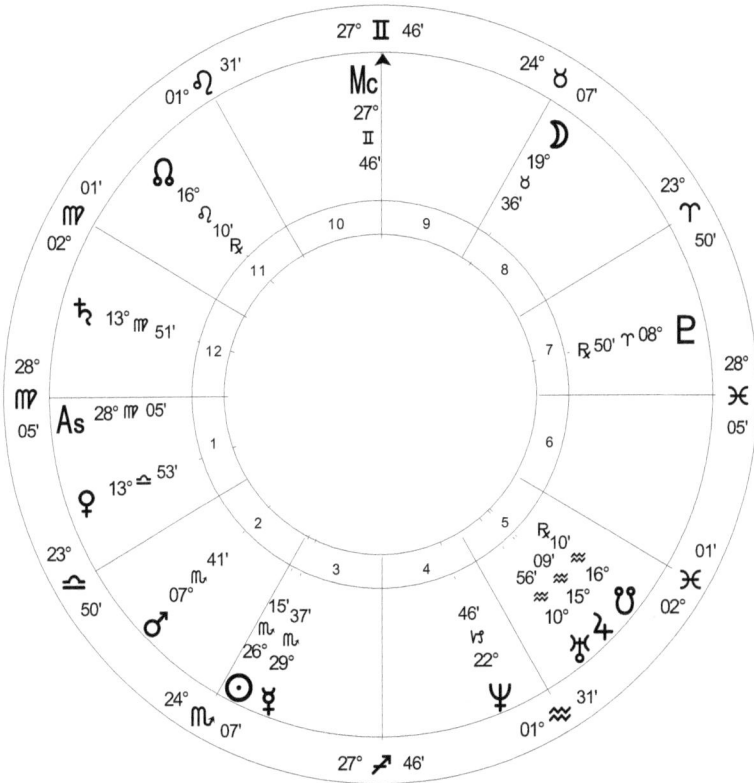

Name	Pt	Long.	Hs	Decl.
Sun	☉	26°♏15'30"	3	−19°20'
Moon	☽	19°♉36'06"	8	+12°49'
Mercury	☿	29°♏37	3	−20°51'
Venus	♀	13°♎53	1	−04°56'
Mars	♂	07°♏41	2	−13°40'
Jupiter	♃	15°♒09	5	−17°12'
Saturn	♄	13°♍51	12	+07°57'
Uranus	♅	10°♒56	5	−18°08'
Neptune	♆	22°♑46	4	−21°04'
Pluto	♇	08°♈50 ℞	7	−12°18'
North Node	☊	16°♌10 ℞	11	+16°00'
South Node	☋	16°♒10 ℞	5	−16°00'
Ascendant	As	28°♍05'39"	1	+00°45'
Midheaven	Mc	27°♊46'53"	10	+23°26'

Chart
James Garfield
Natal Chart
Nov 19 1831 NS, Sat
2:00 am LMT +5:25:55
Orange, Ohio
41°N26'59" 081°W28'51"
Geocentric
Tropical
Placidus
True Node
Rating: A
From his mother

51 Horoscope: James Garfield

We can again see the power of eclipses activating notable patterns in both the U.S. and the president's horoscopes. Before the election, an annular solar eclipse in Cancer on July 7, 1880 fell on the U.S. Sun and squared its Saturn, suggesting upcoming adjustments for the country and its leader. The eclipse also squared Garfield's first house Venus (his physical body) from his tenth house. Before the shooting, a total lunar eclipse in Sagittarius on June 12, 1881 opposed and conjoined the U.S. Mars.

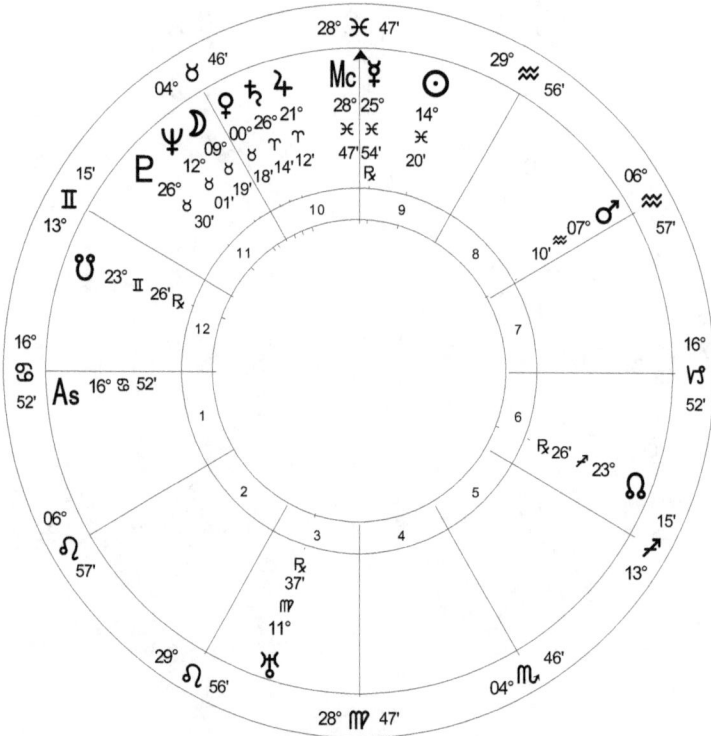

Name	Pt	Long.	Hs	Decl.
Sun	☉	14°♓20'46"	9	-06°09'
Moon	☽	09°♉19'10"	11	+17°56'
Mercury	☿	25°♓54 ℞	9	+01°29'
Venus	♀	00°♉18	10	+14°29'
Mars	♂	07°♒10	8	-19°28'
Jupiter	♃	21°♈12	10	+07°16'
Saturn	♄	26°♈14	10	+07°59'
Uranus	♅	11°♍37 ℞	3	+07°57'
Neptune	♆	12°♉01	11	+13°47'
Pluto	♇	26°♉30	11	+06°19'
North Node	☊	23°♐26 ℞	6	-23°17'
South Node	☋	23°♊26 ℞	12	+23°17'
Ascendant	As	16°♋52'27"	1	+22°23'
Midheaven	Mc	28°♓47'09"	10	-00°28'

Chart
Garfield Inauguration
Natal Chart
Mar 4 1881 NS, Fri
1:05 pm LMT +5:08:09
Washington, DC
38°N53'42" 077°W02'12"
Geocentric
Tropical
Placidus
True Node
Rating: A
"Little after 1:00 Friday"

52 Horoscope: Garfield Inauguration

A few months before Garfield's shooting and a week before the exact parallel of Jupiter and Saturn in March of 1881, Tsar Alexander II was assassinated in Russia. A committee of 22 men and women seeking revolution were successful in executing an elaborate plot to kill the Tsar with home-made nitroglycerin bombs as he returned to the Winter Palace on a Sunday.

The coming years included the Wounded Knee Massacre, where over 250 Lakota Sioux men, women and children were slaughtered in South Dakota in 1890, one of the last major American military attacks on Indigenous groups. The economy continued in depression through the 1890s. However, with the growth of railroads, electricity, the telephone and steel, corporations and the industrial north were on the rise.

William McKinley was re-elected to a second term as president in 1900 and served less than a year more. After giving a speech about the booming economy at the Buffalo, New York World's Fair, McKinley was shaking hands when he was shot by anarchist Leon Czolgosz on September 6, 1901. The president died eight days later. Jupiter and Saturn were exactly conjunct in Capricorn in November of 1901. While the exact Jupiter-Saturn conjunction fell after the inauguration and death dates, the two planets were very close in both declination and longitude during much of the previous year.

McKinley's well-timed birth chart also shows an open enemy (or other significant individual) coming to him as the ruler of his seventh house, Mars, falls in his first in single-minded Scorpio. Like Garfield, McKinley also has Pluto in Aries inconjunct Mars in Scorpio (with McKinley's Pluto conjunct the seventh house cusp). The co-ruler of his Midheaven, the Sun, is placed in its detriment and conjoins the Moon, Jupiter and Neptune in Aquarius, showing a potential loss of position or a noteworthy end of life since the planets are all in his fourth house.

The Mars-Pluto theme is common to many of the zero-year presidents, bringing great intensity, a possible need for control, and the potential for violence into their lives. Harrison, Warren Harding and Ronald Reagan had an opposition; Franklin Roosevelt and George W. Bush a semi-sextile; and John F. Kennedy a semi-square. Thomas Jefferson and James Monroe both had a trine. Depending on its placement in the birth chart, this combination may simply bring tremendous focus, great drive and ambition, strength, or the ability to accomplish goals. Mars-Pluto combinations are also in some of the inauguration charts. Lincoln had a conjunction in 1861, FDR a trine in 1941, JFK a sextile, Ronald Reagan a trine in 1981, and Bush a semi-sextile in 2001.

McKinley's planets are all in South declination, suggesting someone somehow more responsive than active. (Lincoln only had Venus in the North, Garfield the Moon and Saturn, and Zachary Taylor the Moon and Uranus. Warren Harding had the Moon in North declination, along with Uranus, Neptune and Pluto; Reagan the Moon, Saturn, Neptune and Pluto North).

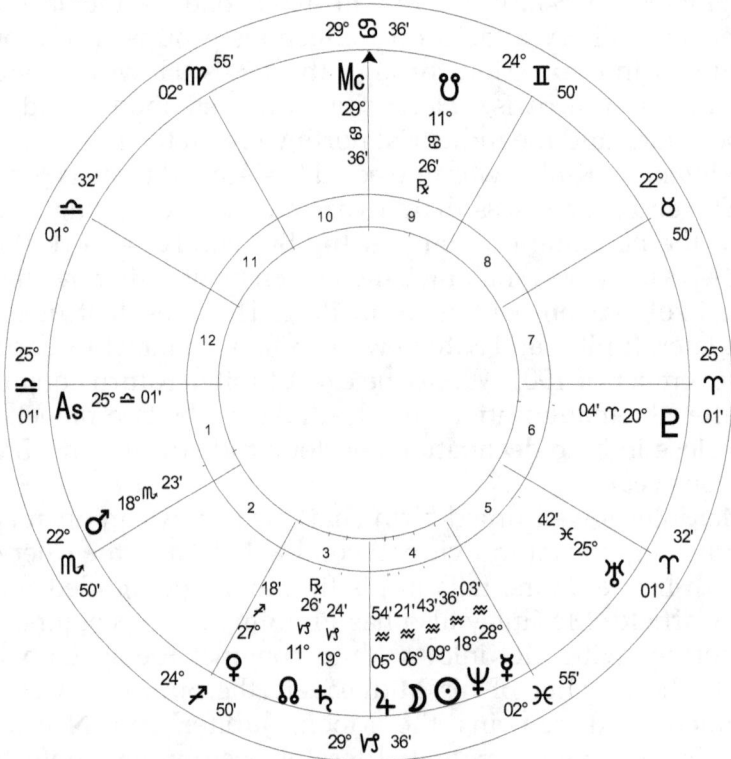

Name	Pt	Long.	Hs	Decl.
Sun	☉	09°♒43'01"	4	-17°49'
Moon	☽	06°♒21'45"	4	-16°33'
Mercury	☿	28°♒03	4	-11°55'
Venus	♀	27°♐18	3	-18°11'
Mars	♂	18°♏23	1	-16°07'
Jupiter	♃	05°♒54	4	-19°17'
Saturn	♄	19°♑24	3	-21°51'
Uranus	♅	25°♓42	5	-02°22'
Neptune	♆	18°♒36	4	-15°30'
Pluto	♇	20°♈04	6	-07°54'
North Node	☊	11°♑26 ℞	3	-22°57'
South Node	☋	11°♋26 ℞	9	+22°57'
Ascendant	As	25°♎01'28"	1	-09°41'
Midheaven	Mc	29°♋36'35"	10	+20°14'

Chart
William McKinley
Natal Chart
Jan 29 1843 NS, Sun
11:32 pm LMT +5:23:04
Niles, OH
41°N10'58" 080°W45'56"
Geocentric
Tropical
Placidus
True Node
Rating: A
From his mother in 1896

53 Horoscope: William McKinley

McKinley's inauguration Sun squares Uranus as well as Pluto, indicating unexpected occurrences and potential challenges for the president. The mutable T-square, along with Neptune, again falls on the U.S. Mars square Neptune, creating a grand cross, similar to Harrison's pattern of sixty years before. And an out-of-sign conjunction of the Moon and Mars on the third house cusp is reminiscent of the squares in Garfield and Harrison's inauguration charts as well.

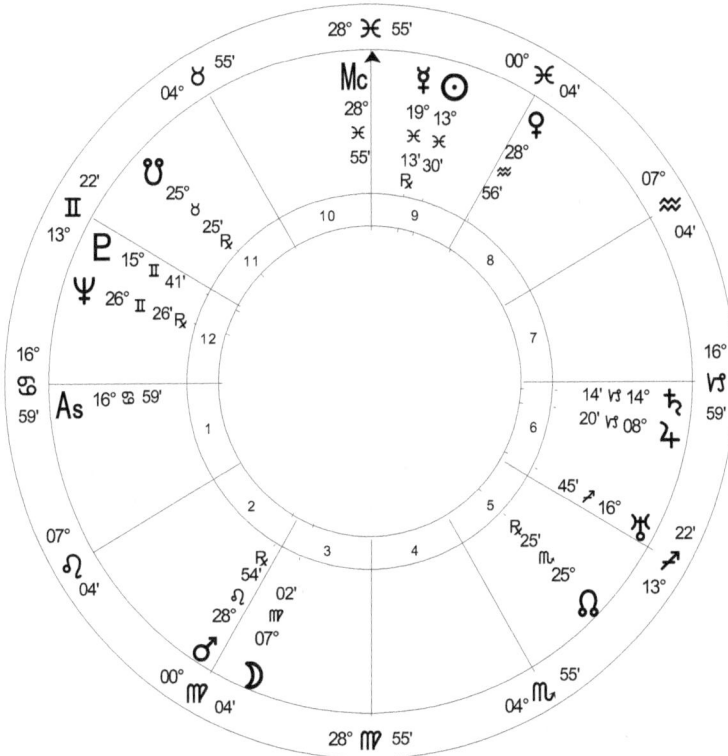

Name	Pt	Long.	Hs	Decl.
Sun	☉	13°✶30'11"	9	-06°29'
Moon	☽	07°♍02'07"	3	+04°21'
Mercury	☿	19°✶13 ℞	9	-00°53'
Venus	♀	28°♒56	8	-12°58'
Mars	♂	28°♌54 ℞	2	+15°50'
Jupiter	♃	08°♑20	6	-22°57'
Saturn	♄	14°♑14	6	-22°08'
Uranus	♅	16°♐45	6	-22°47'
Neptune	♆	26°♊26 ℞	12	+22°11'
Pluto	♇	15°♊41	12	+13°25'
North Node	☊	25°♏25 ℞	5	-19°07'
South Node	☋	25°♉25 ℞	11	+19°07'
Ascendant	As	16°♋59'01"	1	+22°22'
Midheaven	Mc	28°✶55'52"	10	-00°25'

Chart
McKinley Inauguration
Natal Chart
Mar 4 1901 NS, Mon
1:17 pm EST +5:00
Washington, DC
38°N53'42" 077°W02'12"
Geocentric
Tropical
Placidus
True Node
Rating: A
"... oath of office at 1:17"

54 Horoscope: McKinley Inauguration

The pattern of U.S. Saturn contraparallel Neptune suggesting potential loss and suffering is reiterated in McKinley's inauguration, with Jupiter, Saturn and Uranus contraparallel a close Neptune parallel the Ascendant (falling right on McKinley's Saturn-South Node contraparallel). In addition, Mercury and the Midheaven are parallel near 0° declination, and so fall at the midpoint of all the contraparallels. (Harrison and Franklin Roosevelt had natal Saturn conjunct Neptune; Lincoln and Kennedy both had the conjunction on the MC; Garfield had a wide trine (9°); McKinley had the two planets semi-sextile; Harding had them inconjunct (a little wide at 4°); and Reagan had a bi-novile (about 80°).

The McKinley inaugural Nodes in Scorpio and Taurus fall in the U.S. twelfth house and square the MC/IC axis, an unfavorable combination for the chief executive (MC). Saturn conjoins Jupiter in Capricorn and opposes the inaugural Ascendant. It also creates a T-square with the U.S. Sun-Saturn square that may specifically relate to an authority figure.

Astrologer Julius Erickson wrote in the *St. Louis Post-Dispatch* of April 28, 1901, well before the shooting, that,

The President will be in grave danger of illness or accident while on a long journey… An especially serious or vexatious period may be looked for during the early part of June, 1901. He will be in danger of illness or accident about that time. He is in aspect somewhat similar to those in operation while Lincoln and Garfield assumed office.

Erickson must have noticed the Sun-Uranus pattern of hard aspects in the earlier inauguration horoscopes. He had probably linked an attack to transiting Mars in Virgo conjoining the inauguration Moon and creating a grand cross with the inauguration Sun in Pisces and Uranus in Sagittarius along with the transiting Sun in Gemini. We can now see that Pluto in Gemini also featured in the pattern.

In April, McKinley left on a six-week national railroad tour with his wife, Ida. By the time they arrived in San Francisco in mid-May, however, Ida was ill and the president cut the tour short, returning to Washington by the end of the month. His visit to the Buffalo World's Fair (where he was later shot in September), was also delayed. By June, the time the astrologer had highlighted, events had already conspired to alter the president's plans.

In a follow-up report on September 7, 1901, Erickson explained that Uranus had exactly squared the inauguration Sun at the time of the actual shooting, while the transiting Sun had opposed it (six months after taking office). He added that, "The Moon, which is President McKinley's ruling planet during his term, as it was in Lincoln's and Garfield's, was quite seriously afflicted at the time of his inauguration." The Moon was leaving a conjunction with Mars and would go on to form a grand cross with the Sun-Uranus-Pluto T-square in the inauguration horoscope.

All three inaugurations had Cancer rising, with oaths of office between 1:00 and 2:00 p.m., and the Moon had squared Mars for Garfield and Neptune for Lincoln. The astrologer's reference to danger on a long journey could relate to the inaugural Sun in the ninth house of long distance travel, and the emphasis on the Moon in the third.

Eclipses conjoining key placements in the U.S. and the president's charts again signaled important developments. Before the election, a total solar eclipse in Gemini on May 28, 1900 conjoined the U.S. Uranus and opposed transiting Uranus, provoking surprising, unexpected or unusual issues. During McKinley's national tour and before the shooting, a lunar eclipse in Scorpio on May 3, 1901 fell in his first house and conjoined his Mars, while it squared his Sun and Moon and also squared the midpoint of the U.S. Moon and Nodes.

In the following decades, the automobile and air industries developed, the NAACP was founded by W.E.B. DuBois, and the women's suffrage and workers' rights movements attracted more attention. The U.S. Forest Service and Pure Food and Drug Act were established. With the 1898 Spanish-American war over, the U.S. obtained its first territories abroad, took control of the Panama Canal, and emerged as a world power in World War I. The flu pandemic hit the U.S. in 1918.

Warren Harding, born the year that Lincoln died, campaigned on a "return to normalcy" platform after World War I. He was considered a weak candidate, but as a newspaper publisher, he exploited modern advertising techniques and press coverage. Harding was nominated after a nine ballot deadlock at the Republican convention in June of 1920. Elected with Jupiter and Saturn already in Virgo, he served less than two and a half years. (Outgoing President Woodrow Wilson did not appear at the actual ceremony, as he was weak and almost had to be lifted up a flight of steps, reminiscent of Shield Pacal and Chan Balam on the Maya Tablet of the Cross at Palenque, page 89.)

On a tour of Canada, Alaska and the west in 1923, Harding suffered from intestinal cramps, then pneumonia. Many accounts say he died of a heart attack. Some question whether it was poison as the president was enmeshed in complicated personal and political relationships. He died on August 2, 1923.

With Jupiter in Sagittarius in his tenth house also ruling his Pisces Ascendant, Harding's birth chart shows his publishing background, good luck in his career, and a great ability to attract attention to his campaign. But Jupiter forms an out-of-sign opposition to Uranus, which could also indicate reversals of fortune.

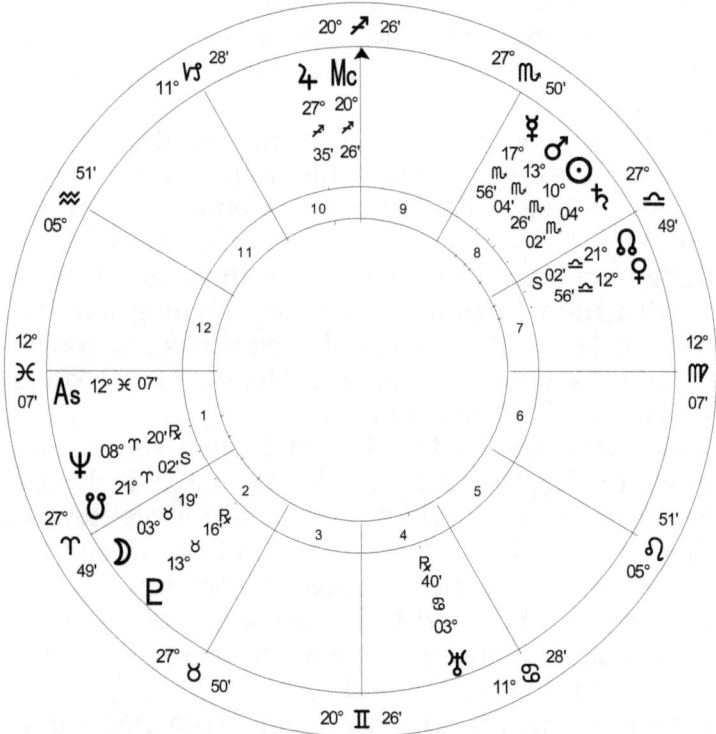

Name	Pt	Long.	Hs	Decl.
Sun	☉	10°♏26'34"	8	−14°57'
Moon	☽	03°♉19'29"	2	+11°34'
Mercury	☿	17°♏56	8	−17°50'
Venus	♀	12°♎56	7	−03°35'
Mars	♂	13°♏04	8	−15°42'
Jupiter	♃	27°♐35	10	−23°21'
Saturn	♄	04°♏02	8	−10°46'
Uranus	♅	03°♋40 ℞	4	+23°39'
Neptune	♆	08°♈20 ℞	1	+01°52'
Pluto	♇	13°♉16 ℞	2	+00°34'
North Node	☊	21°♎02 ℞	7	−08°12'
South Node	☋	21°♈02 ℞	1	+08°12'
Ascendant	As	12°♓07'28"	1	−07°01'
Midheaven	Mc	20°♐26'29"	10	−23°06'

Chart
Warren G. Harding
Natal Chart
Nov 2 1865 NS, Thu
2:30 pm LMT +5:30:52
Blooming Grove, Ohio
40°N42'28" 082°W43'
Geocentric
Tropical
Placidus
True Node
Rating: A
From his father.

55 Horoscope: Warren G. Harding

A businessman, he profited from the Sun, Mercury, Mars and Saturn in Scorpio, all in his eighth house of investments. But their various oppositions to his Moon and Pluto in Taurus suggest a potentially violent and even tragic death. The eighth house dynamics also point toward the tremendous support of his wife, Florence, his romantic affairs while in office, and the complexity of his political partnerships.

Florence Harding's biographer has documented the First Lady's keen interest in astrology. Not unlike Nancy Reagan 60 years later, Mrs. Harding adjusted the scheduled dates for some of her husband's public appearances and meetings with foreign dignitaries. In a reading on May 20, 1920, astrologer Marcia Champney told the First Lady that her husband would win his party's nomination and be elected, but not live out his term as president. Reporter Henry B. Hunt's *Newswire* article in 1920 confirmed the prediction in print. And former president William Howard Taft, who later became Chief Justice of the Supreme Court, wrote a friend on May 2, 1921 about the astrologer's forecasts. He dismissed the prediction of Harding's nomination as "grasping at the obvious," but added that since the inauguration two months before, "… the oracle this time indicated that the President would not see the end of his term." (Anthony p. 288, 448) In doing so, Taft confirmed the forecast over two years before it proved true.

Madame Marcia, as she liked to style herself, was said to have previously forecast President Garfield's assassination and Edith Galt's marriage to President Wilson. But she was also clairvoyant, so we may not know exactly how much of a role astrology played in her accurate prediction.

Harding's inauguration includes the familiar Sun-Uranus combination, now conjoined with Mercury retrograde in Pisces and opposite Jupiter (the Jupiter opposite Uranus also echoes the president's natal pattern). The Sun also opposes Saturn. These afflictions not only point to the potential for unexpected events involving the country's leader, but also the complications of the presidency itself. Mars in Aries is accentuated by its placement in the tenth house and exact opposition to U.S. Saturn. Along with the Moon in Capricorn in the inauguration chart, it creates a grand cross with the country's Sun square Saturn. The inaugural Saturn also activated the U.S. Mars square Neptune. And the Nodes in late Aries and Libra form another grand cross with the U.S. Mercury-Pluto opposition. Not a particularly good time for either the president or the country, though President Harding was popular.

We can begin to see the many cyclic, repeating influences at work in the 20-year inauguration horoscopes. Jupiter and Saturn's conjunctions repeat, as does the Sun in hard aspects to Uranus. The 1921 inauguration chart also features an angular Moon square Mars, and Moon-Mars combinations were also present in Harrison, Garfield and McKinley's inauguration horoscopes.

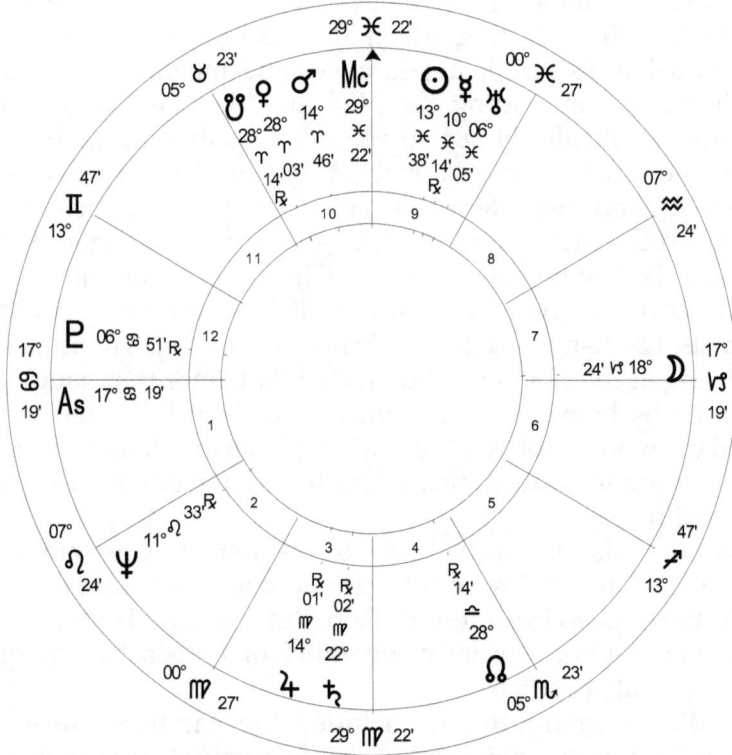

Name	Pt	Long.	Hs	Decl.
Sun	☉	13°✕38'45"	9	−06°26'
Moon	☽	18°♑24'31"	7	−17°09'
Mercury	☿	10°✕14 ℞	9	−04°25'
Venus	♀	28°♈03	10	+14°23'
Mars	♂	14°♈46	10	+05°34'
Jupiter	♃	14°♍01 ℞	3	+07°37'
Saturn	♄	22°♍02 ℞	3	+05°19'
Uranus	♅	06°✕05	9	−09°57'
Neptune	♆	11°♌33 ℞	2	+17°22'
Pluto	♇	06°♋51 ℞	12	+19°49'
North Node	☊	28°♎14 ℞	4	−10°51'
South Node	☋	28°♈14 ℞	10	+10°51'
Ascendant	As	17°♋19'09"	1	+22°19'
Midheaven	Mc	29°✕22'19"	10	−00°14'

Chart

Harding Inauguration
Natal Chart
Mar 4 1921 NS, Fri
1:18 pm EST +5:00
Washington, DC
38°N53'42" 077°W02'12"
Geocentric
Tropical
Placidus
True Node
Rating: A
"oath of office at 1:18 pm"

56 Horoscope: Harding Inauguration

Eclipses played a significant role in Harding's scenario as well. Prior to the election, a total lunar eclipse in Taurus on October 27, 1920 fell on Harding's Sun-Moon-Saturn opposition and squared the U.S. Nodes, suggesting a meeting with destiny. Before he died, a solar eclipse in Pisces on March 17, 1923 fell in his first house and closely squared his tenth house Jupiter and Midheaven.

Harding's administration was solidly pro-business, with lowered taxes and high protective tariffs. The United States continued winding down from the First World War and favored the president's "America First" isolationist policy. An immigration quota system was imposed for the first time, and the Ku Klux Klan revived its power. After Harding's death, a Congressional committee uncovered the Teapot Dome bribery scandal and many others. The growth of the stock market, prohibition of alcohol, organized crime, the Jazz Age youth culture and a growing acceptance of the eugenics movement characterized the 1920s. The Great Depression dominated the '30s.

Franklin Delano Roosevelt was elected in 1940 for his third term in office. During this time, there were three exact conjunctions of Jupiter and Saturn due to Jupiter's retrograde motion: in August and October of 1940 and February 1941. FDR took his third oath of office on the new inauguration date of January 20, 1941. (Presidents would by law now come to power at noon, but could not act until they took the oath of office.) Astrologically, the change in inauguration date alters the destiny of both the president and the country. Roosevelt had the Sun, Mercury and Venus in Aquarius, and inauguration Suns would now be in Aquarius as well.

The president survived his third term during World War II and began his fourth term in 1945 at the age of 63. He suffered from high blood pressure, heart disease and maybe even brain cancer, and died on April 12, 1945 of a cerebral hemorrhage. Some have suggested his death was a result of cyanide poisoning by the Nazis.

Like Lincoln, another Aquarius president, even though he was elected in a term that held the Jupiter-Saturn conjunction, he died in a subsequent term while in office. Like Jefferson, he had a natal conjunction of Jupiter and Saturn (though wide) and was elected in 1940 at the age of 58 near his own Jupiter and Saturn returns and the return of the cyclic conjunction.

Roosevelt was an innovator with Uranus conjunct the Ascendant, and Uranus in the 1940 inauguration chart was conjunct the Ascendant as well. He helped lift the country out of the Great Depression with public funding and his cheerleading fireside chats on the radio.

FDR's natal Jupiter and Saturn had Neptune sandwiched between them, and all variously squared his Aquarius Sun. These show his personal resilience and ability to overcome obstacles (he

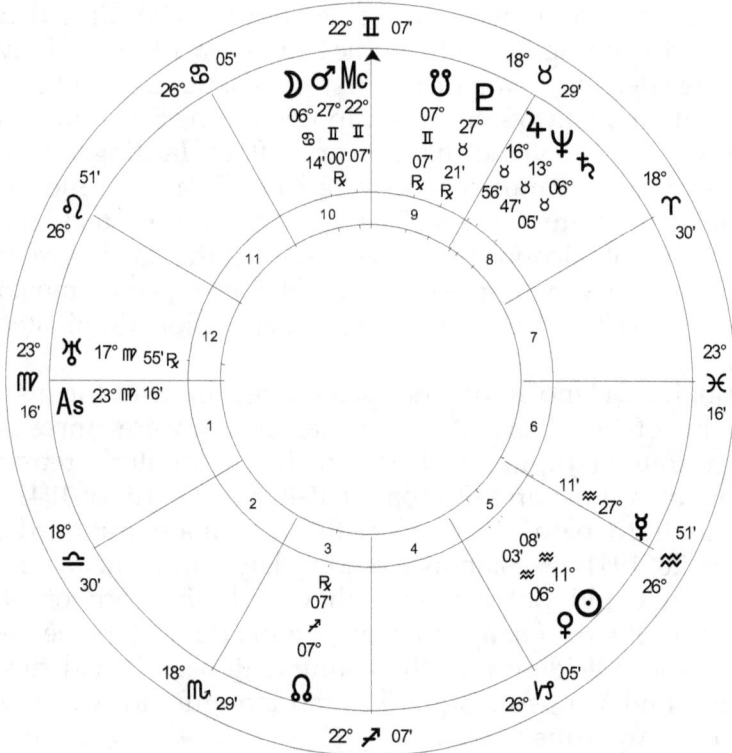

Name	Pt	Long.	Hs	Decl.
Sun	☉	11°≈08'11"	5	-17°26'
Moon	☽	06°♋14'53"	10	+20°50'
Mercury	☿	27°≈11	6	-13°13'
Venus	♀	06°≈03	5	-19°44'
Mars	♂	27°♊00 ℞	10	+26°56'
Jupiter	♃	16°♉56	8	+16°02'
Saturn	♄	06°♉05	8	+11°21'
Uranus	♅	17°♍55 ℞	12	+05°31'
Neptune	♆	13°♉47	8	+14°17'
Pluto	♇	27°♉21 ℞	9	+06°30'
North Node	☊	07°♐07 ℞	3	-21°30'
South Node	☋	07°♊07 ℞	9	+21°30'
Ascendant	As	23°♍16'01"	1	+02°40'
Midheaven	Mc	22°♊07'31"	10	+23°13'

Chart
Franklin D. Roosevelt
Male Chart
Jan 30 1882 NS, Mon
8:45 pm LMT +4:55:44
Hyde Park, NY
41°N47'05" 073°W56'01"
Geocentric
Tropical
Placidus
True Node
Rating: AA
Father's diary

57 Horoscope: Franklin D. Roosevelt

was the first president with a significant physical disability). Born to a wealthy family, Roosevelt remained somewhat dependent upon family resources for much of his life, and the eighth house placements also show the complexity of his relationships.

Roosevelt's out-of-bounds Mars conjunct his Midheaven in Gemini conjoined U.S. Mars and squared its Neptune.

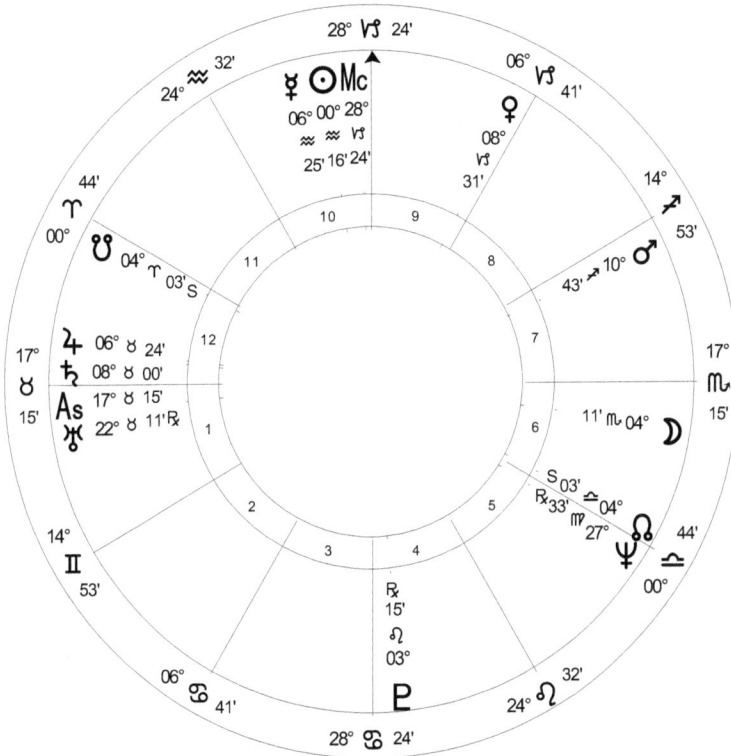

Name	Pt	Long.	Hs	Decl.
Sun	☉	00°≈16'52"	10	-20°05'
Moon	☽	04°♏11'03"	6	-10°30'
Mercury	☿	06°≈25	10	-20°40'
Venus	♀	08°♑31	9	-22°57'
Mars	♂	10°♐43	7	-21°53'
Jupiter	♃	06°♉24	12	+12°38'
Saturn	♄	08°♉00	12	+11°56'
Uranus	♅	22°♉11 ℞	1	+18°04'
Neptune	♆	27°♍33 ℞	5	+02°08'
Pluto	♇	03°♌15 ℞	4	+23°35'
North Node	☊	04°♎03 ℞	6	-01°36'
South Node	☋	04°♈03 ℞	12	+01°36'
Ascendant	As	17°♉15'49"	1	+16°59'
Midheaven	Mc	28°♑24'37"	10	-20°29'

Chart
FDR Inaugural 1941
Natal Chart
Jan 20 1941, Mon
12:11:30 pm EST +5:00
Washington, DC
38°N53'42" 077°W02'12"
Geocentric
Tropical
Placidus
True Node
Rating: A
Exact time reported.

58 Horoscope: Roosevelt 1941 Inauguration

We have seen Saturn conjunct Neptune in both William Henry Harrison and Abraham Lincoln's horoscopes as well as Saturn contraparallel Neptune in the U.S. chart. Roosevelt also had the conjunction, as did John F. Kennedy. We could say these men were all burdened in some way by the circumstances of their presidencies.

Inauguration Uranus in the first house at 22 Taurus squared the U.S. Midheaven/fourth house axis (or MC/IC). Jupiter and Saturn widely conjoin the inauguration Ascendant and closely square the U.S. Nodes. Though Roosevelt had evaded the Sun-Uranus inauguration pattern with the change to a January inauguration date, he came up against the Sun opposite Pluto, signaling the challenges to come in WWII. The Sun-Pluto opposition creates a grand cross in the inauguration horoscope with the Moon, Mercury, Jupiter and Saturn, and activates the U.S. Nodes as well, suggesting the possibility of karma or destiny at work for the country or its leader.

Eclipses are certainly not necessarily harbingers of death, but they do stir up events and may heighten stakes. Before the election, a total solar eclipse in Libra on October 1, 1940 fell in Roosevelt's first house, affecting him personally and creating a grand trine with his Sun, Venus and South Node. The eclipse conjoined the U.S. Saturn and squared its Sun and Jupiter. At the start of his fourth term and near the president's birthday, a total solar eclipse on January 25, 1944 fell on the U.S. South Node (near a U.S. nodal return). Before he died, a solar eclipse of January 14, 1945 conjoined U.S. Pluto and opposed its Mercury.

Following WWII, the U.S. aided Europe and increased its global influence. The arms race and Cold War issues with the Soviets characterized the late 1940s and '50s as the space age began.

John F. Kennedy was elected president in 1960 at the age of 43. He was assassinated at the age of 46 by Lee Harvey Oswald on November 22, 1963.

Kennedy is the fourth president we've seen with Saturn conjunct Neptune in his natal horoscope. Like Lincoln elected 100 years before, the planets are near his Midheaven. The combination explains the imaginative association of the musical "Camelot" with this presidency, and may relate to his medical issues as well as the suggestion of him as a sacrificial victim. Speculation about his death and conspiracy theories continued for many decades. (Other notable leaders of the time who had the Saturn-Neptune combination in their birth charts include Robert F. Kennedy with the square, Martin Luther King with a trine, and Richard M. Nixon with a sextile.)

The potential for a violent end can be seen in Kennedy's seventh house ruler, Mars, placed in the eighth house in its detriment in Taurus, making it more malefic. Mars conjunct Mercury, with both inconjunct the Ascendant and squaring Uranus, show the sudden nature of his demise.

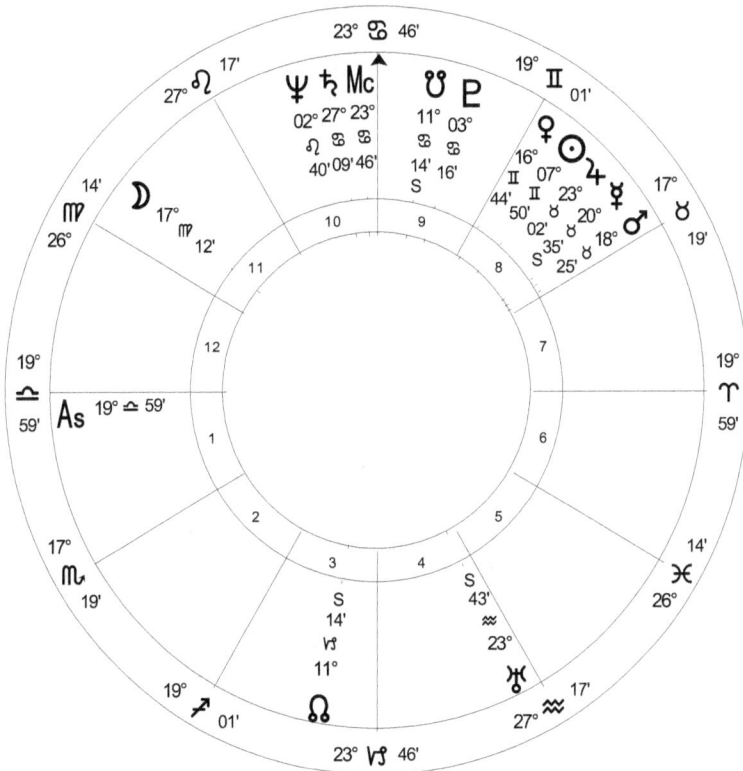

Name	Pt	Long.	Hs	Decl.
Sun	☉	07° Ⅱ50'36"	8	+21°37'
Moon	☽	17° ♍12'32"	11	+00°40'
Mercury	☿	20° ♉35	8	+14°24'
Venus	♀	16° Ⅱ44	8	+23°07'
Mars	♂	18° ♉25	8	+17°03'
Jupiter	♃	23° ♉02	8	+17°44'
Saturn	♄	27° ♋09	10	+21°05'
Uranus	♅	23° ♒43 ℞	4	−14°18'
Neptune	♆	02° ♌40	10	+19°22'
Pluto	♇	03° ♋16	9	+18°50'
North Node	☊	11° ♑14 ℞	3	−22°58'
South Node	☋	11° ♋14 ℞	9	+22°58'
Ascendant	As	19° ♎59'30"	1	−07°49'
Midheaven	Mc	23° ♋46'08"	10	+21°21'

Chart
John F. Kennedy
Natal Chart
May 29 1917, Tue
3:00 pm EST +5:00
Brookline, Massachusetts
42°N19'54" 071°W07'18"
Geocentric
Tropical
Placidus
True Node
Rating: A
Garth Allen quotes his mom

59 Horoscope: John F. Kennedy

The president's packed eighth house also suggests his numerous sexual liaisons and family fortune as well as his notable death.

Astrologer Donald Bradley, writing in *American Astrology* magazine in November of 1963, using a combination of Tropical and Sidereal zodiacs, called attention to Mars on Washington D.C.'s Ascendant at the full Moon of November 1, 1963 with Mars also squaring Uranus in the ninth house. In addition, for the first half of the month,

...the U.S. horoscope which shows a progressed Moon-Mars opposition exact at this time on the heels of which a Moon-Neptune square "matures." In the past, such configurations have coincided with personal danger to our head of state, all the more so in this case in view of the grievous attack by Saturn on the President's natal trio of Mars, Mercury and Jupiter, along with Uranus square his Sun... November is obviously fraught with perils... (Bradley, p. 40, editor stated "News copy received June 3, 1963.")

Astrologer Kelsey Richfield identified the recurrence of the Moon, Mars and Nodal afflictions in U.S. progressed to natal aspects at the time of the presidential deaths, along with those between the fated presidents and U.S. natal horoscope (see Appendix 4). Many of the zero-year presidents as well as some of their inauguration horoscopes also have Moon-Mars aspects. The United States has a trine, as did JFK, FDR had the conjunction in his birth chart, Harrison a sextile, Lincoln a square, and Harding an opposition. (Teddy Roosevelt, who was shot in an assassination attempt in 1912, also had an opposition in his birth chart.) Harrison, Garfield and Harding's inaugurations had cyclic squares between the two planets; and McKinley, Woodrow Wilson in 1913 and the 2021 inauguration have conjunctions.

Transiting Uranus had exactly squared Kennedy's Sun in early October, shortly before his death, and we've already seen the pattern of Uranus afflicting the Sun in several of the inauguration charts for those who died in office.

The president's Ascendant conjoins the U.S. Saturn; his South Node conjoins the U.S. Sun and squares its Saturn, hinting at their fated association. At his inauguration, Jupiter and Saturn in Capricorn conjoined his fourth house cusp, showing a major turning point. At the president's death, transiting Jupiter in Aries squared his Nodes. He was on a half Nodal return, tending toward negative overtones for presidents according to astrologer Ken Negus. Jupiter activated the country's Sun square Saturn too.

Jupiter and Saturn were only 3 degrees apart for Kennedy's inauguration, and exactly conjunct in Capricorn in February of 1961 when they fell on the U.S. Mercury-Pluto opposition. The inauguration Nodes in Virgo-Pisces, with the North Node closely conjunct Pluto, all squared the U.S. Uranus in Gemini in its twelfth house, highlighting a potential for turmoil.

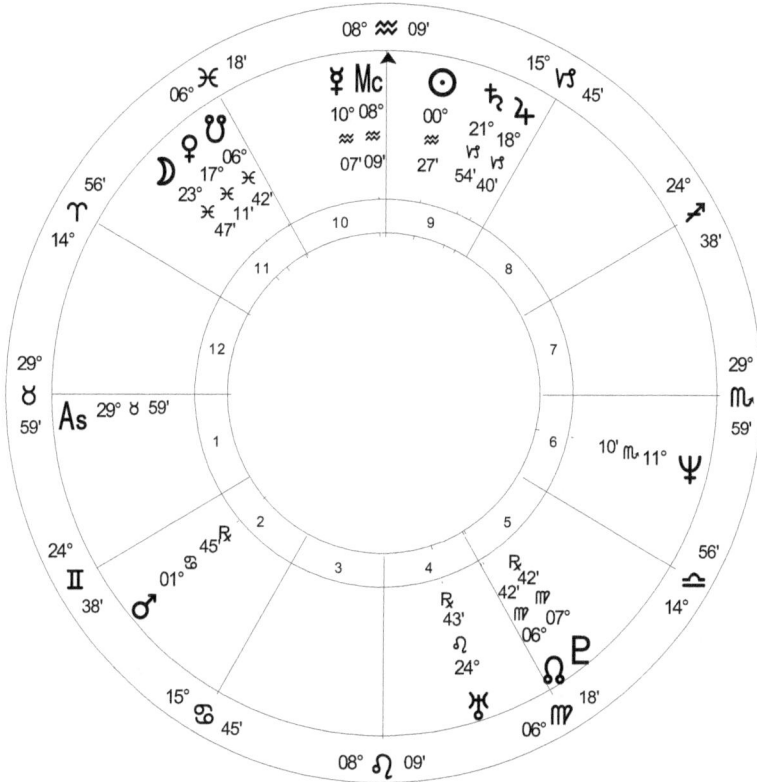

Name	Pt	Long.	Hs	Decl.
Sun	☉	00°≈27'33"	9	-20°03'
Moon	☽	23°♓47'34"	11	-03°52'
Mercury	☿	10°≈07	10	-19°35'
Venus	♀	17°♓11	11	-05°20'
Mars	♂	01°♋45 ℞	2	+27°12'
Jupiter	♃	18°♑40	9	-22°15'
Saturn	♄	21°♑54	9	-21°34'
Uranus	♅	24°♌43 ℞	4	+14°00'
Neptune	♆	11°♏10	6	-13°30'
Pluto	♇	07°♍42 ℞	5	+20°41'
North Node	☊	06°♍42	5	+09°03'
South Node	☋	06°♓42	11	-09°03'
Ascendant	As	29°♉59'00"	1	+20°09'
Midheaven	Mc	08°≈09'36"	10	-18°13'

Chart
Kennedy Inauguration
Natal Chart
Jan 20 1961, Fri
12:51 pm EST +5:00
Washington, DC
38°N53'42" 077°W02'12"
Geocentric
Tropical
Placidus
True Node
Rating: A
Time oath administered.

60 Horoscope: Kennedy Inauguration

The South Node in Pisces was also closely inconjunct the U.S. North Node, perhaps adding another note of destiny to the mix.

Inauguration Uranus at about 25 Leo conjoined the U.S. fourth house cusp and opposed its Midheaven, shaking up the country.

The fixed star Algol can relate to head and neck injuries, and was placed at about 26 Taurus conjunct Kennedy's Jupiter in the eighth house when he was born. It also conjoins the inauguration Ascendant in late Taurus. (This star features in several of the inaugural horoscopes, but its influence is varied and inconsistent. It was conjunct inauguration Pluto in 1881, conjunct the South Node in 1901, conjunct Uranus in 1941, and conjunct Saturn in the first house in 2001.)

We can once again track the role eclipses played in foreshadowing pivotal events during the president's term. A total lunar eclipse in Pisces on September 5, 1960 opposed and conjoined Kennedy's Moon, ruler of his Midheaven, and squared his Sun in the eighth house. It fell in the United States' tenth house and squared its Uranus, presaging unforeseen events. Before Kennedy was shot, a total solar eclipse in Cancer on July 20, 1963 exactly conjoined his tenth house Saturn. It also conjoined U.S. Mercury and closely opposed its Pluto.

The 1960s and '70s were noted for civil rights activism and rebellions against the status quo. The assassinations of leading activist Dr. Martin Luther King, Jr. and presidential candidate Robert F. Kennedy shook the nation in 1968. The U.S. experienced the highest inflation rates in its history, and divisions over the Vietnam War and the Watergate scandal escalated. Astrology and other New Age topics became popular.

As the Jupiter-Saturn conjunction moved to Libra, an air sign, things began to change with the election of Ronald Reagan. There had been nearly 200 years of Jupiter-Saturn conjunctions in earth signs and the combination began to mutate into air. Due to retrograde motion, as we previously saw with Harrison and Franklin Roosevelt, there were three exact conjunctions, hitting for the first time before the inauguration on December 31, 1980, again on March 4, 1981, and finally on July 24, 1981.

Only two months after the inauguration, as Reagan returned to his car from an afternoon speech at the Washington Hilton on March 30, 1981, he was shot and seriously wounded by John Hinkley, Jr., the bullet penetrating his left lung and lodging close to his heart. (Agents had felt no need for the president to wear a bullet-proof vest.) Press Secretary James Brady, a Secret Service officer and a policeman were also wounded.

Near death, the president was rushed to a nearby medical center. He lost an enormous amount of blood but recovered. At 70 years old, the oldest president to date, some commentators have suggested that symptoms of Alzheimer's Disease, which would take his life 23 years later, began at this time. (Reagan died in 2004, during the zero-year presidency of George W. Bush.)

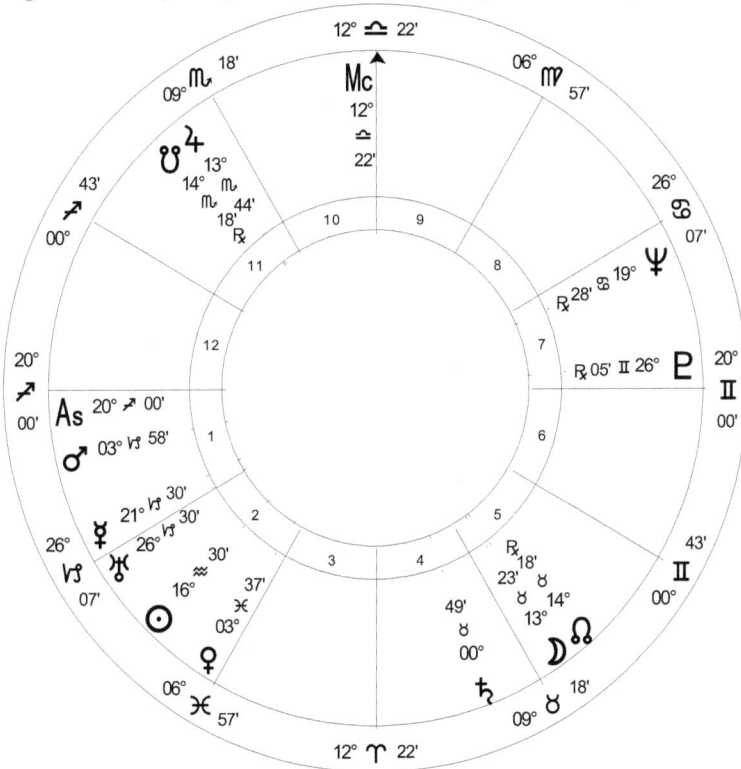

Name	Pt	Long.	Hs	Decl.
Sun	☉	16°≈30'04"	2	−15°53'
Moon	☽	13°♉23'44"	5	+15°47'
Mercury	☿	21°♑30'	1	−21°30'
Venus	♀	03°♓37'	2	−11°34'
Mars	♂	03°♑58'	1	−23°49'
Jupiter	♃	13°♏44'	11	−14°47'
Saturn	♄	00°♉49'	4	+09°32'
Uranus	♅	26°♑30'	2	−21°20'
Neptune	♆	19°♋28' ℞	7	+21°24'
Pluto	♇	26°♊05' ℞	7	+16°41'
North Node	☊	14°♉18 ℞	5	+16°08'
South Node	☋	14°♏18 ℞	11	−16°08'
Ascendant	As	20°♐00'21"	1	−23°04'
Midheaven	Mc	12°♎22'09"	10	−04°53'

Chart
Ronald Reagan
Natal Chart
Feb 6 1911, Mon
3:43 am CST +6:00
Tampico, IL
41°N37'49" 089°W47'10"
Geocentric
Tropical
Placidus
True Node
Rating: DD
Joan Quigley Rectification

61 Horoscope: Ronald Reagan

We do not have a birth time for Reagan, and rectifications have proliferated (astrologer Ed Dearborn collected over 50 of them). Joan Quigley, the president's astrologer hired after the assassination attempt, worked with his chart extensively and rectified it to Sagittarius rising with Mars in Capricorn in the first house. If correct, Reagan shared a similar Mars-Pluto dynamic with James Garfield and William McKinley (though both of the earlier presidents had Pluto inconjunct Mars and Reagan's opposition is a little wide). Quigley's scenario also shows Reagan as stronger than his enemies. Mars rises, exalted in Capricorn, making the president tough and resilient. It is departing from the significator of his adversaries, Pluto. Mercury in Capricorn ruling Pluto and the seventh house is placed in the second house opposite Neptune, signifying the attacker's failure to kill the president. Its conjunction with Uranus might also describe the suddenness of the attack. (We can even see Hinkley's mental instability in these afflictions of Mercury in Reagan's chart.)

Jupiter in Scorpio rules the Ascendant and conjoins the South Node in a T-square with the Sun and Moon (both ruling the eighth). While First Lady Nancy Reagan accepted responsibility for hiring Quigley, Ronald Reagan most likely had an active interest in astrology and metaphysics himself. Hollywood astrologer Carroll Righter was reportedly responsible for Ronald Reagan's inauguration as Governor of California at the unusual hour of 12:02 a.m. (after midnight), strongly hinting that astrology was behind the choice of time.

There was a partial lunar eclipse on Reagan's presidential inauguration day, near a Nodal return for the U.S., alerting us to the potential for dramatic events during the term. (Reagan's natal Sun-Moon square similarly created a T-square with his Nodes.) Jupiter and Saturn had moved to air-sign Libra, a signal that the presidential death cycle might be broken. The conjunction conjoined U.S. Saturn and squared its Sun, activating the danger signs present in the U.S. horoscope. Transiting Pluto also in Libra turned the U.S. Mercury-Pluto opposition into a T-square with an exact square to chart-ruler Mercury.

Saturn is exalted in Libra in the inauguration chart, making it less malefic. In addition, its conjunction with Jupiter and the two planets' various trines to the Sun, South Node, Mercury and Mars all in Aquarius in the tenth house, as well as Jupiter and Saturn's sextile to the Moon, are more indicative of the president's welfare than otherwise.

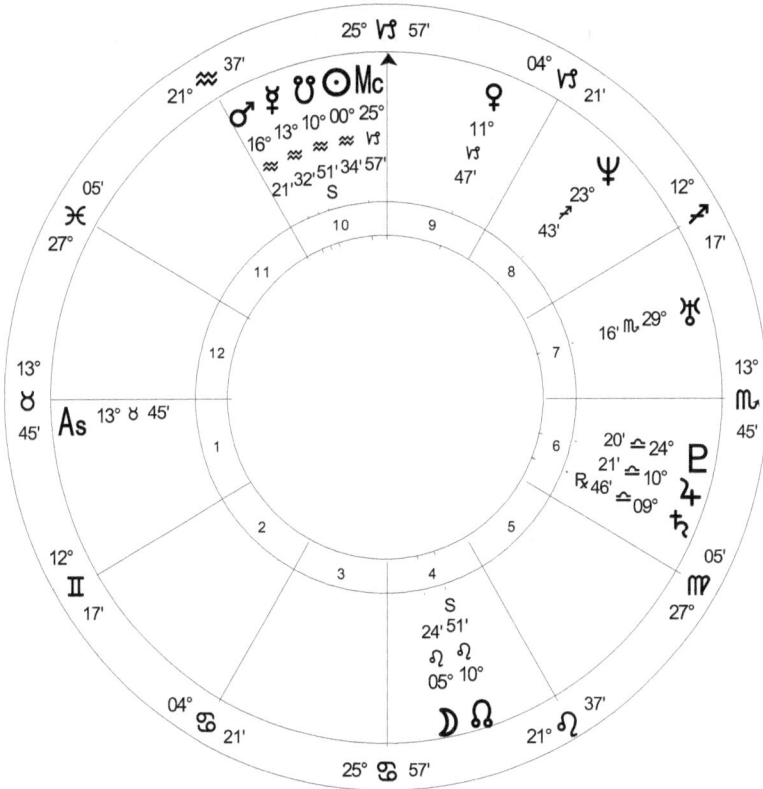

Name	Pt	Long.	Hs	Decl.
Sun	☉	00°≈34'04"	10	−20°01'
Moon	☽	05°♌24'42'	4	+18°25'
Mercury	☿	13°≈32	10	−18°24'
Venus	♀	11°♑47	9	−22°54'
Mars	♂	16°≈21	10	−16°58'
Jupiter	♃	10°♎21	6	−02°49'
Saturn	♄	09°♎46 ℞	6	−01°37'
Uranus	♅	29°♏16	7	−19°46'
Neptune	♆	23°♐43	8	−21°59'
Pluto	♇	24°♎20	6	+06°34'
North Node	☊	10°♌51 ℞	4	+17°30'
South Node	☋	10°≈51 ℞	10	−17°30'
Ascendant	As	13°♉45'17"	1	+15°58'
Midheaven	Mc	25°♑57'21"	10	−20°57'

Chart
Reagan Inauguration
Natal Chart
Jan 20 1981, Tue
12:00 pm EST +5:00
Washington, DC
38°N53'42" 077°W02'12"
Geocentric
Tropical
Placidus
True Node
Rating: A
20th Amendment time

62 Horoscope: Reagan Inauguration

The inauguration Uranus at 29 Scorpio squaring the U.S. MC/IC axis from its sixth house also shows unforeseen events that could change the direction of the country.

Like Harrison and Roosevelt, Reagan is the third president elected in zero years with an out-of-bounds Mars. It closely contraparalleled the U.S. Pluto, accentuating the potential for violence. (Inaugural charts with Mars out-of-bounds include JFK's and the contentious election of Rutherford B. Hayes, along with Lincoln's assassination and the assassination attempt on Harry S. Truman in 1950. The U.S. July 4, 1776 chart has this placement as well.)

Eclipses always tell part of the story, and astrologers could have easily seen the possibility of important developments for the president. Before the election, a total solar eclipse in late Aquarius conjoined the U.S. Midheaven and squared transiting Uranus on February 16, 1980, highlighting unanticipated events for the head of state. Solar eclipses in Leo on August 10, 1980 and Aquarius on February 4 1981 opposed and conjoined the U.S. Moon and Reagan's Sun. The United States experienced a Nodal return in April of 1981, marking a time of change for the country and increasing the likelihood of a reversal of trend by adding to Jupiter and Saturn's influence.

Reagan was a popular president, known for his conservative "trickle-down" economic policies. Taxes were lowered, Cold War defense spending was raised, and businesses grew with deregulation. The coming years featured an economic boom, the proliferation of MBAs, "yuppies," and insider trading scandals, as well as a tremendous national debt. The Internet emerged as a mass medium.

George W. Bush was elected in 2000 in a close, contested race decided by the Supreme Court (the outcome was more easily forecast astrologically). The one-time Jupiter-Saturn conjunction and parallel in the spring of that year occurred well before Bush took office in January of 2001.

While watching an NFL playoff game alone on Sunday evening, January 13, 2002, Bush briefly lost consciousness when he choked on a pretzel. He fell to the floor, bruising his lip and cheek, but was otherwise unharmed. On May 10, 2005, while the president was speaking in Freedom Square in Tbilisi, Soviet Georgia, a would-be assassin threw a live hand grenade toward the president. It did not explode, and the assailant was arrested a few months later. And near the end of Bush's second term, in December of 2008, an Iraqi journalist hurled both of his shoes at the him during a press conference, but the president ducked. These incidents were as close as George W. Bush came to dying while in office.

Colonel John Field, an ancestor of President Bush, was killed at the Battle of Point Pleasant as he fought against the Indigenous coalition led by Chief Cornstalk, where Tecumseh and Tensk-watawa's father had also been killed in 1774.

Intercessors for America, a Christian group, claimed they broke the supposed curse and saved both Reagan and Bush through prayer, reviving the old stereotypical theme of righteous Christians rescuing their own from heathens.

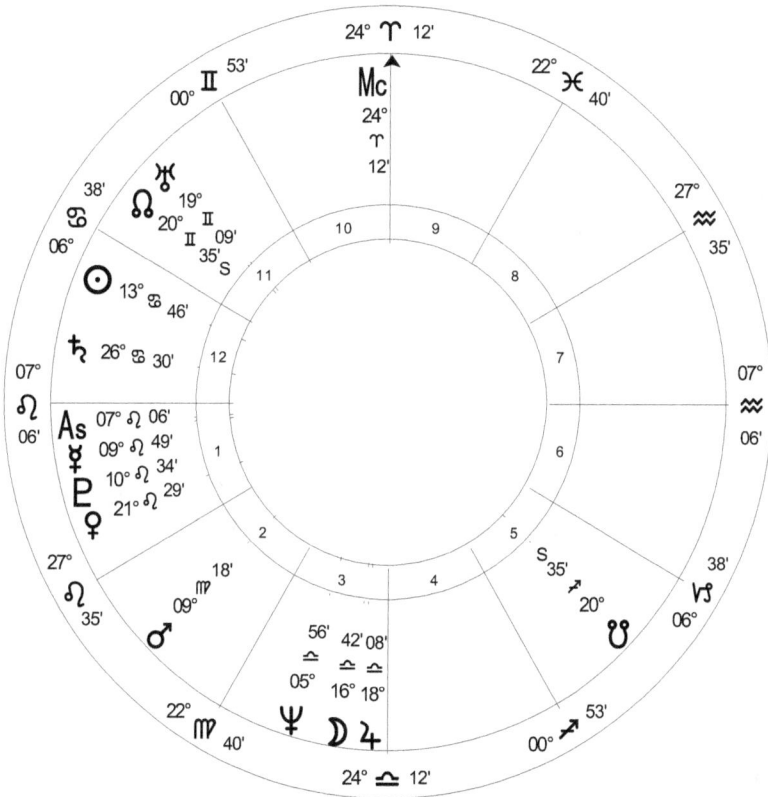

Name	Pt	Long.	Hs	Decl.
Sun	☉	13°♋46'43"	12	+22°43'
Moon	☽	16°♎42'20"	3	−02°12'
Mercury	☿	09°♌49	1	+17°34'
Venus	♀	21°♌29	1	+15°58'
Mars	♂	09°♍18	2	+08°58'
Jupiter	♃	18°♎08	3	−05°56'
Saturn	♄	26°♋30	12	+21°02'
Uranus	♅	19°♊09	11	+23°03'
Neptune	♆	05°♎56	3	−01°00'
Pluto	♇	10°♌34	1	+23°41'
North Node	☊	20°♊35	11	+23°06'
South Node	☋	20°♐35	5	−23°06'
Ascendant	As	07°♌06'49"	1	+18°29'
Midheaven	Mc	24°♈12'35"	10	+09°23'

Chart

George W. Bush
Male Chart
Jul 6 1946, Sat
7:26 am EDT +4:00
New Haven, CT
41°N18'29" 072°W55'43"
Geocentric
Tropical
Placidus
True Node
Rating: AA
Birth record

63 Horoscope: George W. Bush

When I spoke about this topic at a New York NCGR Education Conference in December of 2000, I concluded that Bush would live out his term, as the conjunction had already begun to mutate into air signs, similar to presidents Jefferson (earth) and Monroe (fire) before Jupiter and Saturn were established in earth. Other astrologers at the time believed that the Jupiter-Saturn conjunction would nevertheless bring up notable issues, and they were correct as well.

In keeping with the end of the fateful earth-sign cycle, Bush's natal horoscope does not suggest a serious physical attack, and certainly doesn't foreshadow the possibility of assassination. His dynamic first house, with the Ascendant, Mercury and Pluto all conjunct in Leo, gives him strong instincts for self-preservation.

Saturn, ruler of the seventh house relating to the actions of others for good or ill (public allies or enemies) is placed in Bush's twelfth house and shows that significant others hold a comparatively weaker position in his life. The Sun and Saturn in the twelfth traditionally symbolize unseen enemies, but as they're both ruled by the Moon in the third house conjunct Jupiter, any secret plots would typically be revealed.

If we'd like to consider Uranus as the modern ruler of Bush's seventh house, its placement in the eleventh house conjunct the North Node, with trines to the Moon conjunct Jupiter, likewise brings things out into the open. Jupiter trine Uranus in itself is quite a fortunate combination that would tend to show the president's popularity, and the Moon with this pattern amplifies it. (Astrologer Alan Mayeda has pointed out that three modern presidents, Clinton, Bush and Trump, were all born in 1946 with Jupiter trining an elevated Uranus.)

Aside from an odd placement here or there, all of the presidents who expired with the zero-year pattern, as well as Ronald Reagan, had a notable absence of fire-sign planets in their horoscopes; Bush has abundant fire. (Survivors Jefferson, Monroe and John Tyler all had much fire in their birth charts as well.)

George W. Bush's Sun falls right on the U.S. Sun square Saturn, bringing notable events as well as limitations and challenges to the relationship. The defining events of Bush's presidency were the terrorist attacks of September 11, 2001. While two hijacked planes hit the World Trade Center's Twin Towers, a third crashed at the Pentagon. The crew and passengers were successful in foiling the hijackers' plan on a fourth plane, which crashed in a Pennsylvania field. Al-Qaeda and Osama bin Laden were immediately suspected, with U.S. military forces in Afghanistan for many years. Action in Iraq followed, where the term "regime change" was used: a perfect Jupiter-Saturn phrase.

Astrologer Robert Zoller had forecast "an increasing threat to the U.S. citizens and this is particularly so on the Eastern sea border," (Zoller, p. 1) by interpreting the August 11, 1999 eclipse (a date also associated with a Nostradamus prophecy). The total solar eclipse featured a grand cross of the Sun, Moon, Mars, Saturn and Uranus in fixed signs and its effect would last approximately 2.5 years, based upon the length of totality of nearly two and a half minutes. The eclipsed Sun closely opposed the U.S. Moon.

Bush's inauguration horoscope is also challenging. Jupiter is already in air-sign Gemini, but still within orb of conjoining Saturn (about 7°) in the first house. Traditionally speaking, an aggressive and potentially clandestine attack is symbolized by Mars in Scorpio opposite the Ascendant, in a T-square with Saturn, Mercury and Uranus. Jupiter, ruling the twelfth house of unseen threats, also comes to the country (as the first house represents its identity). The importance of homeland security and overseas defense, as well as phone surveillance of international calls and the registration of those from the Middle East on U.S. soil can also be seen in the Sagittarius Moon's conjunction with Pluto in the eighth house.

Uranus square Saturn conjoins and squares the U.S. Moon and Midheaven, alerting the public to the potential for explosive events during this presidency. The 9/11 attacks occurred less than eight months after Bush came to office, and he received overwhelming public and congressional support for his policies.

Neptune conjoining the Sun in the tenth house of the inauguration chart suggests the possibility of misunderstandings or deception involved, and Neptune closely conjoining the U.S. South Node highlights it further. Certainly both the unforeseen attacks as well as the Administration's allegation that Saddam Hussein was involved with al-Qaeda can both be seen in these combinations. The inaugural Nodes activate the U.S. Sun-Saturn square, suggesting serious issues.

While the Sun conjunct Neptune in the inauguration chart weakens the president's position, the Sun more closely trines Jupiter in the first house (albeit in its detriment in Gemini). Transiting Neptune conjoined Bush's descendant, showing the elusiveness of his enemies. It also opposed his Mercury and Pluto, so it must have been a difficult time for him personally. But as natal Neptune favorably sextiles his first house Mercury, he did not suffer any physical attack himself.

Once again, eclipses alerted us to serious events. Despite their significance, they didn't harm the president himself. Before the contested election, a total lunar eclipse in Capricorn on July 16, 2000 fell on the U.S. Mercury-Pluto opposition, opposed and conjoined Bush's Saturn in the twelfth house, and squared his MC/IC axis.

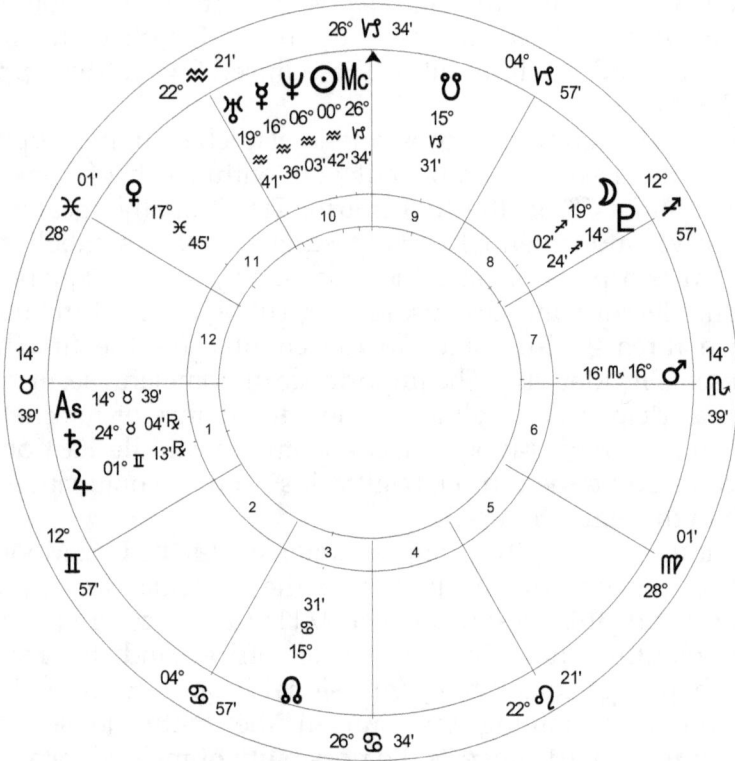

Name	Pt	Long.	Hs	Decl.
Sun	☉	00°≈42'39"	10	–19°59'
Moon	☽	19°♐02'48"	8	–20°37'
Mercury	☿	16°≈36	10	–17°08'
Venus	♀	17°♓45	11	–04°43'
Mars	♂	16°♏16	7	–15°34'
Jupiter	♃	01°♊13 ℞	1	+19°41'
Saturn	♄	24°♉04 ℞	1	+16°44'
Uranus	♅	19°≈41	10	–15°33'
Neptune	♆	06°≈03	10	–18°35'
Pluto	♇	14°♐24	8	–12°14'
North Node	☊	15°♋31	3	+22°32'
South Node	☋	15°♑31	9	–22°32'
Ascendant	As	14°♉39'11"	1	+16°14'
Midheaven	Mc	26°♑34'47"	10	–20°50'

Chart

G. W. Bush Inaugural
Natal Chart
Jan 20 2001, Sat
12:02 pm EST +5:00
Washington
38°N53'42" 077°W02'12"
Geocentric
Tropical
Placidus
True Node
Rating: A
Astrodatabank TV news report

64 Horoscope: G.W. Bush Inauguration

The tech bubble burst in 2000-2001, and Hurricane Katrina, one of the costliest storms on record, hit the New Orleans area in August 2005, drawing attention to climate change. The worldwide financial crisis of 2008 began the most serious recession since the Great Depression; it took the United States many years to recover.

The Jupiter-Saturn conjunction on May 28, 2000 fell at 22 Taurus 43, with the Sun, Jupiter and Saturn all square Uranus in Aquarius. The conjunction had already begun to mutate into air signs 20 years before, and George Bush's inauguration chart included an angular conjunction of Jupiter in air-sign Gemini with Saturn in earth-sign Taurus. The symbolism is unmistakable. The presidential deaths of the earth sign years were rooted in the material plane and the bodies of the presidents. As Jupiter and Saturn mutated into air, the 9/11 attacks and Hurricane Katrina were menaces that arrived in the air; and the dot.com bust, as part of the virtual world, was air-like as well. Bush's loss of consciousness (due to his airway being blocked) is an air sign issue, and even the grenade and shoes thrown at him were tossed into the air.

The exact conjunction for the Bush administration occurred almost eight months before the inauguration. In fact, Jupiter and Saturn were already parallel, too, a month before that. All previous conjunctions in this cycle had occurred after the election or during the presidential term, perhaps yet another reason the chief executive did not expire.

The three conjunctions of the Reagan presidency were all in air-sign Libra. If bodily, physical injury is more of an earthy event, would-be assassin John Hinkley, Jr.'s shooting of Reagan to appeal to his idol, actress Jodie Foster, is a Libra theme played out in a longstanding earth-style manner (Hinckley himself had the Sun and Mercury in Gemini and Neptune in Libra). And while Reagan lived to the age of 93, he had announced his diagnosis of Alzheimer's Disease, an air-sign (thinking) malady, over a decade before.

William Henry Harrison's term represented the transition from fire to earth signs and his life had similarly combined motifs of both: fire-sign exploration and conquest, leading to earth-sign pragmatism and land acquisition for himself and the country. (Jupiter had been in fire-sign Sagittarius and Saturn in earth-sign Capricorn for Harrison's inauguration.)

Ronald Reagan wasn't killed in 1981, but, like generations of Maya leaders, he lost a lot of blood. William Henry Harrison's blood was medically let (as was Taylor's), while Lincoln, Garfield, McKinley and Kennedy were all shot by assassins. Roosevelt died from a hemorrhagic stroke (a ruptured blood vessel in the brain). Harding suffered from congestive heart disease. Blood is ruled by Mars and Jupiter, and the Sun represents the heart. All are closely parallel in the U.S. chart.

For Indigenous people, blood symbolized life, and bloodletting rituals were sacrifices to the Creator to ensure that all flowed as it was intended to. The heart was often an important metaphor. Is bloodletting necessary to offset the current imbalance between the land and the people living on it?

We see blood too often in the contemporary United States, and Mars, of course, also relates to violence. The U. S. has the worst gun violence of any developed country according to the Institute for Health Metrics and Evaluation. The Gun Violence Archive reports that in 2019, there were 417 mass shootings in the U.S (those in which at least four people were wounded by gunshots). The figure has steadily risen, and included 31 mass murders in 2019 alone. The victims are often employees, children or householders going about their daily lives.

These Americans and their leaders may all be considered sacrificial victims. Would prayer, petitions or rituals help balance this horrifying trend? Maybe yes, if people once again felt part of something larger and less alienated from their family, friends, work and spiritual lives.

Chapter 9: In the Air

The Seven Fires Prophecy anticipated these times of unprecedented change in our lives across the globe, and since its warnings were not heeded, many new choices are being forced upon the world at large with great urgency now regarding our relationship with Mother Earth and each other.
– William Commanda, Algonquin (2009)

With the mutation into air signs, is "Tecumseh's Curse" broken? Astrologers agree that the movement of Jupiter and Saturn into air ushers in a new paradigm. About half of the 800-year Jupiter-Saturn Grand Mutation cycle has elapsed since the European conquest of North America began.

Indigenous history and spiritual teachings have come to light in recent decades, and their message seems compelling today. Tobacco and chocolate were once used in moderation by Turtle Islanders for ritual and ceremony, balancing energies and thanking the Manitou for their gifts (they did not inhale tobacco). The use of hallucinogens was sacred, practiced by those trained to utilize them constructively and with community support (today called entheogens, from the Greek for "becoming divine within"). In modern western culture, their use has no meaning and often becomes excessive, hedonistic and addictive. (Similar to the use of alcohol by some Indigenous people who had no cultural connection with it.)

Jupiter and Saturn in earth signs have made materialism and its offshoots, science and technology, dominant forces. Jupiter and Saturn will closely conjoin in earth-sign Capricorn right before both move into Aquarius in December of 2020. This reiterates a final emphasis on earth and suggests that business, markets, real estate and government will all go through an important transition (already begun in the spring with the coronavirus pandemic).

In early 21st century America, there seems to be little consensus. Hate groups abound and once balanced political opinions have been divisive and uncooperative for years. A lack of harmony with the natural world is common in much of the United States. Most people live in cities and suburbs, and family farms have been replaced by vast, specialized agribusinesses. The modern reliance on fertilizers and the genetic engineering of foodstuffs is common. These pollute the earth and manipulate the natural order of things, with genetic modifications deliberately eliminating diversity and endangering species whose existence depends on plant life.

Things need to change and change is often uncomfortable. A lack of balance is especially felt at times of transition, which will usually be the case during a Jupiter conjunct Saturn period of change.

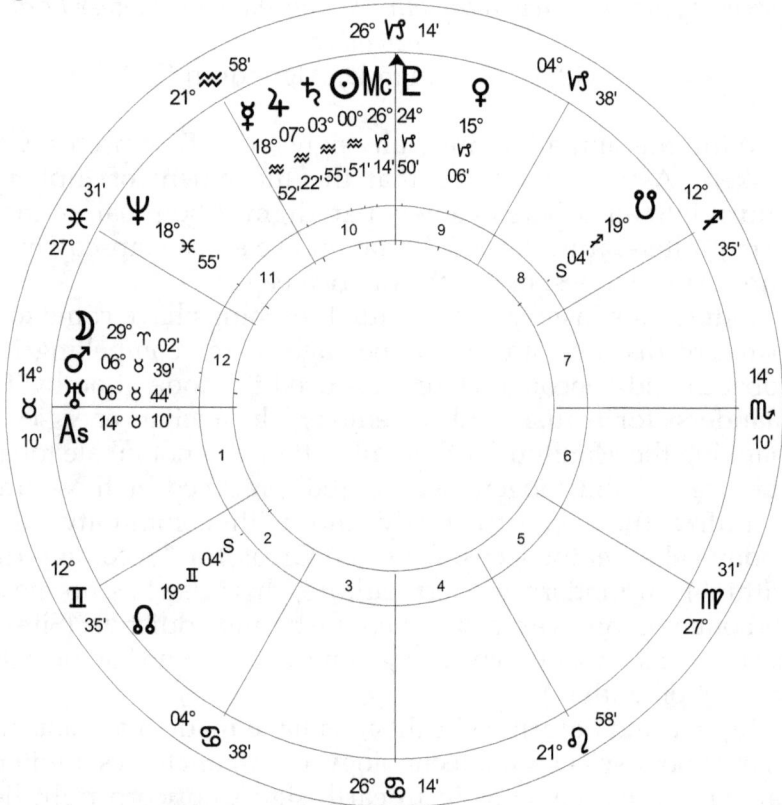

Name	Pt	Long.	Hs	Decl.
Sun	☉	00°♒51'45"	10	−19°57'
Moon	☽	29°♈02'45"	12	+07°24'
Mercury	☿	18°♒52	10	−15°55'
Venus	♀	15°♑06	9	−22°45'
Mars	♂	06°♉39	12	+14°50'
Jupiter	♃	07°♒22	10	−18°55'
Saturn	♄	03°♒55	10	−19°39'
Uranus	♅	06°♉44	12	+13°20'
Neptune	♆	18°♓55	11	−05°22'
Pluto	♇	24°♑50	9	−22°21'
North Node	☊	19°♊04 ℞	2	+22°59'
South Node	☋	19°♐04 ℞	8	−22°59'
Ascendant	As	14°♉10'24"	1	+16°05'
Midheaven	Mc	26°♑14'58"	10	−20°53'

Chart
2021 Inauguration
Natal Chart
Jan 20 2021, Wed
12:00 pm EST +5:00
Washington, DC
38°N53'42" 077°W02'12"
Geocentric
Tropical
Placidus
True Node

65 Horoscope: Biden Inauguration

What lies ahead? The Sun in Aquarius for all presidential inaugurations since 1937 allows us to see how Aquarian ideals and public hopes (U.S. Moon in Aquarius) play out in each administration. The 2021 inauguration horoscope points toward many challenges for the country.

André Barbault's Cyclic Index, based upon times when the outer planets are clustered more closely together, foretells periods of the greatest change in civilization. As Jupiter moved into Capricorn in late 2019, it joined Saturn and Pluto in that sign. With Uranus in Taurus and Neptune in Pisces, the outer planets are confined to less than 120 degrees (a third of the zodiac), escalating the pace of change. With Pluto in late Capricorn, Jupiter and Saturn in Aquarius and Uranus in early Taurus in January of 2021, the orb is reduced to a little more than a square (about 100 degrees). So we continue to be in a period of momentous change and even upheaval that may disrupt society.

This shows up clearly in the 2021 inauguration chart. There's a nice trine between Venus and the Ascendant with sextiles to Neptune, and Mercury also closely trines the North Node. But most of the planets square one another, and Neptune also squares the Nodes. These patterns suggest some turmoil or even loss during the 2021 term. Certainly there should be many noteworthy events in the following four years, and we also appear to be moving definitively into a new and different situation. Uranus and Mars conjoining the first house suggests that the country demands innovation and change from its leaders.

With the Sun, Jupiter and Saturn conjunct and parallel in Aquarius, and a prominent Uranus in the inauguration horoscope, some may be tempted to correlate it with the Age of Aquarius. Much idealism accompanies that concept, and we should remember that each sign has both positive and negative expressions.

The Moon conjoins Mars, and we've regularly seen aspects between these planets in several presidents' natal charts as well as their inaugurations.

Modern inauguration Midheavens fall in Capricorn, favoring a mature leader or one of senior years. But Pluto in Capricorn also conjoins the Midheaven, and the Sun conjunct Saturn adds weight to a senior executive. The Sun is also closely parallel Saturn. Joe Biden, who has an angular Saturn, was 78 when he took the oath of office, older than any president who had served before.

The eighth through twelfth houses are all traditionally ruled by Jupiter and Saturn. They conjoin the Sun and are also accentuated by their placement in the tenth house. Traditionally, Saturn is the final dispositor of the horoscope, making its placement even more significant.

United States presidents eventually escaped the cyclic disruption of the Sun in hard aspect to Uranus with the change of inauguration date to January, but the two cycles do not exactly line up. And so the Sun is once again squaring not only Uranus but also Mars, which may also signal an abrupt change for the country or the head of state.

Joe Biden was elected president on November 3, 2020. Born during World War II, the era's characteristic Saturn-Uranus conjunction straddles his Descendant as it opposes his Sun, Venus and Ascendant. The oppositions have contributed to the ups and downs in his life and career, but six planets in fixed signs give a consistency of purpose. Neptune in his tenth house trines and sextiles the oppositions, balancing the energies and making him a career public servant. A yod with the Moon at its apex and inconjunct aspects to the Ascendant, Venus and Neptune may have also added to the elusiveness of his presidential bids in the past.

The obvious question is: will he survive his term of office?

Biden has a fortunate horoscope in many ways. Sagittarius rises, with Venus and the Sun conjunct the Ascendant, and all are trine Ascendant-ruler Jupiter, giving him vitality, optimism and a strong constitution. The Sun is hyleg (giver of life) in his chart, and while its placement in Scorpio is peregrine (without essential dignity), this sign is known for its recuperative abilities. First house ruler Jupiter exalted in Cancer in his eighth house also makes him a survivor, and he eventually gained enormous public support.

Mars in its own sign of Scorpio is a final dispositor (disposing every other planet in the chart). Though not strongly placed on the twelfth house cusp, it also shows vigor and perseverance. Biden appears to have channeled it into behind-the-scenes government work for 36 years in the Senate and 8 years as Vice President. The twelfth is often connected with "self-undoing," but in this case, seems more in keeping with the personal tragedies he's experienced: losing his wife and infant daughter in an auto accident in 1972 and his eldest son to brain cancer in 2015 (as Mars rules his fifth and twelfth houses, he lost those he loved).

Venus conjoining the Ascendant rules Biden's sixth and eleventh houses, so community work is a natural outlet. The Sun conjoining the Ascendant rules the ninth house, and high-level positions have easily come to him. He is also said to be a religious man, and is only the second Catholic (after John F. Kennedy) elected to the U.S. presidency.

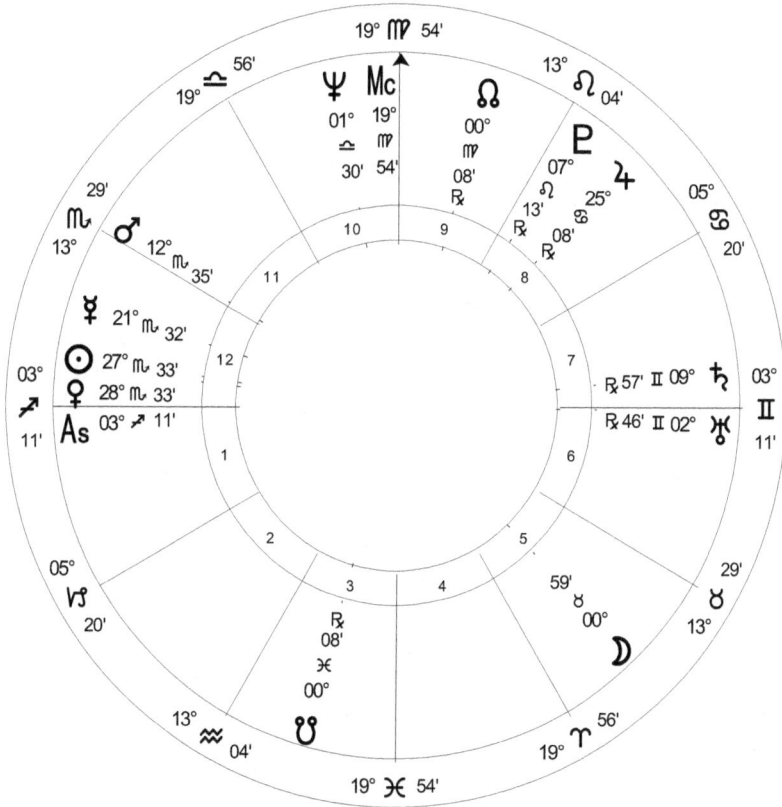

Name	Pt	Long.	Hs	Decl.
Sun	☉	27°♏33'33"	12	-19°37'
Moon	☽	00°♉59'05"	5	+07°43'
Mercury	☿	21°♏32	12	-17°47'
Venus	♀	28°♏33	12	-19°27'
Mars	♂	12°♏35	11	-15°19'
Jupiter	♃	25°♋08 ℞	8	+21°15'
Saturn	♄	09°♊57 ℞	7	+20°00'
Uranus	♅	02°♊46 ℞	6	+20°33'
Neptune	♆	01°♎30	10	+00°36'
Pluto	♇	07°♌13 ℞	8	+23°17'
North Node	☊	00°♍08 ℞	9	+11°25'
South Node	☋	00°♓08 ℞	3	-11°25'
Ascendant	As	03°♐11'31"	1	-20°48'
Midheaven	Mc	19°♍54'38"	10	+03°59'

Chart
Joe Biden
Natal Chart
Nov 20 1942, Fri
8:30 am EWT +4:00
Scranton, PA
41°N24'32" 075°W39'46"
Geocentric
Tropical
Placidus
True Node
Rating: A
From him to Celeste Longacre

66 Horoscope: Joe Biden

As people are living longer and presidents have immediate medical care available, there does seem to be a good chance that Joe Biden could survive his term in office. Saturn conjunct Uranus in Gemini opposing his Ascendant, Sun and Venus make a stroke or heart attack possibilities at some time in his experience, as they're in keeping with his chart and susceptibility increases with age.

Could Biden be assassinated? Probably not. Abraham Lincoln's Sun rising in its detriment in Aquarius ruled his seventh house, while it also trined Mars in its detriment in Libra in his eighth house, a more malefic combination than Biden's rising Sun trining Jupiter in his eighth house. His horoscope also lacks some of the other patterns associated with presidential deaths. Most importantly, Jupiter and Saturn are now in air signs, which so far don't seem to align with the cyclic pattern. While Biden's chart does not have much fire, his rising sign of Sagittarius trines Pluto in Leo in his eighth, so the fire he has is highlighted. And like George W. Bush, he has a strong survival instinct.

Biden has a Moon-Mars opposition, but it's wide and not a dominant part of his horoscope. He also lacks a close aspect between Saturn and Neptune in his chart (a trine by sign), so he does not appear to fit the sacrificial victim pattern.

Most of the presidents who have died in office also had the Sun in the ninth house in their inauguration charts (in 1941 FDR had the Sun in the tenth). Moving into air signs, zero-year presidents Reagan and Bush also had their inaugural Suns in the tenth house. The tenth is stronger and more prominent than the ninth, though the ninth house is considered fortunate. Perhaps the Sun in the ninth for the zero-year presidencies also represents their escape to the spiritual realm, while the tenth house presidents were symbolically tied to their duties.

Since Joe Biden has been in public office for decades, we also have ample evidence of the patterns in his life. His adversaries are represented by Saturn and Uranus in Gemini conjoining his seventh house cusp and their opposition aspects. He has mainly experienced verbal attacks (Gemini) which have lacked consistency and staying power (mutable sign dynamics).

Quoting British Labour leader Neil Kinnock without attribution at a Democratic presidential primary debate in 1987 probably ended Biden's first bid for the presidency (a Saturnian delay). But criticism of his treatment of sexual harassment witness Anita Hill in Justice Clarence Thomas's 1991 Senate hearing did not do much to harm his career path. Similarly, Kamala Harris' denunciation of his lack of support for busing to integrate schools in a 2019 Democratic primary debate seemed to ultimately do him no harm. And as we know, Harris eventually became Biden's Vice President. Since all planets are disposed of by Mars in Scorpio, including Biden himself (first house) as well as his adversaries (seventh house), sometimes they may even come together.

Donald Trump's 2019 investigation of Biden's son Hunter's Ukrainian connections backfired, leading to his own impeachment by Congress, and the release of incriminating emails allegedly found on Hunter Biden's old laptop (Uranus in Gemini) likewise didn't appear to affect the candidate.

Joe Biden's Sagittarian gaffes and lack of speaking polish (he was a stutterer when young) have also not impeded his career.

Two weeks before the 2020 presidential election, a young man was arrested in North Carolina on a concealed weapons charge. Alexander Treisman had collected numerous firearms and explosives as well as child pornography. Evidence also showed a plan to assassinate candidate Biden. While this example comes closer to a Mars in Scorpio threat, it was also neutralized. The Jupiter trines seem very protective. And Mars does not afflict the Ascendant or first house planets, so does not directly attack the president.

Nevertheless, Jupiter and Saturn in Aquarius, along with Uranus in fixed sign Taurus, will square and oppose Biden's Scorpio planets in the early 2020s, beginning with his final dispositor, Mars in Scorpio. His progressed Sun at 17 Aquarius in January of 2021 conjoins the U.S. Moon but also squares his natal Mercury (ruler of his tenth and seventh houses) for the next several years. The progressed Sun is conjoined by transiting Saturn in 2022 and squared by transiting Uranus in 2022-'23, the same time the U.S. experiences these transits to its Moon. We can be rather certain that the president, like the country, will experience many challenges in his term of office. Pluto in Aquarius will also square his Moon throughout 2024. Joe Biden had suggested he will not run again, and this transit coincides with a move or departure after four years.

We can get a better idea of what we might expect in the future by looking back through history. While no inauguration horoscope is as focused or dramatic as in 2021, various elements repeat themselves from previous administrations. Pluto conjoins the Sun (6 degrees apart on January 20, 2021) and is closely conjunct the MC. This combination has not appeared often in U.S. inaugural history.

Pluto can relate to financial issues, power, essential trans-formation, and intervention or even manipulation. Pluto with the Sun or Midheaven in an inauguration horoscope may show the president's experience with these issues during the term. Let's look at what actually characterizes Sun-Pluto presidencies.

The acrimonious 1796 presidential race between Federalist John Adams and Democratic-Republican Thomas Jefferson had been a close one, with Adams winning by only three electoral votes. Jefferson then served as Vice President, an odd pairing due to their alliances with different political parties. Jefferson won the next election in 1800 in a tie with Aaron Burr that was decided by Congress the following February. Burr then became Vice President. At his inauguration, Jefferson spoke for unity and cooperation.

The Sun conjoins Pluto in the 1801 inauguration chart, but the Sun moves ahead to form a grand trine with tenth house ruler Jupiter (exalted in Cancer) and Neptune in Scorpio. The intense divisiveness of Pluto had already passed and led to the reforms of the Twelfth Amendment, so that the President and Vice President would not come from the same party in the future.

Jefferson cut the budget and notably reduced the national debt. He effected the Louisiana Purchase, which he, himself, considered unconstitutional. However, the administration wanted to quickly accept Napoleon's offer and the Senate approved the transfer. One might imagine that the chief executive could abuse his power with the Sun conjunct Pluto, but the aspect is somewhat wide and departing, and the Sun in Pisces is not aggressive. As we know, Jefferson agreed in the end.

One of the most dramatic events of this administration was Vice President Burr's shooting of his longstanding political rival Alexander Hamilton in their famous duel of July 1804. If the chief executive is represented by the tenth house, we may look to the twelfth house (the third house from the tenth, or a multiple of the tenth) for his successor. The twelfth house also seems appropriate as vice presidents are often considered to have little power. Mars in the twelfth squares Pluto and the Sun, hinting at the violence of this event. Burr was off the ticket in the next election.

James Monroe also had the Sun conjunct Pluto in Pisces for his first inauguration in 1817. Pluto may have conjoined the Midheaven (the time is a relative estimate), and the Sun was approaching its conjunction this time. The opposing Federalist candidate had lost by a wide margin and support for that party fell, leading to a transformation in politics that had been growing for years. Monroe, too, strove to eliminate divisiveness.

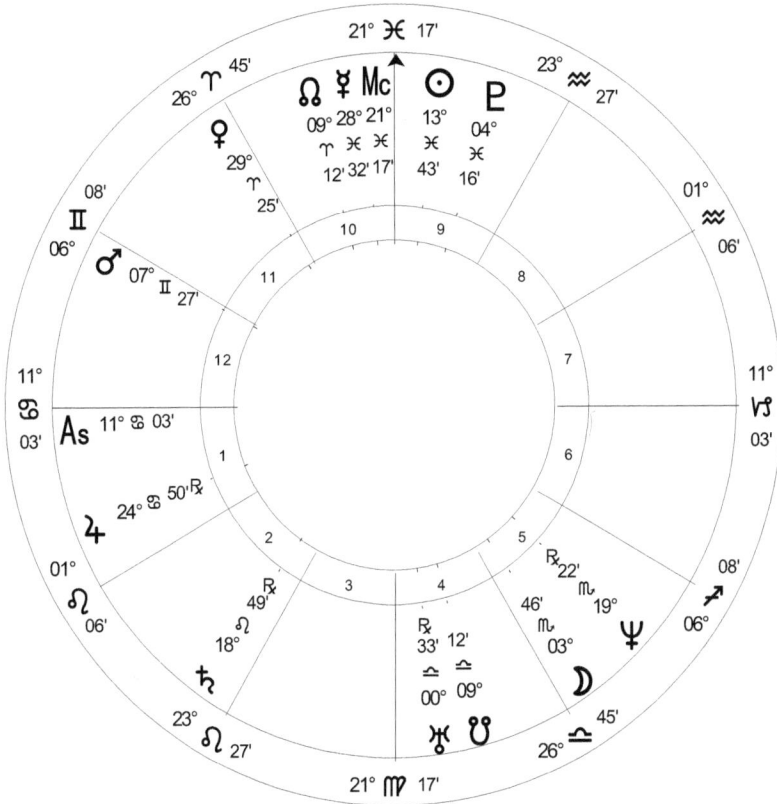

Name	Pt	Long.	Hs	Decl.
Sun	☉	13°♓43'20"	9	−06°24'
Moon	☽	03°♏46'01"	5	−14°50'
Mercury	☿	28°♓32	10	−00°21'
Venus	♀	29°♈25	11	+12°57'
Mars	♂	07°♊27	12	+23°22'
Jupiter	♃	24°♋50 ℞	1	+21°48'
Saturn	♄	18°♌49 ℞	2	+16°29'
Uranus	♅	00°♎33 ℞	4	+00°29'
Neptune	♆	19°♏22 ℞	5	−15°51'
Pluto	♇	04°♓16	9	−21°22'
North Node	☊	09°♈12	10	+03°39'
South Node	☋	09°♎12	4	−03°39'
Ascendant	As	11°♋03'51"	1	+23°00'
Midheaven	Mc	21°♓17'38"	10	−03°27'

Chart
Jefferson Inaugural
Natal Chart
Mar 4 1801 NS, Wed
12:40 pm LMT +5:08:09
Washington, DC
38°N53'42" 077°W02'12"
Geocentric
Tropical
Placidus
True Node
Rating: A
Estimate based on description

67 Horoscope: Jefferson 1801 Inauguration

Pluto-ruled financial issues were also prominent, and Uranus closely squaring the Sun added more disruption. Monroe faced the Panic of 1819 and a serious recession. Banks and small businesses failed, there were bankruptcies, foreclosures and high unemployment. The government funded infrastructure projects.

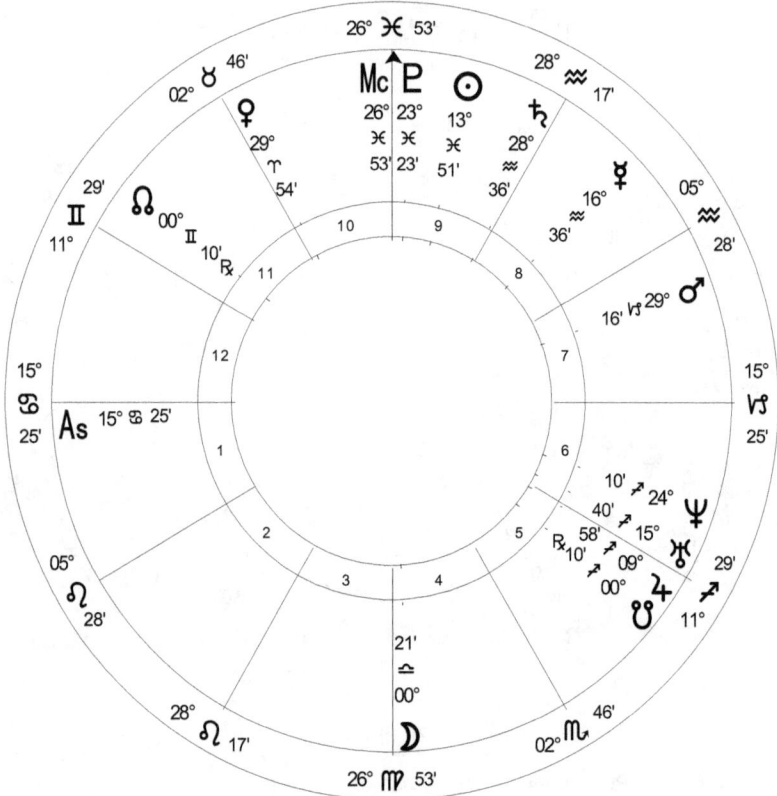

Name	Pt	Long.	Hs	Decl.
Sun	☉	13°♓51'27"	9	−06°21'
Moon	☽	00°♎21'21"	4	+03°50'
Mercury	☿	16°♒36	8	−16°01'
Venus	♀	29°♈54	10	+13°20'
Mars	♂	29°♑16	7	−21°12'
Jupiter	♃	09°♐58	5	−21°07'
Saturn	♄	28°♒36	9	−13°11'
Uranus	♅	15°♐40	6	−22°41'
Neptune	♆	24°♐10	6	−22°01'
Pluto	♇	23°♓23	9	−16°42'
North Node	☊	00°♊10 R	11	+20°12'
South Node	☋	00°♐10 R	5	−20°12'
Ascendant	As	15°♋25'08"	1	+22°34'
Midheaven	Mc	26°♓53'01"	10	−01°14'

Chart

Monroe Inauguration I
Natal Chart
Mar 4 1817 NS, Tue
1:00 pm LMT +5:08:09
Washington, DC
38°N53'42" 077°W02'12"
Geocentric
Tropical
Placidus
True Node
Rating: A
Estimate based on description

68 Horoscope: Monroe 1817 Inauguration

The Sun in the ninth house squares Jupiter, Uranus and (widely) Neptune, all in Sagittarius, emphasizing legal decisions, foreign affairs and long distances. Monroe went on two tours of the country, travelling more than previous presidents. He resolved some border disputes with Great Britain and Spain, and supported the Missouri Compromise, which attempted to equalize slave-holding and free states. Monroe approved funding for Liberia, the American colony in West Africa founded by free Blacks and former slaves. He officially recognized South American countries.

Monroe's inauguration chart has notable squares, but it was strengthened by essential dignity. The Sun may be the general significator for a leader, but if we consider the president to be primarily indicated by the Midheaven, its ruler Jupiter is dignified, and tenth house co-ruler Mars is exalted. Though the Sun closely squares Uranus in Sagittarius, this planet, too, is disposed by Jupiter. While there was much change in the country, the afflictions didn't harm the president himself: he ran virtually unopposed in the next election.

In William McKinley's first term, he had annexed Pacific islands and Puerto Rico, and acceded to popular sentiment for a war to liberate Cuba. With the economy in good shape, the president handily won the 1900 contest against William Jennings Bryan, but lived only six months into his second term. His March 1901 inauguration featured the Sun and Mercury in the ninth house in a T-square with Uranus and Pluto, and his spring tour of the country had been cut short by his wife's illness.

With the Sun's aspects to both Uranus and Pluto, McKinley's inauguration is not unlike the Monroe chart. However Jupiter, ruling the Sun, Midheaven and Uranus, is in its detriment in Capricorn and conjoins Saturn conjunct the Descendant, the place of the setting Sun. (In contrast, we might say that Jupiter is somewhat buoyed by its conjunction with Uranus in the Monroe inauguration.) Jupiter's cosmic state and aspects for McKinley's second term are more in keeping with both Mrs. McKinley's health concerns, the limiting of public appearances, and finally his death. Mars, co-ruler of the tenth house, is intercepted, inconjunct the Midheaven, square the Nodes and is one of the least elevated planets in the horoscope.

The close Sun-Uranus-Pluto T-square led to a radical change in the status quo. While McKinley had very little power and seemed to be the victim of circumstances during his short second term, his successor's experience was very different. When Theodore Roosevelt ascended to the presidency after McKinley's assassination, he had already served as Assistant Secretary of the Navy, won fame leading the Rough Riders into Cuba, and was governor of New York for only two years when party bosses had thrust him into the Vice Presidency to get him out of their way.

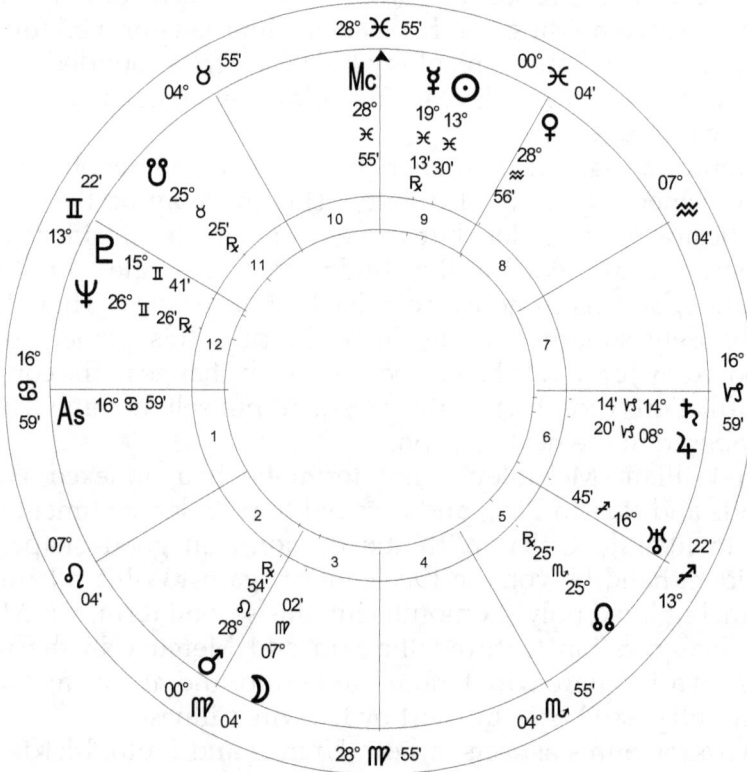

Name	Pt	Long.	Hs	Decl.
Sun	☉	13°♓30'11"	9	−06°29'
Moon	☽	07°♍02'07"	3	+04°21'
Mercury	☿	19°♓13' ℞	9	−00°53'
Venus	♀	28°♒56'	8	−12°58'
Mars	♂	28°♌54' ℞	2	+15°50'
Jupiter	♃	08°♑20'	6	−22°57'
Saturn	♄	14°♑14'	6	−22°08'
Uranus	♅	16°♐45'	6	−22°47'
Neptune	♆	26°♊26' ℞	12	+22°11'
Pluto	♇	15°♊41'	12	+13°25'
North Node	☊	25°♏25' ℞	5	−19°07'
South Node	☋	25°♉25' ℞	11	+19°07'
Ascendant	As	16°♋59'01"	1	+22°22'
Midheaven	Mc	28°♓55'52"	10	−00°25'

Chart
McKinley Inauguration
Natal Chart
Mar 4 1901 NS, Mon
1:17 pm EST +5:00
Washington, DC
38°N53'42" 077°W02'12"
Geocentric
Tropical
Placidus
True Node
Rating: A
"... oath of office at 1:17"

69 Horoscope: McKinley Inauguration

A vigorous man, he prosecuted monopolies, instituted regulations for railroads, food and drugs, and expanded national parks. Roosevelt recognized Panama and obtained a perpetual lease for the Canal Zone. Supporting both business and labor, he successfully mediated a bitter coal strike.

Astrology encyclopedist Nicholas deVore shared that the President had an interest in astrology:

Theodore Roosevelt, speaking of his Horoscope, said:

'I always keep my weather-eye on the opposition of my Seventh House Moon to my First House Mars.'

He was ten years old when his first horoscope was drawn for him by the father of [Chinese diplomat] Li Hung Chang... Roosevelt had his horoscope mounted on a chess board which always stood on a table in his room in the White House.

(DeVore, p. xii. Roosevelt did have a Moon-Mars opposition but the chart's houses differ in a western chart — data in chart notes.)

While he would have his own inauguration chart, Roosevelt's first term is at least somewhat subsumed in the 1901 inauguration. Rather than the Sun in Pisces, he was more specifically represented by the Pluto end of the T-square (as twelfth house successor, appropriate as he was Scorpio with the natal Sun opposite Pluto). He translated the horoscope's squares into his "Square Deal" policy with great activity and many reforms, balancing the needs of business and consumers, and was extremely popular, leading to his re-election.

Franklin Delano Roosevelt won his second term in a landslide as his New Deal programs had already improved the economy and the depression had eased. But his 1937 inauguration had the Sun conjunct the tenth house in a grand cross with Uranus and the Moon in Taurus, Mars in Scorpio, and Pluto conjunct the fourth house cusp. So once again, like the Monroe and McKinley inaugurations, the Sun is caught up in hard aspects with both Uranus and Pluto, quite a difficult pattern. (The Sun-Moon-Mars-Uranus-Pluto pattern is similarly reiterated in the 2021 inauguration chart, near a Uranus return to 1937's.)

Roosevelt continued to face economic issues as the depression worsened from 1937 to '38. But as we might expect from the horoscope, the situation was even more complicated. The Supreme Court struck down New Deal laws as unconstitutional. FDR sought to remake the Court itself by adding members who favored his policies. Congress justifiably saw this as an overreach, though Roosevelt was able to appoint several Supreme Court justices to fill vacancies in the following years.

The build-up of power overseas also impacted this presidential term. The country was already aware of the expansionist interests of Germany, Italy and Japan. With World War II beginning in Europe by 1939, Roosevelt persuaded Congress to support Great

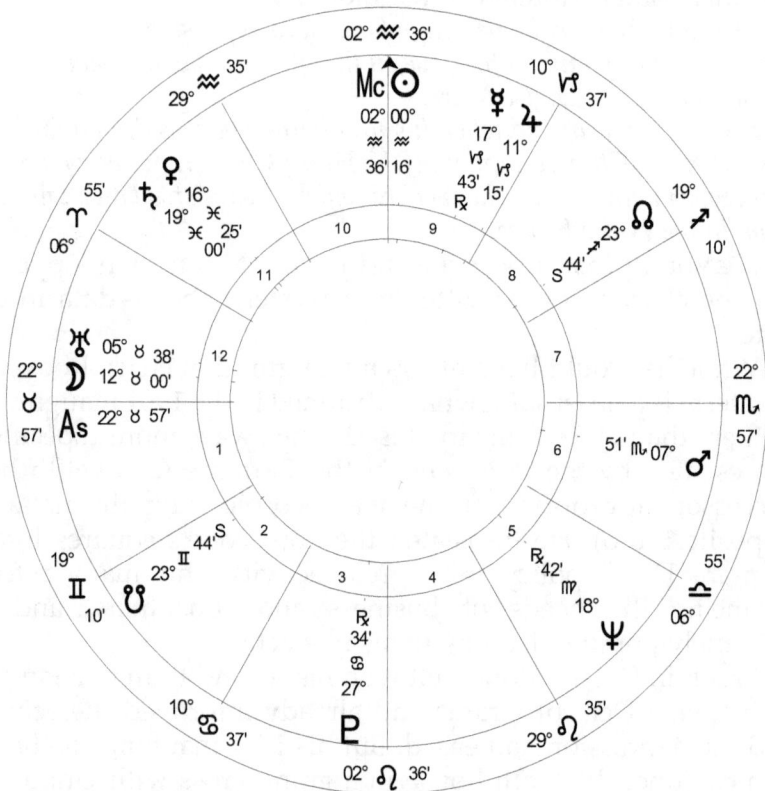

Name	Pt	Long.	Hs	Decl.
Sun	☉	00°≈16'27"	9	−20°05'
Moon	☽	12°♉00'39"	12	+18°44'
Mercury	☿	17°♑43' ℞	9	−18°51'
Venus	♀	16°♓25'	11	−05°50'
Mars	♂	07°♏51'	6	−12°40'
Jupiter	♃	11°♑15'	9	−22°55'
Saturn	♄	19°♓00'	11	−06°13'
Uranus	♅	05°♉38'	12	+12°59'
Neptune	♆	18°♍42' ℞	5	+05°27'
Pluto	♇	27°♋34' ℞	3	+23°10'
North Node	☊	23°♐44'	8	−23°17'
South Node	☋	23°♊44'	2	+23°17'
Ascendant	As	22°♉57'28"	1	+18°31'
Midheaven	Mc	02°≈36'02"	10	−19°35'

Chart

FDR Inaugural '37
Natal Chart
Jan 20 1937, Wed
12:29 pm EST +5:00
Washington, DC
38°N53'42" 077°W02'12"
Geocentric
Tropical
Placidus
True Node
Rating: A
Recorded time

70 Horoscope: Roosevelt 1937 Inauguration

Britain and France. In September of 1940, men were required to register for the draft, a first for peacetime.

Roosevelt's second term Vice President, Henry Agard Wallace, indicated by Uranus in Taurus in the inauguration's twelfth house, was interested in astrology, Theosophy and yoga, and wasn't nominated for the following term, due in part to his uncommon beliefs.

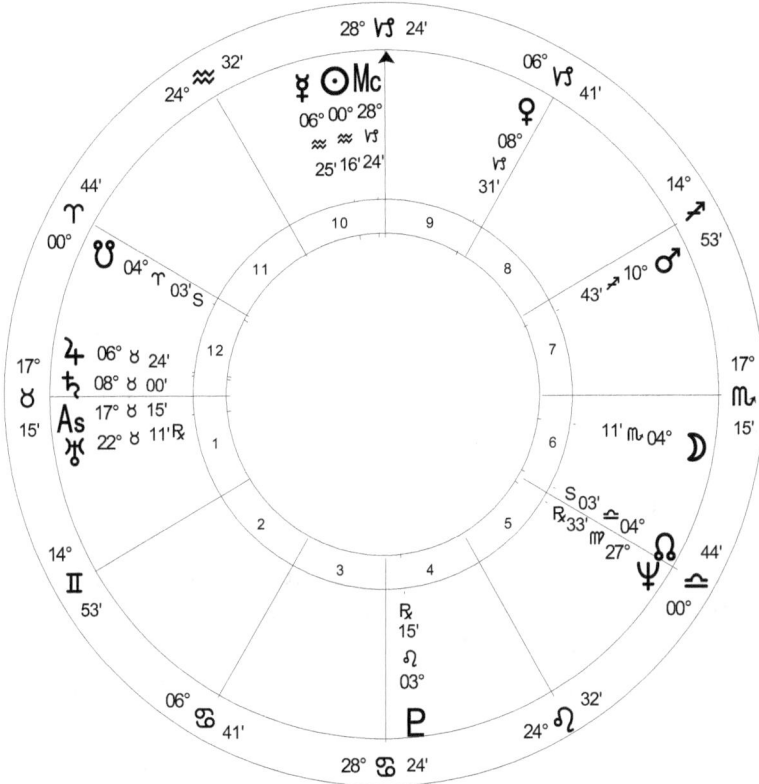

Name	Pt	Long.	Hs	Decl.
Sun	☉	00°≈16'52"	10	−20°05'
Moon	☽	04°♏11'03"	6	−10°30'
Mercury	☿	06°≈25	10	−20°40'
Venus	♀	08°♑31	9	−22°57'
Mars	♂	10°♐43	7	−21°53'
Jupiter	♃	06°♉24	12	+12°38'
Saturn	♄	08°♉00	12	+11°56'
Uranus	♅	22°♉11 ℞	1	+18°04'
Neptune	♆	27°♍33 ℞	5	+02°08'
Pluto	♇	03°♌15 ℞	4	+23°35'
North Node	☊	04°♎03 ℞	6	−01°36'
South Node	☋	04°♈03 ℞	12	+01°36'
Ascendant	As	17°♉15'49"	1	+16°59'
Midheaven	Mc	28°♑24'37"	10	−20°29'

Chart
FDR Inaugural 1941
Natal Chart
Jan 20 1941, Mon
12:11:30 pm EST +5:00
Washington, DC
38°N53'42" 077°W02'12"
Geocentric
Tropical
Placidus
True Node
Rating: A
Exact time reported.

71 Horoscope: Roosevelt 1941 Inauguration

Roosevelt was the only president to serve more than two terms. His unprecedented 1941 inauguration also had a fixed angular grand cross: the Sun conjoining Mercury in Aquarius in the tenth approached an opposition to Pluto in the fourth house. Both sides then squared the Moon in Scorpio in the sixth and Jupiter and Saturn in Taurus in the twelfth house. On December 8, 1941, Congress declared war on Japan after its attack on Pearl Harbor, and the remainder of the term was preoccupied with World War II. Congress continued blocking the president's domestic priorities. Financially, however, war manufacturing provided for greater employment and lifted the economy.

Roosevelt signed an executive order authorizing internment of Japanese Americans and others, many of them U.S. citizens. The Sun square Jupiter, which conjoins tenth-house ruler Saturn, seems in keeping with the forced confinement.

The 1941 inauguration horoscope is similar to the 2021 chart in that the Sun, Moon, Jupiter, Saturn and Pluto are all linked by hard aspects.

Ronald Reagan had won the 1980 election in a landslide, and his first inauguration had the Sun, Moon and Nodes (a penumbral lunar eclipse) squaring Pluto. As in 2021, the Sun and Moon were both departing from their squares. But in 1981, Mars in the tenth house (signifying the administration) also approached a trine to Pluto in the sixth, and Plutonian themes were evident. Reagan was able to wield both financial and political power.

The president inherited a troubled economy with high unemployment and inflation. His Reaganomics policies cut taxes, raised military spending and increased the Federal debt. Reagan's quest to oppose communism around the globe led to the popular invasion of Grenada, aid to Central America and Afghanistan, and even covert arms sales to Contra rebels in Nicaragua. His characterization of the Soviet Union as an evil empire eventually ended in cooperation with Mikhail Gorbachev after the Russian came to power in 1985.

Reagan easily won re-election to a second term, and was the oldest president to date, confirming the strength of Saturn exalted in Libra and its favorable aspects in his first inauguration chart. His memorable debate quote that, "I am not going to exploit, for political purposes, my opponent's youth and inexperience," resonated with voters.

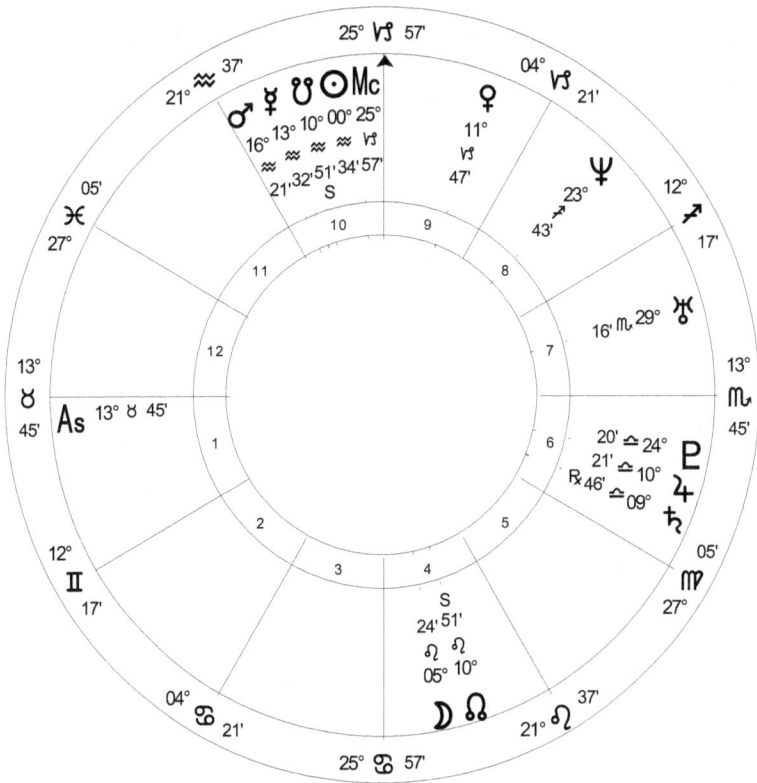

Name	Pt	Long.	Hs	Decl.
Sun	☉	00°≈34'04"	10	-20°01'
Moon	☽	05°♌24'42"	4	+18°25'
Mercury	☿	13°≈32	10	-18°24'
Venus	♀	11°♑47	9	-22°54'
Mars	♂	16°≈21	10	-16°58'
Jupiter	♃	10°♎21	6	-02°49'
Saturn	♄	09°♎46 ℞	6	-01°37'
Uranus	♅	29°♏16	7	-19°46'
Neptune	♆	23°♐43	8	-21°59'
Pluto	♇	24°♎20	6	+06°34'
North Node	☊	10°♌51 ℞	4	+17°30'
South Node	☋	10°≈51 ℞	10	-17°30'
Ascendant	As	13°♉45'17"	1	+15°58'
Midheaven	Mc	25°♑57'21"	10	-20°57'

Chart
Reagan Inauguration
Natal Chart
Jan 20 1981, Tue
12:00 pm EST +5:00
Washington, DC
38°N53'42" 077°W02'12"
Geocentric
Tropical
Placidus
True Node
Rating: A
20th Amendment time

72 Horoscope: Reagan 1981 Inauguration

To summarize, we can see that most of the Plutonian administrations were notable victories for the presidents elected. They all sought to unite the country in various ways, and often succeeded. (Joe Biden, too, when he was inaugurated in 2021, also spoke for unity.) The political parties themselves also underwent change either in their evolution or due to reforms or other pressing issues taking precedence. Developments in the country's territory, alliances and antagonisms came to the forefront. Financial affairs were often highlighted, with important changes in policies and trends during the terms of office. The presidents were either forced into utilizing more fiscal or political power, or chose to do so.

We can see that the addition to Uranus to the Sun-Pluto pattern made things more complex, and that both crisis and reform were experienced in these administrations.

Hard aspects from Uranus to the Sun in the inauguration horoscopes created surprising and unforeseen circumstances in the administrations begun with them. They coincided with danger to the chief executive as well as some of the shortest of presidential terms. Harrison served for a month (Sun conjunct Uranus). Garfield (Sun opposite Uranus) and McKinley (Sun square Uranus) only eked out about six months apiece. And Harding served for about two and a half years (Sun opposite Uranus). The Civil War raged throughout Lincoln's Sun square Uranus 1861 term, with a tempestuous and chaotic situation for the entire country. (These examples were all in Jupiter-Saturn conjunction years, too.)

Another notable Sun square Uranus presidency was James Monroe's first term, discussed earlier (see pps. 150-153). He did not suffer from the transit of Jupiter conjunct Saturn at this time, and the earth-sign "curse" was not yet in effect. (In Harrison's inauguration, Jupiter in Sagittarius in the sixth closely squared the Sun and Uranus in the tenth house, and Saturn in Capricorn trined Pluto and the MC. For McKinley, the Sun formed a T-square with Uranus and Pluto, and Jupiter and Saturn in Capricorn conjoined the Descendant.) Perhaps the Sun and Pluto's various squares to Jupiter, Uranus and Neptune in Sagittarius made them less destructive for Monroe. When heavy planets combine there is a synergism of their effects. In 1817, the diffusion of Neptune might had muted some of the natural volatility or intensity of Pluto, for example.

A concern for 2021 is Uranus conjoining the inaugural Ascendant (less than 7½ degrees). Uranus was in the first house for the presidential terms of Ulysses S. Grant in 1869 and Franklin Roosevelt in 1941. Roosevelt was forced to confront the constant unpredictability of war during his entire third term, and the country was radically changed as a result (though Uranus in Taurus was solidly in the first house that year).

Despite a challenging Sun square Saturn, Ulysses S. Grant's first term featured a grand trine in fire signs, with Uranus rising closely trining the Sun, quite a flowing pattern. Grant had served as General of the U.S. Army at the close of the Civil War. At 47, he was the youngest president to date and a reformer who supported Reconstruction in the south, and civil rights for women, African

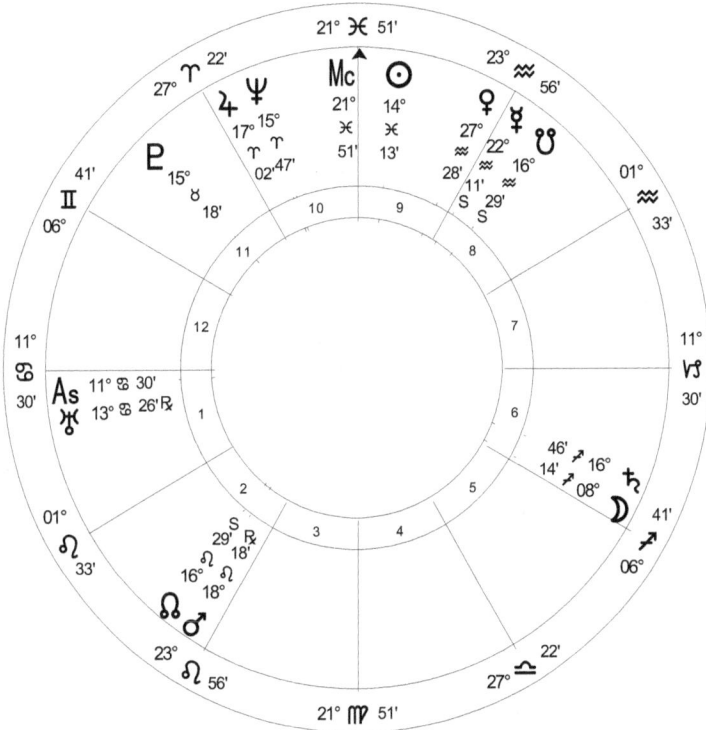

Name	Pt	Long.	Hs	Decl.
Sun	☉	14°♓13'42"	9	-06°12'
Moon	☽	08°♐14'19"	6	-16°52'
Mercury	☿	22°♒11	8	-12°34'
Venus	♀	27°♒28	9	-13°26'
Mars	♂	18°♌18 ℞	2	+19°18'
Jupiter	♃	17°♈02	10	+05°41'
Saturn	♄	16°♐46	6	-21°09'
Uranus	♅	13°♋26 ℞	1	+23°12'
Neptune	♆	15°♈47	10	+04°45'
Pluto	♇	15°♉18	11	+01°56'
North Node	☊	16°♌29 ℞	2	+15°54'
South Node	☋	16°♒29 ℞	8	-15°54'
Ascendant	As	11°♋30'17"	1	+22°57'
Midheaven	Mc	21°♓51'44"	10	-03°13'

Chart

Grant Inauguration
Natal Chart
Mar 4 1869 NS, Thu
12:40 pm LMT +5:08:09
Washington, DC
38°N53'42" 077°W02'12"
Geocentric
Tropical
Placidus
True Node
Rating: A
Estimate based on description

73 Horoscope: Grant 1869 Inauguration

Americans, Indigenous and Jewish people. He made progress in these areas, stabilized the economy and established Yellowstone, the first national park. There was, however, reshuffling of officials due to scandals and corruption, and Grant's second term was more problematic.

The 2021 inauguration, with its Sun-Jupiter-Saturn square Uranus and Mars in its detriment in Taurus, gives it the potential for volatility and even violence. (The storming of the Capitol on January 6th by protesters objecting to the election's outcome may be reflected in the Moon's previous square to Pluto.) Uranus' meaning is always difficult to pinpoint since it so often correlates with unforeseen and unexpected events. But with an angular Sun square Uranus, and in light of the earlier inaugural history, we may expect the following: the president will likely face some surprises during the 2021 term. Popular movements can impact the coming years, leading to reform and even some sort of crisis or upheaval that shakes up the country in a significant way. Like FDR, the president may also need to respond to developments abroad as the country's relationships are re-evaluated and reorganized (Mars rules the seventh house), with the possibility of some kind of revolutionary change or global transformation impacting on the U.S. in some way.

Uranus also squaring Saturn in the tenth house accentuates the breakdown of old structures and movement into a new phase. Unanticipated events might even impact the president personally.

Many presidential elections/inaugurations with hard aspects between Saturn and Uranus have coincided with a change in the president's political party. We can consistently see this in the transitions from James Buchanan to Lincoln, Hoover to FDR, Truman to Eisenhower, Ford to Carter, Clinton to George W. Bush and Bush to Obama. The same pattern is in the 2021 inauguration chart, and Democrat Joe Biden prevailed against incumbent Donald Trump (Republican).

Contemporary astrologers tend to emphasize aspects. But while squares may represent conflict, they also suggest much action and activity. Essential dignity is more important than aspects. Mars ruling the intercepted twelfth and seventh houses points toward enemies or allies in a weakened but more malefic condition (Mars in detriment in Taurus in the twelfth). Mars also rules the Moon, so may point toward public opinion. But with the Moon in the last degree of Aries, this should change. Mars is ruled by Venus in the ninth, so ultimately any plots or conspiracies should be revealed and addressed by authorities or the courts. And the Ascendant (the country) trines Venus.

Using traditional rulers, Saturn in Aquarius is also the final dispositor of this inauguration horoscope, ultimately ruling both Mars and Uranus as well as the Sun, which it closely conjoins. We need to review previous Sun-Saturn administrations for more information. Only a few chief executives began their terms with the Sun actually conjunct Saturn; following are three of them.

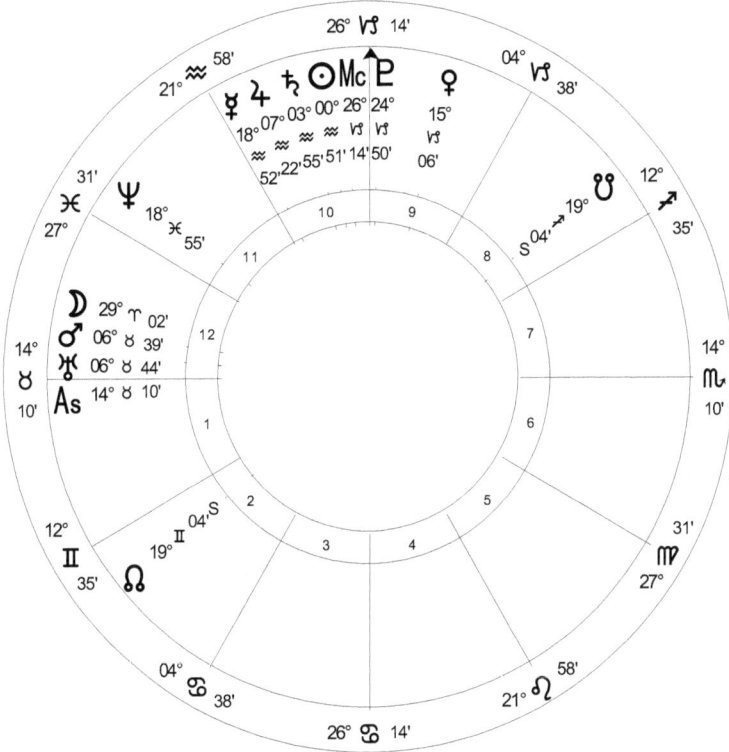

Name	Pt	Long.	Hs	Decl.
Sun	☉	00°≈51'45"	10	-19°57'
Moon	☽	29°♈02'45"	12	+07°24'
Mercury	☿	18°≈52	10	-15°55'
Venus	♀	15°♑06	9	-22°45'
Mars	♂	06°♉39	12	+14°50'
Jupiter	♃	07°≈22	10	-18°55'
Saturn	♄	03°≈55	10	-19°39'
Uranus	♅	06°♉44	12	+13°20'
Neptune	♆	18°♓55	11	-05°22'
Pluto	♇	24°♑50	9	-22°21'
North Node	☊	19°♊04 ℞	2	+22°59'
South Node	☋	19°♐04 ℞	8	-22°59'
Ascendant	As	14°♉10'24"	1	+16°05'
Midheaven	Mc	26°♑14'58"	10	-20°53'

Chart
2021 Inauguration
Natal Chart
Jan 20 2021, Wed
12:00 pm EST +5:00
Washington, DC
38°N53'42" 077°W02'12"
Geocentric
Tropical
Placidus
True Node

74 Horoscope: Biden Inauguration

Zachary Taylor was the only president not elected in a zero year to die in office; he won with a majority and served a little over a year. The 1849 inauguration Sun conjoined both Saturn and the South Node in the ninth house, the president faced contentious issues, and his administration was limited in time and due to circumstances. Over a decade before the Civil War, the slavery debate had created partisan divisions, and southern leaders threatened succession. Taylor himself opposed slavery in new territories, but did not live long enough to act.

With Uranus and Pluto in the tenth house and a fixed T-square involving the Moon, Venus, Mars and to a lesser extent, Pluto, the country's divisions were deep. When Vice President Millard Fillmore took office in July of 1850, Taylor's entire cabinet immediately resigned. Fillmore personally opposed slavery, but felt the 1850 Compromise necessary to preserve the union. He conceded to the south with the possibility of slavery in Utah and New Mexico and Federal enforcement of the Fugitive Slave Act. The Act instituted a return of runaway slaves with no due process. The agreement angered both sides, and Fillmore was not nominated for a second term. We may see his dilemma in the inauguration chart as Mercury ruling the twelfth house could represent the Vice President (the executive's successor). And Mercury is weak: retrograde and conjunct Neptune.

Rutherford B. Hayes came to the presidency in 1877, another challenging period in American history. True to the Sun conjunct Saturn in Pisces, Hayes was described as dignified and he announced in advance that he'd only serve one term.

With a long history of public service, Hayes was an experienced leader and had been an attorney, a Civil War Union Army General, a Congressman and a three-term Governor of Ohio. His wife, Lucy (coincidentally born in the Shawnee homeland of Chillicothe, Ohio) was an advocate for temperance, and spirits were not served in the White House ("dry" of is course a very Saturnine word). The two were both abolitionists who supported Reconstruction efforts in the south and believed in equal rights.

Hayes' election was one of the most hotly disputed in U.S. history. He lost the popular vote, but electoral votes in Florida, Louisiana and South Carolina were contested amidst charges of fraud and Black voter suppression. A congressional commission was appointed to sort it out, with a deal finally brokered only days before the scheduled inauguration. Democrats agreed to give

Hayes the White House, but insisted upon an end to southern Reconstruction.

But inauguration day, March 4, fell on a Sunday and Hayes was a religious man who would not take an oath on the Sabbath. Given the electoral crisis and the tardiness of the agreement, the new president was sworn in at a private gathering at the White House on Saturday evening, March 3. (The public ceremony followed on Monday.)

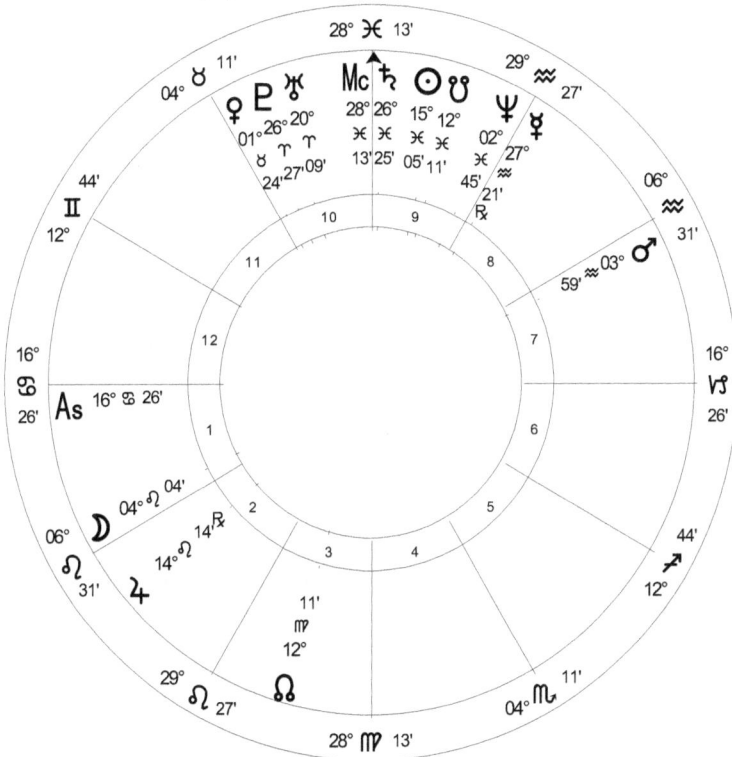

Name	Pt	Long.	Hs	Decl.
Sun	☉	15°♓05'56"	9	−05°52'
Moon	☽	04°♌04'44"	1	+16°04'
Mercury	☿	27°♒21 ℞	8	−10°14'
Venus	♀	01°♉24	10	+14°25'
Mars	♂	03°♒59	7	−20°13'
Jupiter	♃	14°♌14 ℞	2	+17°33'
Saturn	♄	26°♓25	9	−03°18'
Uranus	♅	20°♈09	10	+07°20'
Neptune	♆	02°♓45	9	−11°06'
Pluto	♇	26°♈27	10	−05°22'
North Node	☊	12°♍11	3	+06°59'
South Node	☋	12°♓11	9	−06°59'
Ascendant	As	16°♋26'52"	1	+22°26'
Midheaven	Mc	28°♓13'33"	10	−00°42'

Chart
Taylor Inauguration
Natal Chart
Mar 5 1849 NS, Mon
1:00 pm LMT +5:08:09
Washington, DC
38°N53'42" 077°W02'12"
Geocentric
Tropical
Placidus
True Node
Rating: A
Estimate based on description

75 Horoscope: Taylor Inauguration

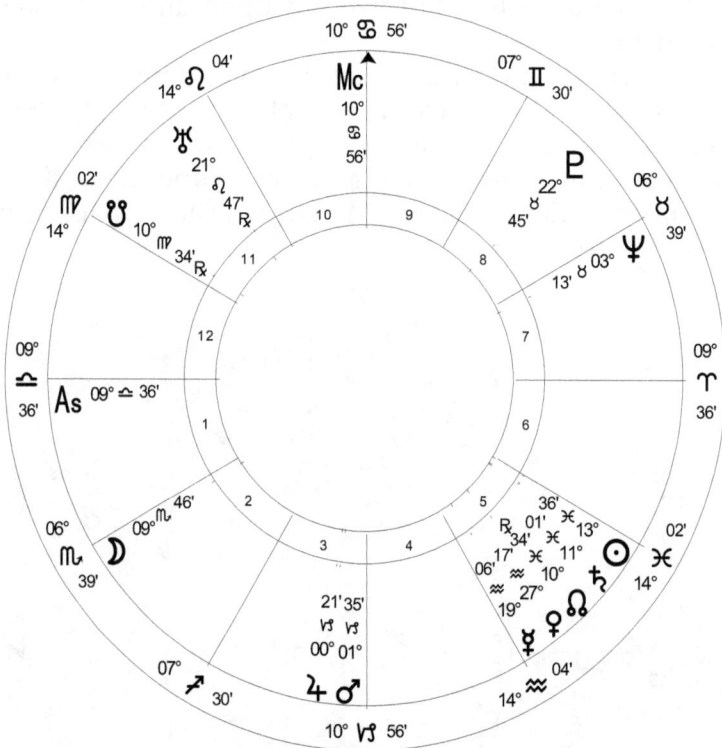

Name	Pt	Long.	Hs	Decl.
Sun	☉	13°✕36'20"	5	−06°27'
Moon	☽	09°♏46'13"	2	−19°03'
Mercury	☿	19°♒06	5	−16°29'
Venus	♀	27°♒17	5	−13°30'
Mars	♂	01°♑35	3	−23°36'
Jupiter	♃	00°♑21	3	−23°02'
Saturn	♄	11°✕01	5	−08°59'
Uranus	♅	21°♌47 R	11	+14°58'
Neptune	♆	03°♉13	7	+10°57'
Pluto	♇	22°♉45	8	+04°51'
North Node	☊	10°✕34 R	5	−07°36'
South Node	☋	10°♍34 R	11	+07°36'
Ascendant	As	09°♎36'21"	1	−03°48'
Midheaven	Mc	10°♋56'41"	10	+23°00'

Chart
Hayes Inauguration I
Natal Chart
Mar 3 1877 NS, Sat
8:00 pm LMT +5:08:09
Washington, DC
38°N53'42" 077°W02'12"
Geocentric
Tropical
Placidus
True Node
Rating: A
Estimate based on description

76 Horoscope: Hayes Inauguration I

Saturnine themes continued. Hayes inherited a depression and followed the scandals of the second Grant administration. While he had pledged his support for Blacks and trusted the south to do the right thing, Federal troops would be removed from Louisiana and South Carolina, ultimately leading once again to voter suppression. Hayes was often blocked by a Democratic Congress, but in what appears to be a methodical manner, he made appointments based on merit, began civil service reforms and addressed Postal Service corruption.

The Sun conjunct Saturn in Capricorn in the ninth house limited both John F. Kennedy's influence and the length of his administration. He had won a close contest against Richard Nixon, but despite Democratic control of both houses, many of his proposals were blocked by those with a more conservative bent.

The Sun is departing from its conjunction with Saturn. The president accelerated spending and increased the national debt, and was able to relieve the country of a recession.

The Kennedy years are remembered for the Cold War with the Soviet Union and Cuba ("cold" is another fitting Saturnine adjective). With the Sun, Jupiter and Saturn in the ninth house of international relations, the administration supported the ill-fated Bay of Pigs attempt to remove Fidel Castro from office, and had better luck with the Cuban Missile Crisis stand-off. Spending for arms and nuclear weapons, the beginning of military involvement in South Vietnam, and conflicts with the Soviets over the division of Germany and the building of the Berlin wall were all attempts to contain Communism.

Civil rights were a crucial issue during the Kennedy years, with Martin Luther King, Jr's arrests in Atlanta and Birmingham, and the March on Washington all in the early '60s. Kennedy's civil rights legislation had been cleared by the House and Senate but did not pass until after his death.

As all three previous Sun conjunct Saturn administrations have addressed Black inequality, and with the Black Lives Matter movement at the forefront in 2020, it seems probable that racial justice will once again feature during the 2021 administration. The Sun-Saturn combinations reiterate the Sun-Saturn affliction in the U.S. horoscope.

To review what we've learned from analyzing similar inaugurations of the past, the Sun-Pluto charts represented notable victories for the presidents, who sought to unite the country. (They included some of the most memorable chief executives in history.) The political parties themselves underwent change. Developments in the country's territory, alliances and antagonisms came to the forefront. Financial affairs were often highlighted, with important changes in policies and trends. (In 2021, the country faces a recession and an exponentially rising national debt.)

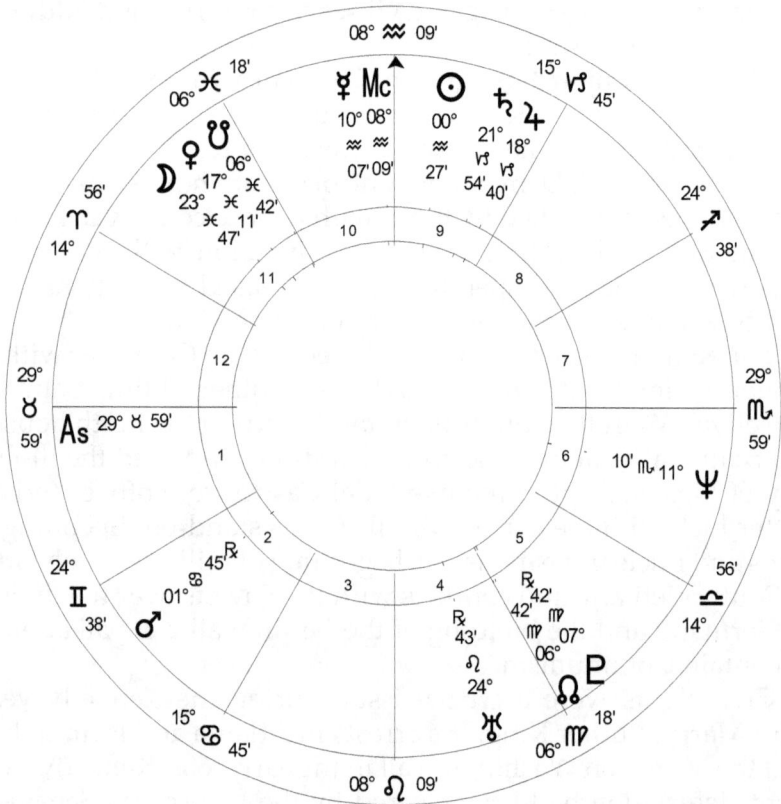

Name	Pt	Long.	Hs	Decl.
Sun	☉	00°≈27'33"	9	-20°03'
Moon	☽	23°♓47'34"	11	-03°52'
Mercury	☿	10°≈07	10	-19°35'
Venus	♀	17°♓11	11	-05°20'
Mars	♂	01°♋45 ℞	2	+27°12'
Jupiter	♃	18°♑40	9	-22°15'
Saturn	♄	21°♑54	9	-21°34'
Uranus	♅	24°♌43 ℞	4	+14°00'
Neptune	♆	11°♏10	6	-13°30'
Pluto	♇	07°♍42 ℞	5	+20°41'
North Node	☊	06°♍42	5	+09°03'
South Node	☋	06°♓42	11	-09°03'
Ascendant	As	29°♉59'00"	1	+20°09'
Midheaven	Mc	08°≈09'36"	10	-18°13'

Chart
Kennedy Inauguration
Natal Chart
Jan 20 1961, Fri
12:51 pm EST +5:00
Washington, DC
38°N53'42" 077°W02'12"
Geocentric
Tropical
Placidus
True Node
Rating: A
Time oath administered.

77 Horoscope: Kennedy Inauguration

Hard aspects from Uranus to the Sun in Jupiter-Saturn inauguration horoscopes created unforeseen circumstances in the corresponding administrations. Abraham Lincoln and Franklin Delano Roosevelt faced tempestuous and chaotic years, and the 2021 administration also has indications of unpredictability and the prospect of involvement in overseas conflicts, with the country potentially re-evaluating its relationships.

Uranus squaring Saturn in the tenth house in the 2021 inauguration highlights the breakdown of old structures and the opening of a new phase. (Biden reversed many of his predecessor's executive orders in his first days in office.) Change and progress should be inevitable, but as before, the president could be limited to some extent by public opinion, opposing parties and international relations. Popular movements should impact the coming years, leading to reform or even some sort of crisis or upheaval that shakes up the country in a significant way. Uranus and Mars conjoining the first house in 2021 suggest a new identity and perspective for the country. Mars also holds the possibility of volatility or perhaps even violence.

An inaugural Sun conjunct Saturn has correlated with contentious issues and administrations that were limited in time or by circumstances. In the past these have brought civil rights and racial injustice to the forefront, and it seems likely that these issues will continue to be addressed.

An inauguration chart generally provides the outlook for one or two terms. Other cyclic factors will show trends or developments over longer periods of time. As Indigenous people knew, eclipses are harbingers of change. Their influence may be more pronounced when total or when actually passing over a location. The June 16, 1806 eclipse that Tenskwatawa predicted was at 25 Gemini, conjoined the U.S. Mars and Ascendant, and sliced through the country from Arizona through Ohio and into Maine. That year, the Lewis and Clark expedition reached the west coast as Indigenous people continued to be pushed west. In 1811, a tremendous earthquake split the country vertically down its center. Within 20 years, Turtle Islanders were ordered west of the Mississippi.

A total solar eclipse at 17 Gemini also conjoined the U.S. Mars and Ascendant on June 8, 1918, with its path cutting the country in half from Washington State through Florida. It similarly signaled major developments. That week, the Senate passed the 19th Amendment, allowing women the right to vote. In November an armistice was signed ending World War I in Europe, though the influenza pandemic had already killed more people than the war by that time. And Prohibition, an unpopular rule that nevertheless gained traction, was enacted in January of 1919.

On August 21, 2017, a total solar eclipse at 29 Leo 52 conjoined the U.S. IC. Its shadow of totality lasted for over three and a half minutes as it crossed the country from Oregon to South Carolina, splitting it horizontally. It reminded us of the divisions of north and south in the Civil War and exacerbated the country's schisms between liberal and conservative groups. By the spring of 2020, the Black Lives Matter movement had gained momentum in the U.S. and spread around the world.

An annular eclipse at 21 Libra will conjoin U.S. Saturn and square its Mercury on October 14, 2023. A solar ring around the Moon's shadow will be visible for over five minutes through its central path from Oregon through Texas, Central and South America. Another total solar eclipse at 19 Aries will square the U.S. Mercury and oppose Saturn in Libra on April 8, 2024. Its path crosses the country as it falls over Mexico, Arizona, Ohio and New York through Maine. These eclipses will surely stimulate some notable events and renew long-standing issues to be addressed once again. The United States cannot escape its natal chart with its emphasis on Jupiter square Saturn in Libra, indicating the continued struggle between opportunity and equality, as well as a need for compromise between tolerance for one another's views with protection of what we all value.

The cyclic earth-sign presidential "curse" is probably broken as we move into air signs. But we don't yet know enough about what Jupiter and Saturn in Aquarius, Libra and Gemini represent in order to project a pattern for future presidents or the United States itself. What can we learn from the past?

The Jupiter-Saturn Great Mutations represent larger historic shifts. As Bruce Scofield and Barry C. Orr discussed in their book on Mayan astrology,

The last Great Mutation [into fire signs] occurred in 1603, and the pioneering astronomer Johannes Kepler himself wondered what kind of new age it would bring, knowing that 800 years earlier, Charlemagne restored the Holy Roman Empire and 800 years before that Christ walked the Earth. (Scofield and Orr, p. 107)

History has recorded numerous events that may be associated with the long-term influence of Jupiter conjunct Saturn in Aquarius. In another air-sign era, they conjoined around the years 551, 610 and 670 CE. Beginning about 550, the Bhakti movement in India began to spread. Adherents believed in one God and that all were created equal, and supported doing away with the caste system. They advocated direct communication with God, and worship through good deeds and a simple life. These ideas reflect Aquarian intellectual and humanitarian ideals.

The Christian Byzantine Emperor Justinian, in an act of intellectual authoritarianism, closed the Neoplatonic School of Athens around 529, resulting in astrologers and other so-called pagan philosophers leaving what was left of the Roman Empire.

Justinian also obtained the first silkworm eggs from China around 552, which soon marked the advent of the East Roman Empire silk industry. Silk was an unusual, light and airy fabric for the west. Plague in the Byzantine Empire had subsided by the 590s. In 610, the prophet Muhammad had his first revelation, in which the angel Gabriel appeared to him. Angels are often depicted as human-like, Aquarian-style beings.

Jupiter and Saturn next came together in Aquarius in 1226, 1286 and 1345. The beginning of the Sixth Crusade was in 1228, but the First had started in 1096. By the time the crusaders gave up the last of their territory in the Middle East in 1291, a period of approximately 200 years had elapsed, ending the Catholic Church's ideological campaign against Muslims for the Holy Land.

When Genghis Khan, leader of the Mongols, died in 1227, he left the largest empire in history in Asia and China. Around the same time, the first Zen Buddhist school was introduced in Japan. This study, about controlling the mind and connecting with transpersonal powers in a quest to attain enlightenment, seems very much in keeping with the airy nature of Aquarius.

Khan's grandson, Kublai Khan, reigned from 1260 to 1294. By 1345, the time of the third Jupiter-Saturn conjunction of the series, the Mongol Empire was breaking up, representing a literal reorganization of world power.

Other notable turning points in civilization coincided with the Aquarian years. The Aztecs established their capital Tenochtitlán in what is now Mexico City around 1325. The Hundred Years War between the English and French lasted from approximately 1346 to 1453 (when Constantinople also fell). And from 1347 to 1357, over 25 million died from bubonic plague in Europe. The Middle Ages ended and the Renaissance began as Florentines rediscovered Greek and Roman classics around 1350. Their brand of humanism advocated the Aquarian ideals of independent study, education and community involvement.

The most recent Jupiter-Saturn conjunction in Aquarius occurred in 1405. This coincided with the translation of Ptolemy's *Geography* into Latin, restoring ancient knowledge to Europe as the Roman Empire approached its end. Money enriched the community as the first modern public bank was founded in

Genoa in 1407. It would last for about 400 years, another long Jupiter-Saturn conjunction period. The bank sold shares to cover the city's public debt, collected taxes, borrowed from and lent to merchants, and soon accepted deposits. It developed accounting systems still in use today. The Aquarian symbolism of community involvement and shared responsibility is reflected in its innovations.

All of these historic developments are so far-reaching that it's nearly impossible to realistically imagine what major shifts in various movements, religions and even civilizations will follow.

The first Jupiter-Saturn conjunction in air-sign Libra was in 1980-1981. Personal computers went mainstream in the '80s. The Internet, websites and blogs became popular in the '90s and social media followed in the 2000s. As Saturn entered Aquarius for the first time in the spring of 2020, the coronavirus pandemic swept the world, communicated through the air. Internet meetings and classes became commonplace and transactions increasingly moved online. These are just a few examples of how things have already developed.

Jupiter and Saturn conjoined exactly at 0° Aquarius on December 21, 2020. Aquarian concerns will surely be evident in 2021 and 2022 as Jupiter and Saturn transit this sign, and should give us more of an idea of what we can expect from the combination. Aquarius rules original thinking, which often leads to cultural change, alternative lifestyles, social experiments, reform or even revolution.

The theme of cooperation is highlighted, as individuals become more involved as part of groups. So we may see more of socialized medicine, co-op home ownership, apartment living, an updated use of public space, increased employee business ownership, and a greater role for collective bargaining. The general consensus should evolve, so democratic elections, political representation, human and civil rights are all emphasized, as well as the possibility of broader global guidelines to address climate change and environmental pollution. On the other hand, since Aquarius is as much about independence as community, states' rights and views of national independence could also change, with the development of various international associations.

Aquarians are often interested in developing the mind, and the coming years should provide advances in education, intellectual freedom, and the use of logic and independent thinking. Distance learning will likely continue, as will the use of keyboards over pen, paper and longhand. New Age subjects, astrology and esoteric belief systems should flourish. But as Aquarius is a fixed sign, many differences of opinion can also follow. Minority or partisan voices may be raised ("I can't breathe" invokes air), and some issues could be controversial. Various communities may feel alienated, with rebellions against the status quo, the development of fringe groups, and ideological battles.

Aquarius also relates to modern developments, technology and electronics. We may expect even more in the way of online social media, mass marketing and public relations, electronic financial transactions and the further development of the airwaves, cryptocurrencies, 3-D printing, robotics, artificial intelligence and electric cars; expansion of the use of alternative forms of energy like wind power and nuclear power (maybe cold fusion); innovations in space flight, passenger airlines and satellites; medical advances in treating nervous system disorders (like spinal cord injuries and Alzheimer's Disease), the use of non-invasive treatments, radiation and ultrasound surgery, and new remedies for diabetes; as well as more carbon-neutral heating, air conditioning and ventilation systems.

With the possibility of technology as a greater part of regular life, people could become more detached from personal relationships and emotional connections, and lose touch with silence, the interior life or even the soul. A dependence on the grid makes any interruptions of service problematic. Increasing numbers of satellites can block out the stars, with advanced technologies consuming more energy and further depleting the Earth's resources. Technology can also be abused, as for example, genetic engineering or the development of an intellectual elite.

The Jupiter-Saturn conjunctions will continue in air signs: Libra in 2040, Gemini in 2060, Aquarius again in 2080 and Libra once more in 2100.

While astrology can identify times when the repetition of a cycle will be felt in the larger community, when looking ahead for longer periods, we ultimately find it difficult to forecast exactly what will happen. But the coming years should bring major change to individuals, the U.S. and other countries around the globe. 2020 is, quite simply, the beginning of a new age.

Technology, unfortunately, does not rank high among Indigenous values. It represents an element of the other path, the one that Tenskwatawa and the elders warned us of, that leads away from spirituality and toward a damaged Earth. The Midewiwin have preserved their understanding of a long-term cycle that relates specifically to Turtle Island/North America and that virtually reiterates the Jupiter-Saturn Grand Mutation period. So the Seven Fires Prophecies may offer more insight into the future.

Algonquin historian Evan T. Pritchard has shared that the wisdom keepers anticipated the whites at the halfway point in their cycle, or the beginning of the Fourth Fire (around 1608 – see Appendix 2 for more). With Jupiter in Gemini and Saturn in Aquarius, Henry Hudson landed in New York Harbor in September of 1609, within the year or so of signs and omens following the August 10, 1608 annular eclipse that marked the beginning of the new phase. This occurred as western astrology's Jupiter-Saturn conjunctions were mutating into fire signs, representing discovery and exploration. (The full Seven Fires cycle began around 1216, near the previous Jupiter-Saturn mutation into air.)

The ancient prophets had said,

...*if these the eastern visitors did indeed come in brotherhood, all would be well and a new 'rainbow' race would emerge on Turtle Island (their name for North America), a mingling of the four colors of humanity, which the elders say was known because of the four colors of the birches, red, brown, white and yellow. However if the visitors came with weapons of war, their arrival could lead to disaster at the end of the seven fires, unless the fears and misunderstandings could be worked out. If both types of visitors came together... It would bring a series of difficult tests for the native people of Turtle Island.* (Pritchard, p. 10-11)

The end of the Midewiwin cycle in the year 2000 was followed by the destruction of the World Trade Center towers on 9/11 in Manhattan, within the thirteen Moons for signs and omens following the partial solar eclipse of Christmas 2000. The eclipse was visible in Nova Scotia, where the ancients originally received the prophecies, and where Henry Hudson had also landed. The Nodes fell on the U.S. Venus and Jupiter, bringing up issues involving relationships and cultural values. If we take the 2001 events as a sign for the future era based upon Hudson's arrival nearly 400 years before, it does not seem promising.

According to Ojibway elder Edward Benton-Banai, whether an Eighth Fire can be lit, bringing peace, harmony and respect for all, is an open question and largely depends on the attitude of the white cultural society. A period of purification may be needed for the Eighth Fire (a spiritual and not literal concept) to be lit at all.

The island is a vortex for a creative power in the universe; we don't know why, but the brighter that light gets the more the darkness will try to destroy it. And the more dark and dangerous it gets, the greater and more miraculous will be the deeds of those who would be heroes. You ask what will happen at the end of the seven fires? ...The light from this island will light the world, and its darkness will engulf the world. In the last days, the greatest villains will come here and take everything with their trickery, and then the greatest of heroes will appear and take it all back in the name of the people. There will be great wealth and equal poverty. There will be brilliant leaders and unbelievably stupid ones as well...

What the prophecies say is absolutely true, that if enough people choose to walk in balance, and tend good fires at night, awaken to the power of Manitou within them, and live and die for love and brotherhood, then we will all walk in the light and we will all ignite the glow of the eighth fire which will last 784 years. But... if enough people lose hope and plunge themselves into destruction and the sleeping state of awareness... then the whole planet shall suffer for it, and no one will be able to light the eighth fire in the winds that will blow then. (Pritchard, p. 247, 2009)

However as most astrologers believe in free will, there is always hope:

If all the people of Turtle Island could embrace racial and cultural diversity and the process of negotiation through loving communication that brings peace, it will be a sign of great hope for the lighting of the eighth fire, and will help bring peace to all the world. (Pritchard, p. 20)

Though other steps must also be taken, for,

If we lose indigenous knowledge and the Native American way of life, which is centered on continuing with and listening to the mother earth, we will not be able to survive the purification that must still happen before the lighting of the eighth fire. (Pritchard, p. 135)

Astrology teaches us that time's events and characteristics can be anticipated, that our experiences are cyclical and repeat themselves. Jupiter and Saturn began their mutation into air signs in 1980, and became established in air signs in 2020. It's an end but also a new beginning. Things will change, won't they?

Today we have gathered and we see that the cycles of life continue. We have been given the duty to live in balance and harmony with each other and all living things. So now, we bring our minds together as one as we give greetings and thanks to each other as people.

Now our minds are one.

We gather our minds to greet and thank the enlightened Teachers who have come to help throughout the ages. When we forget how to live in harmony, they remind us of the way we were instructed to live as people. With one mind, we send greetings and thanks to these caring Teachers.

Now our minds are one.

Now we turn our thoughts to the Creator, or Great Spirit, and send greetings and thanks for all the gifts of Creation. Everything we need to live a good life is here on this Mother Earth. For all the love that is still around us, we gather our minds together as one and send our choicest words of greetings and thanks to the Creator.

Now our minds are one.

(Excerpts from Mohawk version of Haudenosaunee Thanksgiving Address, or *The Words that Come Before All Else*.)

Appendix 1: Tecumseh and Tenskwatawa Charts

The data for Tecumseh is rather consistent for March 9, 1768. As he was named for a shooting star, his biographer Allan W. Eckert claims he was born at the same moment as the meteor, but his book is fictionalized and no documented facts support this conclusion.

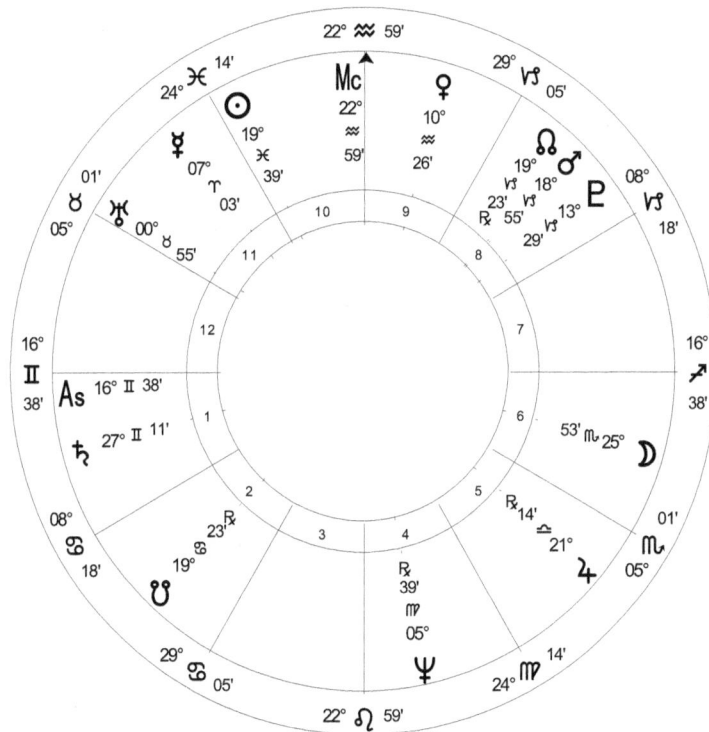

Name	Pt	Long.	Hs	Decl.
Sun	☉	19°♓39'05"	10	-04°06'
Moon	☽	25°♏53'58"	6	-23°13'
Mercury	☿	07°♈03	11	+03°57'
Venus	♀	10°♒26	9	-17°29'
Mars	♂	18°♑55	8	-22°49'
Jupiter	♃	21°♎14 ℞	5	-06°51'
Saturn	♄	27°♊11	1	+22°38'
Uranus	♅	00°♉55	11	+11°21'
Neptune	♆	05°♍39 ℞	4	+10°13'
Pluto	♇	13°♑29	8	-21°11'
North Node	☊	19°♑23 ℞	8	-22°03'
South Node	☋	19°♋23 ℞	2	+22°03'
Ascendant	As	16°♊38'29"	1	+22°47'
Midheaven	Mc	22°♒59'27"	10	-13°52'

Chart

Tecumseh
Natal Chart
Mar 9 1768 NS, Wed
10:30 am LMT +5:31:56
Chillicothe, Ohio
39°N19'59" 082°W58'57"
Geocentric
Tropical
Placidus
True Node
Rating: X
Time is speculative

78 Horoscope: Tecumseh

Tecumseh was born with Uranus in Taurus and Pluto in Capricorn, energies we're familiar with. His crusading Sun in Pisces trine Moon in Scorpio gave him a mission, and the fact that he got as far as he did is a testament to his commitment. His Mars-Pluto-North Node conjunct and parallel show his ability to work shrewdly and strategically, and the squares to Jupiter in Libra made diplomacy important for him, too.

For a more immediate impression of some of the energies of his chart, we can look to Supreme Court Justice Ruth Bader Ginsburg, who shared the Sun in Pisces, Moon in Scorpio and Mercury in Aries. But her Mars in Virgo conjoined Neptune and the South Node, so she lived by the pen while he died by the sword. Tecumseh's Venus was at 10° and Ginsburg's Saturn at 12° Aquarius, and both worked for community and special interests.

Like his older brother, Tenskwatawa was born with Uranus in Taurus, Neptune in Virgo and Pluto in Capricorn. But the Prophet's grand trine in earth included Venus, Jupiter and Pluto in Capricorn, a fitting signature in the earth-sign era. His Jupiter and Pluto are also closely parallel in declination, giving his activism even more of a boost. While his birth data remains a question, it's likely he was a 1771 Aquarius.

The Prophet's tight Sun-Saturn-Uranus T-square shows not only the loss of his father before his birth, but also the many dramatic changes he experienced in life. The Sun and Saturn are both in signs of their detriment, but their mutual reception strengthens them somewhat. His full Moon in Leo gave him the ability to command attention.

We can see the Shawnee's prophetic abilities in Neptune's important trines, its inconjunct aspect to the Sun in Aquarius and square to Mars in Gemini (which falls on the U.S. Mars-Neptune square). Mercury retrograde square the North Node in Scorpio helped him turn his mind inwards.

Tenskwatawa had a yod in his birth chart (also called the "Finger of God" pattern for its seemingly fatalistic influence). Mars sextiles Saturn and both planets are quincunx Jupiter in Capricorn. Venus and Pluto in Capricorn fall on either side of Jupiter and their midpoint conjoins it, strengthening the pattern. Tecumseh's Mars-Pluto conjunction in Capricorn fell near the same point. It creates a T-square with the U.S. Sun-Saturn square.

When the Prophet predicted the eclipse of June 16, 1806, it fell at 25° Gemini, closely trining his natal Mercury. He was nearing a Jupiter return as his influence expanded.

Astrologer Donna Cunningham identified Saturn-Uranus aspects as a signature for astrologers, and along with his Sun and Mercury in Aquarius, the close square in his chart makes me think Tenskwatawa may have been one. Jupiter in Capricorn is also a placement common to astrologers. But in 1824 he told ethno-grapher C. C. Trowbridge that the Shawnees held "no ceremonies upon the appearance of a new Moon, nor do they calculate the time of its reappearance." (Kinietz and Voegelin, p. 38)

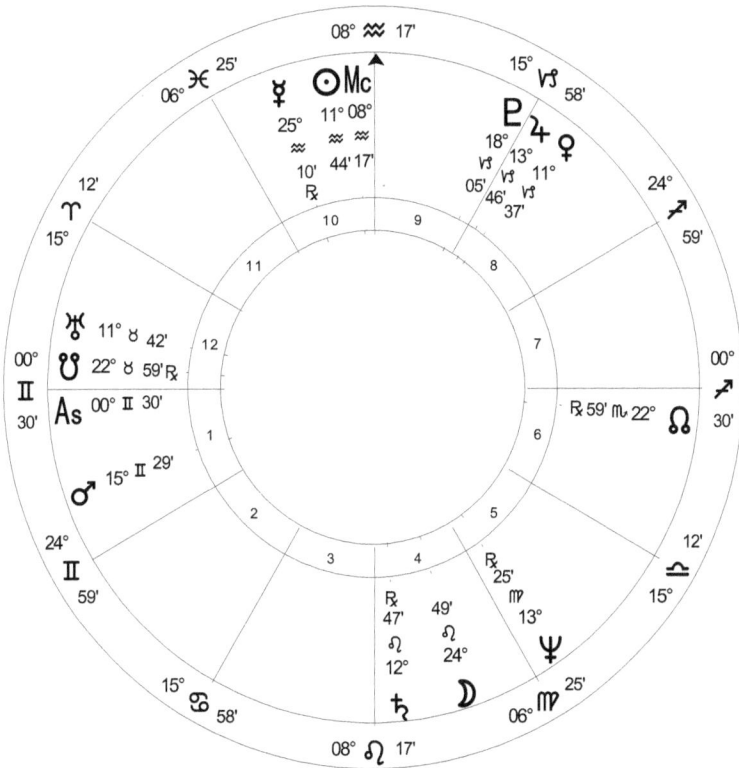

Name	Pt	Long.	Hs	Decl.
Sun	☉	11°≈44'54"	10	-17°17'
Moon	☽	24°♌49'47"	4	+08°32'
Mercury	☿	25°♑10 ℞	10	-10°58'
Venus	♀	11°♑37	8	-16°06'
Mars	♂	15°♊29	1	+25°40'
Jupiter	♃	13°♑46	8	-22°46'
Saturn	♄	12°♌47 ℞	4	+17°57'
Uranus	♅	11°♉42	12	+15°01'
Neptune	♆	13°♍25 ℞	5	+07°27'
Pluto	♇	18°♑05	9	-22°18'
North Node	☊	22°♏59 ℞	6	-18°32'
South Node	☋	22°♉59 ℞	12	+18°32'
Ascendant	As	00°♊30'33"	1	+20°16'
Midheaven	Mc	08°≈17'14"	10	-18°12'

Chart
Tenskwatawa
Natal Chart
Jan 31 1771 NS, Thu
12:00 pm LMT +5:31:56
Chillicothe, Ohio
39°N19'59" 082°W58'57"
Geocentric
Tropical
Placidus
True Node
Rating: XX
Ancestry.com Coutu Family Tree

79 Horoscope: Tenskwatawa

The fact remains that no one else in the area (including William Henry Harrison) anticipated the eclipse. Some Shawnees belonged to the Midewiwin society that had more information. I believe they may have kept the facts private for political or religious reasons.

Appendix 2: The Seven Fires Prophecy Cycle

Algonquin historian Evan T. Pritchard reconstructed the timeline of the Seven Fires prophecy cycle in his book *Henry Hudson and the Algonquins of New York* (pages 272-277). Each 112-year life walk cycle can be divided in half, creating two periods of 56 years. A year of signs and omens follows the start of each phase of the cycle, and eclipses punctuate them. Pritchard suggests a beginning on the new Moon of September 12, 1216 at the time of an intermeshing of the solar and lunar calendars. I share some of his timeline, but have not confirmed the information.

1216: First Fire begins September 12. First solar year ends September 11, 1217; first lunar year ends October 1, 1217, outlining the first year of signs and omens.

Sept. 1272: Midpoint of the First Fire, 56 years completed. Year of signs and omens ends September 1273.

1328: Second Fire begins.

1384: Midpoint of the Second Fire.

1440: Third Fire begins. Cornplanter's Eclipse January 28, 1451.

1492: Columbus' first voyage.

1496: Midpoint of the Third Fire. John Cabot's eclipse, August 8.

1552: Fourth Fire begins. Saskatchewan eclipse, July 10, 1553.

1608: John Smith's eclipse, August 10, 1608. Close alignment of the Sun-Moon calendars, September 8-11, 1608. End of the first half of the Seven Fires cycle (392 years).

Henry Hudson lands at Manhattan Island September 11, 1609.

1664: Fifth Fire begins. James Bay eclipse, September 1, 1664.

1720: Midpoint of the Fifth Fire. Pontiac born.

1776: After Staten Island Peace Conference, Adams and Franklin commit to revolution last day of Fifth Fire, September 11.

Sixth Fire begins September 12.

1777: U.S. Articles of Confederation adopted November 15, 1777.

1832: Midpoint of Sixth Fire.

1834: Trail of Tears eclipse, November 30, 1834.

1888: Seventh Fire begins.

1889: Wovoka's eclipse January 1, 1889.

1890: Wounded Knee massacre December 29, 1890.

1944: Midpoint of the Seventh Fire.

1945: Long House eclipse July 9, 1945. Hiroshima bombed August 6, 1945.

1991: Fifth Sun begins for Maya, July 11, 1991.

1999: Solar and lunar calendars coincide September 11-12.

2000: End of Seventh Fire (784 year cycle).

2001: World Trade Center destroyed September 11, 2001.

.

Appendix 3: Presidents Elected in Zero Years

President	Election/ Inauguration	Jupiter-Saturn	Dates Exact	Died in Office
Jefferson	10/31/1800 3/4/1801	5 Virgo 08 11 N 59	7/17/1802 6/26/1802	No d. 7/4/1826
Monroe	11/3/1820 3/5/1821	24 Aries 38 6 N 23	6/19/1821 5/20/1821	No d. 7/4/1831
Harrison	10/30/1840 3/4/1841	8 Capricorn 54 22 S 21 22 S 20 22 S 41	1/26/1842 3/24/1841 4/22/1841 10/24/1841	4/4/1841 (2/28/44 - Explosion)
Lincoln	11/6/1860 3/4/1861	18 Virgo 22 7 N 12	10/21/1861 9/29/1861	4/15/1865
Garfield	11/2/1880 3/4/1881	1 Taurus 35 8 N 43	4/18/1881 3/21/1881	9/19/1881
McKinley	11/6/1900 3/4/1901	13 Capricorn 59 22 S 44	11/28/1901 12/5/1900	9/14/1901
Harding	11/2/1920 3/4/1821	26 Virgo 35 4 N 23	9/10/1921 8/16/1921	8/2/1923
Roosevelt	11/5/1940 1/20/1941	14 Taurus 27 12 Taurus 27 9 Taurus 07 13 N 03	8/7/1940 10/19/1940 2/15/1941 6/22/1940	4/12/1945
Kennedy	11/8/1960 1/20/1961	25 Capricorn 12 20 S 50	2/18/1961 3/2/61	11/22/1963
Reagan	11/4/1980 1/20/81	9 Libra 30 8 Libra 06 4 Libra 56 0 S 44	12/31/1980 3/4/1981 7/24/1981 11/21/80	3/30/1981 (Shot) d. 6/5/04
G.W. Bush	11/7/2000 1/20/2001	22 Taurus 43 15 N 19	5/28/2000 4/23/2000	No
Biden	11/3/2020 1/21/2021	0 Aquarius 29 20 S 19	12/21/2020 12/25/2020	

Appendix 4: U.S. and Presidents' Aspects to U.S.

Kelsey Richfield rejected the idea of Jupiter-Saturn conjuncttions for presidential deaths and concluded that the answer was in progressed to natal U.S. aspects (usually involving the Moon, Mars and the Nodes) at the same time as presidents with afflictions to the U.S. chart were in office. A 2:17 a.m. chart for the U.S. was used (Uranus rising in Gemini) and the argument has some merit. I share the data published in 1980 but have not confirmed it.

U.S. Progressed to Natal Aspects at time of Death

1. Harrison – Venus square Mars
2. Taylor – Saturn trine Mars (but square Taylor's Saturn)
3. Lincoln – Mars opposite Moon
4. Garfield – Moon opposite Mars
5. McKinley – Moon opposite Mars
6. Harding – Mars square Mars
7. Roosevelt – Moon square Mercury, Mercury square Mars
8. Kennedy – Moon opposite Mars

President to U.S. Aspects

1. Harrison – Moon square Mars
2. Taylor – Saturn quincunx Mars
3. Lincoln – Nodes square Nodes
4. Garfield – Mars square Nodes
5. McKinley – Mars square Moon
6. Harding – Saturn/Sun midpoint square Nodes
7. Roosevelt – Saturn square Nodes
8. Kennedy – Mars square Moon

Chart Notes

Charts and other astrological data were calculated with Solar Fire Gold version 8.1.5, Esoteric Technologies Pty Ltd, January 16, 2014. I obtained much of the presidents' birth data from *Astrodata-bank.com* and used Lois Rodden's rating system for the horoscopes in this book.

AA is based upon original birth records.

A is birth data from a family member's memory or a news report.

B is from biographical works, generally researched by the authors.

C recommends caution, as this data is either from an undocumented source or rectified from an approximate time.

DD stands for "dirty data" for two or more conflicting times available.

X is used when there is no time of birth. I usually use noon charts for this category.

XX refers to conflicting dates.

I've adapted these guidelines for the event charts. In the 19th century, presidents often gave their inaugural addresses first, taking the oath of office after that, almost always around mid-day. In the 20th century, the oaths generally came first. In 1933, the 20th Amendment to the Constitution changed the inauguration date from March 4 to January 20, and set the time for the new president to officially take office at noon. When I have found the time of the oath, usually a few minutes later, I use it, as presidents cannot officially act until they take the oath.

Not all of the inauguration times are exact. While reporters sometimes mentioned exactly when the president took the oath of office, they more often conveyed an exact time the president-elect entered the hall, began speaking, departed, etc. In these cases, sometimes within 15 minutes to a half hour, I still rate them "A" with the caveat that it is estimated. Additional details on the charts and sources are below.

Palenque Anniversary: This is the initiation date of Chan Bahlum provided in Susan Milbrath's *Star Gods of the Maya*, pps. 298-99. The date comes from correlating the inscriptions with our calendar, so may be variable. I chose a time when Jupiter and Saturn would be visible.

United States: I use Evangeline Adams' July 4, 1776, 3:03 a.m. chart (data in *Astrology for Everyone*, p. xix). *Astrodatabank.com* lists R.A. Billington, B.J. Loewenborg, S.H. Bruckheimer's *The United States* (1947) as "just after 3 a.m." as the source of the U.S. chart Adams used, but there is no original source for this data. Adams' time is also close to Laurie Efrein's rectified chart for the U.S. (2:52:10 a.m. quoted by Al H. Morrison). C.E.O. Carter in *An Introduction to Political Astrology* gives a 20 Gemini

11 rising chart, also close to the one Adams used, and attributes it to Mr. C. Hey (p. 67).

William Henry Harrison: No birth time is available, I used Isaac Starkman's rectification which seemed appropriate with Ascendant ruler Venus conjunct Pluto, an angular Uranus and Pluto, and the Sun and Jupiter in the eleventh house. (Doris Chase Doane used a similar time in *Horoscopes of U.S. Presidents* but did not provide a data source.)

Harrison Inauguration: The *Jeffersonian Republican* of Stroudsburg, Pennsylvania on 3/4/1841 stated the ceremony would be at noon. Paul F. Boller, Jr. in *Presidential Inaugurations* says that Harrison spoke for an hour and 40 minutes (the longest inaugural address in history).

John Tyler (chart not shown): March 29, 1790, 6:04:12 a.m. in Charles City, Virginia, rectified by Isaac Starkman, *Astrodatabank* gives it a "DD" rating for conflicting times.

Zachary Taylor (chart not shown): November 24, 1784, 10:56:51 a.m., Barboursville, Virginia, *Astrodatabank* rates "C," citing *Horoscopes of the U.S. Presidents* by Doris Chase Doane. It appears to be a rectified time.

Abraham Lincoln: Carl Sandburg says "just about sunup" in his 1926 biography of Lincoln, from the midwife (p. 22).

Lincoln Inauguration: Lincoln commenced his inaugural address at 1:30, followed by the oath of office according to the *New York Herald* on 3/4/1861. I estimated the length of Lincoln's speech from its text to between 10 and 25 minutes and used 1:45 p.m.

James Garfield: *Astrodatabank* sources *Astrology and the Occult Sciences*, Fall 1942, which quotes Charles Latimer, a family friend, who was given the data by Garfield's mother.

Garfield Inauguration: The Jackson, MI *Citizen-Patriot* on 3/7/1881: the president took the oath at "a little after 1 o'clock Friday." I estimated 1:05 p.m.

William McKinley: *Astrology and the Occult Sciences* of Spring 1943 quotes his mom in 1896 with the time of 11:32 pm.

McKinley Inauguration: The Hornell, NY *Evening Tribune* of 3/4/1901 said that "McKinley took the oath of office at 1:17 and immediately began his inaugural address."

Warren Harding: *Modern Astrology* of December 1920 indicates the data was from his father.

Harding Inauguration: An Associated Press report in the Harrisburg, PA *Patriot* stated that "Mr. Harding took the oath of office at 1:18 p.m., exactly eight years to the minute from the time the same words of obligation were spoken by Mr. Wilson in his first inauguration."

Franklin Roosevelt: *Astrodatabank* cites his birth record in *Sara and Eleanor* by Jan Pottker, 2005, pg. 59. Father James detailed the labor and birth in mother Sara's diary, saying that, "At quarter to nine my Sallie had a splendid large boy."

Roosevelt 1941 Inauguration: The Riverside CA *Daily* of 1/20/41 stated that after the Vice Presidential oath, the chief justice "gave Mr. Roosevelt his oath for the third time at 12:11½ p.m."

John F. Kennedy: *Astrodatabank* cites several sources for the con-sistent time of birth. Garth Allen quoted his mother in *American Astrology* of May, 1960, and the same data is found in *The Fitzgeralds and the Kennedys* by Doris Kearns Goodwin, p. 274.

Kennedy Inauguration: I used the exact time of the president's oath, though Kennedy officially became president at noon. The oath was administered at 12:51 pm according to the *Washington Post* of January 21, 1961, p. A01 and other sources.

Ronald Reagan: There is no authenticated birth time for Reagan, so I've used Joan Quigley's rectification as she worked with his chart exten-sively. Ed Dearborn collected over 50 times published by astrologers, from midnight to 3:30 p.m., some reportedly from the Reagans to astrologers, others speculative or rectifications. Edmund Morris' fiction-alized biography provides a fictional time. Read the *Astrodatabank* entry online for more. This is truly "Dirty Data," (the day is not in question).

Reagan Inauguration: The Springfield, IL *State Journal-Register* of 1/20/81 says that, "After reciting the 35-word oath of office at noon." I've used noon, but it could be a few minutes later.

George W. Bush: Hospital and birth certificate records.

Bush Inauguration: Lois M. Rodden quotes news reports at the time for 12:02 p.m.

Biden Inauguration: As per the 20th Amendment, at noon. Biden took the oath of office at 11:49 a.m. as per *The New York Times* on 1/20/21. However he is not legally president until noon.

Joe Biden: *Welcome to the Planet Earth* of April 1987 included Celeste Longacre's data from him. Sy Scholfield also cited his birth notice in The Scranton, Pennsylvania *Times-Tribune* of 11/20/1942 (p. 26), which confirms the date and morning time: "A son was born this morning in St. Mary's Hospital to Mr. and Mrs. Joseph R. Biden of Baltimore, Md."

Thomas Jefferson 1801 Inauguration: For the first inauguration in Washington D.C. *The New York Weekly Museum* of 3/14/1801 says "At 12 o'clock, Thomas Jefferson... repaired to the Capitol." Following his entry, seating and a few moments of silence, he spoke, sat again for a short time, then took the oath. Since his speech wasn't particularly long, I estimated 12:40 for the oath.

James Monroe 1817 Inauguration: According to the *Philadelphia Gazette* of 3/7/1817, "The President reached the Congress Hall a little before 12..." First the vice president took his oath and gave an address, then Monroe spoke followed by the oath. His talk was longer than Jefferson's, but the 1:00 p.m. time is again an estimate.

Theodore Roosevelt (chart not shown): A letter from Roosevelt's grandmother in *The Life and Times of Theodore Roosevelt* by Stefan Lorant (p. 19), states the time of birth was "a quarter to eight in the evening" on October 27, 1858 in New York, NY.

Franklin Roosevelt 1937 Inauguration: *The Seattle Daily Times* of 1/20/37, p. 2 reported that, "the president took the oath at 12:29 p.m."

U.S. Grant 1869 Inauguration: *The Philadelphia Inquirer* on 3/5/1869 reported that Grant entered at noon, the vice president and new senators were sworn-in, then the president. The ceremony was "over in fifteen minutes from the time the General came out of the Senate," and his oath came before his address. I have estimated 12:40 p.m.

Zachary Taylor Inauguration: *The New York Herald* reported on 3/8/1849 that Taylor entered at 12:30 p.m. He came down the aisle, sat, conversed briefly with the chief justice, then gave a 15-minute address and finally took his oath of office. He arrived at the White House by 1:30 after the procession had left. I estimate about 1:00 p.m. for his oath.

Rutherford C. Hayes Inauguration: Paul F. Boller, Jr. describes "a real crisis" in *Presidential Inaugurations*. Hayes won 185-184 electoral votes and the Congressional committee made their final choice on Friday, March 2. Democrats called the decision partisan fraud, and some spoke of blocking it. As March 4 was a Sunday, the public ceremony was postponed until Monday the 5th since Hayes did not want to take a Sunday oath. With time of the essence, Hayes and outgoing President Grant agreed to a Saturday evening, March 3rd private ceremony. 36 guests "began assembling at 7:30" at the White House (Boller, p. 25-26) for a brief proceeding. Estimate is for approximately 8:00 p.m.

Tecumseh's birth date of March 9, 1768 is consistent in the literature, though no time is available. I have speculated a tenth or eleventh house Sun, as he was so highly regarded, with Saturn rising in Gemini, since he consistently acted and spoke with forethought.

Tenskwatawa's birth data is more confusing. There is no time available and many sources provide conflicting dates. I used the January 31, 1771 date from the *Coutu Family Tree* on *Ancestry.com*, as descendants did extensive research into all of his siblings. (Though January 30 also appears elsewhere, as does 1775.) I used a noon chart for the Prophet, and I like the way his Mars rising squares Neptune, just as we find in the U.S. chart.

Bibliography

Adams, Evangeline. *Astrology, Your Place Among the Stars*. New York: Dodd, Mead and Company, 1930.

Anthony, Carl Sferrazza. *Florence Harding: The First Lady, the Jazz Age, and the Death of America's Most Scandalous President*. New York: William Morrow & Co., 1998.

Ashmand, J.M., transl. *Ptolemy's Tetrabiblos or Quidripartite being the Four Books of the Influence of the Stars*. North Hollywood, CA: Symbols & Signs, 1976.

Aveni, Anthony F. *Skywatchers of Ancient Mexico*. Austin: University of Texas Press, 1980.

Baires, Sarah E., "White Settlers Buried the Truth about the Midwest's Mysterious Mound Cities," *Smithsonianmag.com*, February 23, 2018.

Barbault, Andre, and Johnston, Kate, transl., "An Overview of Pandemics," *The Astrological Journal*, May/June 2020.

Barbault, Andre and Johnston, Kate, transl. *Planetary Cycles Mundane Astrology*. London: The Astrological Association CIO, 2016.

Barber, John Warner, compiler, "Indian Eloquence: Speech of Logan, a Mingo Chief," in *United States Book, or Interesting Events in the History of the United States*. New Haven: L.H. Young, 1833.

Benton-Banai, Edward. *The Mishomis Book: the Voice of the Ojibway*. Minneapolis: University of Minnesota Press, 2010.

Bluhm, Raymond K., "Battle of Tippecanoe" in *Brittanica.com*.

Boller, Paul F., Jr. *Presidential Inaugurations*. San Diego, New York and London: Harcourt, Inc., 2001.

Bomboy, Scott, "What Really Killed the First President to Die in Office?" *Constitution Center Blog*, April 4, 2018.

Boner, Patrick J., transl., "Kepler on the New Star: De stella nova, Chapters 7-9," *Culture and Cosmos: Kepler's Astrology*, Dorian Gieseler Greenbaum, ed., Volume 14, No. 1 and 2, 2010.

Bradley, Donald a/k/a Allen, Garth a/k/a McIntyre, Leslie, "Tomorrow's News," *American Astrology*, November 1963.

Brau, Jean-Louis, Weaver, Helen and Edmands, Allan, "Comet," in *The Larousse Encyclopedia of Astrology*. NY: New American Library, 1980.

Brokenleg, Isaiah and Torres, Elizabeth, eds. *Walking Toward the Sacred: Our Great Lakes Tobacco Story*. Lac du Flambeau, WI: Great Lakes Inter-Tribal Council, 2013.

Broughton, Luke D. *Elements of Astrology*. New York: 1898.

Calvin, William H. *How the Shaman Stole the Moon: In Search of Ancient Prophet-Scientists from Stonehenge to the Grand Canyon*. New York: Bantam Books, 1991.

Cartwright, Mark, "The Aztec New Fire Ceremony," in *Ancient History Encyclopedia*, February 17, 2016.

Caterine, Darryl V., "Heirs Through Fear: Indian Curses, Accursed Indian Lands, and White Christian Sovereignty in America," *Novo Religio: The Journal of Alternative and Emergent Religions*, Volume 18, Issue 1, 2014.

Chaudhuri, Jean and Joyotpaul. *A Sacred Path: The Way of the Muscogee Creeks*. Los Angeles: UCLA American Indian Studies Center, 2001.

Christino, Karen. *What Evangeline Adams Knew*. Brooklyn, NY: Stella Mira Books, 2002.

Commanda, William, "Letter to Governor General of Canada," May 8, 2009.

Connery, William S., "The Zero-Year Presidential Curse: Might Tragedy Strike?" *The World and I,* April 14, 2003.

Cramer, Diane. *Managing Your Health and Wellness: A Guide to Holistic Health*. Woodbury, MN: Llewellyn Publications, 2006.

Cunningham, Donna. *Being a Lunar Type in a Solar World*. York Beach, ME: Red Wheel Weiser, 1982.

Daniels, Gary C., "Were Creek Indians from West Mexico?" *LostWorlds.org*, February 27, 2011.

Demmons, Doug. "Creek Medicine Man Lifts 'Curse' from Talladega Superspeedway," *Birmingham News*, October 22, 2009.

deVore, Nicholas. *Encyclopedia of Astrology*. New York: Philosophical Library, 1947.

de Vos, Gail. *What Happens Next? Contemporary Urban Legends and Popular Culture*. Santa Barbara, CA: Libraries Unlimited, 2012.

Drake, Benjamin. *Life of Tecumseh and of His Brother the Prophet: with a Sketch of The Shawanoe Indians*. Cincinnati: H. M. Rulison; 1856.

Eckert, Allan W. *A Sorrow in Our Heart: the Life of Tecumseh*. New York: Bantam Books, 1992.

Edmonson, Munro S., transl. *The Ancient Future of the Itza: The Book of Chilam Balam of Tizimin*. Austin: University of Texas Press, 1982.

Edmunds, R. David. *The Shawnee Prophet*. Lincoln, NE and London: University of Nebraska Press, 1983.

Farnell, Kim. *The Little Book of Comets and Astrology*. London: Kim Farnell, 2020.

Flatley, Helen, "Mesopotamian Rulers Appointed 'Substitute Kings' During Solar Eclipses," *The Vintage News*, March 27, 2019.

Foote, Rev. William Henry, "Cornstalk, the Shawanee Chief," in *The Southern Literary Messenger*, John R. Thompson, ed., Vol. 16, Issue 9, September 1850.

Forbes, Jack D., "Indigenous Americans: Spirituality and Ecos," *Daedalus*, Fall 2001.

Grignon, Antoine. *Recollections*. Franklin Classics 2018 reprint of 1914 original.

Gruzinski, Serve. *The Aztecs: Rise and Fall of an Empire*. New York: Harry N. Abrams, Inc., 1992.

Hancock, Jonathan Todd. *A World Convulsed: Earthquakes, Authority and the Making of Nations in the War of 1812 Era*. Chapel Hill: University of North Carolina dissertation, 2013.

Hazelrigg, John. *Astrosophic Principles*. Los Angeles: Llewellyn Publications, 1917.

Hively, Ray and Horn, Robert, "Geometry and Astronomy in Prehistoric Ohio," *Archaeoastronomy* No. 4 (*Journal of the History of Astronomy* xiii, 1982).

Howe, Henry. *Historical Collections of Virginia: Containing a Collection of the Most Interesting Facts, Traditions, Biographical Sketches, Anecdotes &c.* Charleston, SC: W. R. Babcock, 1849.

Hunter, John Dunn. *Memoirs of a Captivity Among the Indians of North America*. Richard Drinnon, ed. New York: Schocken Books, 1973 reprint of 1824 original.

Irving, Kenneth, editorial note to "American Presidents – a 20-Year Death Pattern?" by Benjamin F. Wells, *American Astrology*, February 2001.

Irwin, Lee. *Coming Down from Above: Prophecy, Resistance and Renewal in Native American Religions*. Norman: U. of Oklahoma Press, 2008.

Jansky, Robert Carl. *Interpreting the Eclipses.* San Diego: Astro Computing Services, 1979.

Jefferson, Thomas, "An Appendix Relative to the Murder of Logan's Family" in *Notes on the State of Virginia.* Boston: H. Sprague, 1802.

Johansen, Bruce E., "Dating the Iroquois Confederacy," *Akwesasne Notes New Series,* October-December 1995, Volume 1, #3 and 4.

Johnson, Kenneth, "The Symbolism of the Mayan Fire Ceremony," *Maya-Portal.net,* June 30, 2011.

Jortner, Adam. *The Gods of Prophetstown.* New York: Oxford University Press, 2011.

Jung, Jim, "The Mississippians," *The Waterman & Hill Traveller's Companion Nature Almanac,* 2004.

Kauffman, Bill, "Flashback: He Died of the Presidency," *American Enterprise Institute,* April 1, 2006.

Kinietz, Vernon and Voegelin, Erminie W., eds. *Shawnese Traditions C. C. Trowbridge's Account.* Ann Arbor: University of Michigan Press, 1939.

Lakomaki, Sami. *Gathering Together: The Shawnee People through Diaspora and Nationhood, 1600-1870.* New Haven: Yale U. Press, 2014.

Lepper, Bradley T., "The Archaeoastronomy of the Newark Earthworks," *OhioHistory.org,* December 22, 2013.

Little, Gregory L., Little, Lora and Van Auken, John. *Mound Builders: Edgar Cayce's Forgotten Record of Ancient America.* Memphis: Eagle Wing Books, 2001.

Lodge, David, "Traveling Through Time – 1600s," *Shelby County Historical Society,* Sidney, Ohio, 1997.

Louis, Anthony, "Will Coronavirus Kill Astrology?" *Anthony Louis – Tarot & Astrology Blog,* June 4, 2020.

Lounsbury, Floyd G., "A Palenque King and the Planet Jupiter," in *World Archaeoastronomy,* A.F. Aveni, ed. Cambridge University Press, 1989.

Lucas, David M., "Our Grandmother of the Shawnee: Messages of a Female Diety," *Semantic Scholar,* 2001.

Katne, Seldes with assistance from Cook, Catherine, "An Overview of Tribal Magic" *The Sugar Quill,* July 16, 2002.

McEvoy, Frances, "Jupiter-Saturn Conjunctions in U.S. History," *The Astrologer's Newsletter*, December 2000.

_____. "A Roll Call of Presidents," *The Geocosmic Journal*, Volume 21, Fall 1996.

McHugh, Jane, "What Really Killed William Henry Harrison?" *New York Times*, March 31, 2014.

McKenney, Thomas Loraine and Hall, James. *History of the Indian Tribes of North America, with Biographical Sketches and Anecdotes of the Principal Chiefs*. Philadelphia: U.S. Department of the Interior, Bureau of Indian Affairs and Frederick W. Greenough, 1838.

McWhirter, Louise. *McWhirter Theory of Stock Market Forecasting*. Tempe, AZ: American Federation of Astrologers, 2008 reprint of 1938 original.

Martin, Frederick, "Venus and the Dresden Codex Eclipse Table," *Journal for the History of Astronomy, Archaeoastronomy Supplement*, Volume 26, 1995.

Martin, Joel and Birnes, William J. *The Haunting of the Presidents: a Paranormal History of the U.S. Presidency*. Old Saybrook, CT: Konecky & Konecky, 2003.

Mayeda, Alan, "Great American Eclipses and Presidents of the United States: an Astrological Perspective," *ISAR International Astrologer*, August, 2017.

Merriman, Raymond, A., "The Great Mutation and the Start of a New Era: Jupiter and Saturn," from *Forecast 2020 Book*. Scottsdale AZ: MMA Inc., 2019.

Milbrath, Susan. *Star Gods of the Maya: Astronomy in Art, Folklore and Calendars*. Austin: University of Texas Press, 1999.

Miller, Gregory M., "Shawnee Culture," *GreatAmericansClass. blogspot.com*, January 25, 2012.

Mitchell, Chris, "How Medieval Astrologers Knew What You Really, Really Wanted," *Astrological Journal*, July/August 2020.

Mize, Jamie Myers. *Sons of Selu: Masculinity and Gendered Power in Cherokee Society*, 1775-1846. Greensboro: University of North Carolina Press, 2017.

Negus, Kenneth, "Nodal Returns," New York National Council for Geocosmic Research lecture, December 8, 1996.

Norman, Michael and Scott, Beth. *Historic Haunted America*. New York: Tor Books, 1995.

O'Neill, Fred, "Cornstalk's Curse and Other Area Legends," *Marietta Ohio Times*, Marietta, July 7, 2014.

Orr, Marjorie, "U.S. Presidents – Tecumseh's Curse – Jupiter-Saturn," *star4cast.com*, January 3, 2019.

Pohl, Robert S. *Urban Legends & Historic Lore of Washington, DC.* Charleston, SC: History Press, 2013.

Poling, Jim, Sr. *Tecumseh: Shooting Star, Crouching Panther.* Toronto: Dundurn Press, 2009.

Pritchard, Evan T. *Henry Hudson and the Algonquins of New York: Native American Prophecy & European Discovery 1609.* San Francisco and Tulsa: Council Oak Books, 2009.

Raymond, Ethel T. *Tecumseh.* Toronto: Glasgow, Brook & Co., 1915.

Redish, Laura, ed., "Native American Panther Mythology," *Native-Languages.org*

Redmond, Timothy, "The Presidential Curse and the Election of 2020," *Skeptical Inquirer*, Volume 43, No. 6, November-December 2019.

Reitwiesner, William Addams, "Ancestry of George W. Bush." *wargs.com/political/bush.html*

Richardson, John, "The Fate of Tecumseh," *Smithsonian*, July 1995.

Richfield, Kelsey, "The Presidential Death Cycle: Myth and Reality," *CAO TIMES*, Volume 4, No. 2, 1980.

Romain, William F. *Mysteries of the Hopewell: Astronomers, Geometers, and Magicians of the Eastern Woodlands.* University of Akron Press, 2000.

Roos, Dave, "Human Sacrifice: Why the Aztecs Practiced This Gory Ritual," *History.com*, October 11, 2018.

Roys, Ralph L., transl. *The Book of Chilam Balam of Chumayel.* Norman: University of Oklahoma Press, 1967.

Sea, Geoffrey, "History Got it Wrong: Scientists Now Say Serpent Mound as Old as Aristotle," *IndianCountryToday.com*, April 27, 2017.

Schele, Linda and Friedel, David. *A Forest of Kings.* New York: William Morris & Co., 1990.

Scofield, Bruce, "Saturn Conjunct Pluto and the Return of Quetzalcoatl," *The Mountain Astrologer*, June/July 2019.

Scofield, Bruce and Orr, Barry C. *How to Practice Mayan Astrology: the Tzolkin Calendar and Your Life Path.* Rochester, VT: Bear & Co., 2007.

Siebert, Frank T., Jr., "Review of Shawnese Traditions by C.C. Trowbridge," *American Anthropologist*, N.S., 42, 1940.

Smith, William Henry. *The History of the State of Indiana*. Whitefish, MT: Kessinger Publishing, LLC, 2010 reprint of 1897 original.

Steel, Duncan. *Eclipse: The Celestial Phenomenon that Changed the Course of History*. Washington, DC: Joseph Henry Press, 2001.

Stuek, Adam. *A Place Under Heaven: Amerindian Torture and Cultural Violence in Colonial New France, 1609-1729*. Milwaukee: Marquette University dissertation, 2012.

Sugden, John. *Tecumseh: A Life*. New York: Henry Holt and Co., 1997.

Sutherland, A., "Sacred Medicine Bundle with Relics of the First Ancestors or Given by the Gods," *AncientPages.com*, September 15, 2016.

Tate, Carolyn, "The Use of Astronomy in Political Statements at Yaxchilan, Mexico," in *World Archaeoastronomy*, A.F. Aveni, ed. Cambridge University Press, 1989.

Tate, Cassandra, "Smohalla," *HistoryLink.org*, July 11, 2010.

Thompson, Dan Rokwaho, Stokes, John and Kanawahienton, Benedict. *Thanksgiving Address: Greetings to the Natural World*. Onchiota, NY: Six Nations Indian Museum and the Tracking Project, 1993.

Thornton, Richard, "Native American History of Oconee County, Georgia," from *People of One Fire*, *AccessGenealogy.com*, 2010-2013.

Watters, Barbara H. *Horary Astrology and the Judgment of Events*. Washington DC: Valhallah Paperbacks, Ltd., 1973.

Westin, Leigh. *Beyond the Solstice by Declination*. Brookhaven, MS: Gheminee, 1999.

Zoller, Robert, "Nuntius," August 2000.

"Bottle Creek Indian Mounds," Alabama Historical Commission, Montgomery, AL,

"The Cornstalk Curse," *AmericanHauntingsInk.com*.

"Earthquakes and Native American Spirituality," *NativeAmerican Roots.net*, April 8, 2010.

"Earthworks/Mounds, Chillicothe," *Ohio Visitors Bureau*.

"Hopewell Indian Mounds Located Near Chillicothe, Ohio," *Hopewell Culture National Historic Park, TouringOhio.com*

"Living Maya Time: Sun, Corn and the Calendar," *Smithsonian National Museum of the American Indian.*

"Mexicans to Light Aztec Sacred Fire," *New York Times*, March 14, 1925.

"Napoleon's and Tecumseh's Comet," *AstroCoins.MrCollector.eu.*

"North and South America," *Portal to the Heritage of Astronomy.*

"Strange Happenings During the Earthquakes," City of New Madrid, Missouri.

"Tippecanoe," *American Battlefield Trust.*

"Tyler Narrowly Escapes Death on the USS Princeton," *History.com*, November 16, 2009.

Reference Works:

Astrodatabank

GenealogyBank

History.com

Infoplease World History

Ohio History Central

Wikimedia Commons

Wikipedia

World History Timeline

Acknowledgments

Research was important to this project, and I was gratified to discover a wealth of writing on Indigenous history and culture published in recent decades, with much available on the Internet, including scans of older texts. When I began looking into this topic over 20 years ago, I could not answer many of my questions and found limited resources. Historians of the 21st century have the good fortune to more easily discover materials that illuminate the past.

This book was enriched by the observations, ideas and suggestions of many friends and colleagues. I especially benefitted from Joan Aldrich's critical eye and lifelong experience in anthropology, religion and astrology; Adam Kraar's support, open mind and unique perspective; Connie di Marco's enthusiasm, insight and candor; and Christopher Renstrom's feedback and historical understanding. Scott Silverman's comprehensive knowledge of astrological techniques and the literature, his incisive Pluto in Virgo take on declination and chart patterns, and his Indigenous perspective all gave me a more holistic view.

I'd also like to thank the FaceBook group *Astrological Declinations and OOB Objects (in Celebration of Kt Boehrer)* for helping keep declinations on my mind with regular information and feedback on some of my thoughts. Moderators Marij Franken-Norden and Wendy Guy, Jan Kampherbeck, Astrid Fallon and many other members continue to enhance my understanding of this topic.

Others who contributed to the work by sharing their knowledge and resources (from 2000 through 2020) include Tom Callanan, Ronnie Dreyer, Sonja Foxe, Smiljana Gavrancic, Philip M. Graves and the Astrolearn Astrology Library, Ken Irving, John Marchesella and the New York Chapter of the National Council for Geocosmic Research, Olga Morales, Martha E. Ramsey, Barbara Shafferman, and Amy Winchester of the University of Michigan Museum of Anthropological Archaeology. The many fine astrologers on FaceBook and Twitter also help keep me up-to-date with fresh and provocative information.

Many thanks also to those tech-savvy astrologers on the *Solar Fire* FaceBook page who have helped me with the program: Pam Crane, Martina Erskine, Miguel Etchepare, Mary Clare Fritzsche, Wendy Guy, Lynn Koiner, Uroš Laban, Chris Mitchell, Michael O'Reilly and Daya Ryelle, and if I have overlooked you please know that I appreciate all program help!

Astrodatabank.com was a very helpful resource for presidential birth data.

All photos are courtesy of *Wikimedia Commons* unless credited otherwise.

Index

About the Author

Karen Christino has written eight books about astrology, as well as horoscope columns for *Glamour, Cosmopolitan* and *Life & Style* magazines, and features for *Marie Claire, Seventeen* and numerous astrology journals. She was the astrologer for *Modern Bride* for nearly ten years and wrote the "Choose Your Career" column for *American Astrology* throughout the '90s. Karen has a B.A. from Colgate University, also studied at Columbia University, and is professionally certified by the National Council for Geocosmic Research. See below for her books, and read her blog and more about her work at *KarenChristino.com*.

Other Astrology Books by Karen Christino

Foreseeing the Future:
Evangeline Adams and Astrology in America

A world-famous astrologer in the 1920s, Evangeline Adams popularized astrology in the U.S. *Foreseeing the Future* chronicles her life and forecasts and illuminates the history of astrology. Adams defied convention and made a lasting impression on American culture. She wrote four books and had a top-rated radio show in the early '30s, battled legal authorities in New York City, married a man over 20 years her junior and made stunning predictions. J.P. Morgan, Tallulah Bankhead and Joseph Campbell were just a few of her renowned clients. This book will fascinate those interested in cultural history, women's studies or astrology – skeptic and believer, expert and novice alike.

What Evangeline Adams Knew:
A Book of Astrological Charts and Techniques

The astrological secrets of America's most famous astrologer: how Adams predicted World War II and the stock market crash of 1929, foresaw death for Enrico Caruso and Rudolph Valentino, and chose presidential winners, travel and wedding dates. Includes chapters on Evangeline's work with the magician Aleister Crowley and for clients like Joseph Campbell, Eugene O'Neill and Tallulah Bankhead, along with court transcripts of her famous New York City fortunetelling trial.

The Precious Pachyderm:
An Evangeline Adams Mystery

Manhattan, 1926. A wealthy businessman found dead. A priceless elephant figurine from an extravagant Indian prince gone missing. And famous astrologer Evangeline Adams is a primary suspect. To save their jobs, Adams' assistants Mary Adler and Clara Cosentino investigate the astrologer's classy clients, oddball employees and offbeat associates to help discover who really committed the crime. And Evangeline solves her first case with the help of astrology in this funny, fast-paced whodunit.

The Best of Al H. Morrison

The collected works of one of the most brilliant and innovative astrologers of the 20th century—Morrison's thoughts on Chiron and the minor planets, the Void of Course Moon, Declination, and a wide array of other topics in astrology and beyond.

Regal Brides: The Astrology of Five American Women and their Royal Marriages

The Duchesses of Marlborough and Windsor, Princess Grace of Monaco, the Queen of Sikkim and Queen Noor of Jordan, each born in the United States, became royalty through their marriages. See what astrological factors made them exceptional, their wedding horoscopes and compatibility with their royal husbands.

Your Wedding Astrologer

Filled with wedding tips for each sign of the zodiac, *Your Wedding Astrologer* helps brides plan the perfect affair and understand a new spouse, in-laws and sexuality. There's even a chapter on choosing wedding dates astrologically.

www.ingramcontent.com/pod-product-compliance
Lightning Source LLC
LaVergne TN
LVHW051050080426
835508LV00019B/1801